REVIEW IS INSIDE LAST PAGE

Tommy
Goes
to
War

Tommy
Goes
to
War

Malcolm Brown

J. M. Dent & Sons Ltd
LONDON TORONTO MELBOURNE

First published 1978
© Malcolm Brown 1978
All rights reserved. No part of this publication may be
reproduced, stored in a retrieval system, or transmitted, in
any form or by any means, electronic, mechanical,
photocopying, recording or otherwise, without the prior
permission of J. M. Dent & Sons Ltd.

Made in Great Britain
by Butler & Tanner Ltd
Frome and London
for J. M. Dent & Sons Ltd
Aldine House, Albemarle Street, London

This book is set in 10 on 13 pt Monophoto Times

British Library Cataloguing in Publication Data

Tommy goes to war.
1. European War—Campaigns—Western
2. European War, 1914–1918—Personal narratives
I. Brown, Malcolm, b. 1930
940.4′144′0922   D530

ISBN 0–460–04327–7

Title page photograph The survivors of a
raiding party return: the puffs of cloud
behind them are in fact the explosions of
a covering artillery barrage.

Right: A trench scene of January 1918:
men of the 1/4th Battalion East Lancashire
Regiment in a sap-head at Givenchy.

Contents

Acknowledgments

The basic elements of this book were created sixty years ago on the Western Front, which is just another way of saying that the most important acknowledgment of all must be to the soldiers themselves, who, frequently in conditions of squalor and danger, wrote the remarkable letters and diaries on which *Tommy Goes To War* is largely based. With them I must include the *ex*-soldiers who in their memoirs and reminiscences tried to capture after the war the essence of their experiences during it. My gratitude to these men cannot be overstated. And from this it follows that my second most important acknowledgment must be to the people who preserved these letters and diaries and memoirs—and the photographs, the documents and the drawings of which I have been privileged to make use—realizing that they were not mere ephemera to be glanced at and thrown away, but that, quite apart from their personal value, they were the stuff of history. It is quite obvious that I am in their debt; more significantly, the nation is in their debt too, for they have kept for future generations the small print and the fine detail of one of the most important episodes of our national life.

On a more personal level, I must make acknowledgment to my employers, the BBC, for letting me make my documentary film *The Battle of the Somme* in 1976 and for subsequently giving me permission to compile this book; to *Radio Times* for publishing my appeal, made in connection with that film, for authentic First World War material, and to Monica Boggust, Barbara Cumming and Josette Nichols of BBC Television Documentary Department for helping me to sort the hundreds of letters and packages that were sent in response.

I must also make honourable mention of my family, for being patient with a house strewn for many months with books and papers, and to my wife Betty for undertaking a score of valuable tasks of which not the least significant was the correcting of the proofs; also to my son Martin for drawing the diagram on page 77. And in the context of my own family it would not be out of place to mention my own father, who appears occasionally in this book as Private W. G. Brown, 2/3rd Field Ambulance, 59th (North Midland) Division. My many talks with him about the war over the years helped to awaken what has become a long-standing interest in this momentous subject and he had happily survived to read, discuss and add one or two of his own experiences to these pages, but, sadly, died while the book was being printed.

6

Of my friends at the Imperial War Museum who have suggested and advised throughout this enterprise I cannot speak too highly. I could mention many names but will content myself with three: Rose Coombs, Special Collections Officer, whose grasp of the minutiae of the Great War is surely unrivalled and who, among many other generous acts, first introduced me to the Western Front at Vimy Ridge on the bitterly cold morning of Remembrance Day 1975; Mike Willis, of the Department of Photographs, who dealt courteously, inventively and good-humouredly with my numerous requests; and Roderick Suddaby, Keeper of the Department of Documents, who, aided by his helpful and patient staff, introduced me to a whole series of superb collections of letters, diaries and reminiscences. These three have helped me well beyond the call of duty and have not only fed my knowledge but endlessly recharged my enthusiasm with theirs.

Finally I must acknowledge a very special debt to Shirley Seaton, who volunteered to share with me the enormous amount of research that the book entailed, who became my first reader and my first critic, and without whom *Tommy Goes To War* would be, quite literally, half the book it is.

The author and publishers wish to thank the following for permission to reproduce photographs or other visual material:
Mr A. L. Atkins, 47–9, 101 *top left & right*, 149 *bottom*; Mr & Mrs R. E. Babidge, 212–13, 214 *top left & right*; Miss Doris Bateman, 185–7; Mrs Ann Beal, 234; Mr John Boggust, 214 *bottom*; Mrs Kathleen Brown, 53; Mr W. Carson Catron, 37 *top left & right*; Mr W. H. Coates, 113; Mr W. N. Collins, 210, 211; Miss Rose E. B. Coombs, 18 *left*, 42 *bottom*, 114–15; Mr Mark Crocker, 60 *top*, 64, 129, 140, 152, 197, 206 *left*, 260, 261; Mrs Vera Dendy, 28 *bottom*, 30, 31; Brigadier Cyril Drummond, 41, 70, 101 *bottom*, 119 *bottom*; Mr & Mrs F. V. Eyles, 228, 229; Mr A. W. Ford, 28 *top*; Mr A. Foreman, 93; Mrs I. J. Giles, 167; Mr John Green, 266 *top*; Mr Malcolm Greenhill, 100; Mr J. H. Harrison, 246, 247; Mrs Grace Hayward, 266 *bottom*; Mrs Colin Hoare, 146; Mrs F. E. Home, 34 *top*, 38; Illustrated Newspapers, 126, 127, 171, 237; Imperial War Museum, 2–3, 4–5, 11, 12, 15, 22, 24–5, 42 *top*, 44–5, 50, 52, 56–7, 59, 62–3, 65, 68, 69, 74, 76, 77, 79, 80, 82, 84, 85, 86, 91, 94, 98–9, 102, 106, 107, 108, 111, 122, 134–5, 138, 139, 142–3, 149 *top*, 150–1, 154, 158, 159, 160, 161, 166, 172, 176–7, 179, 181 *top*, 188, 191, 198–9, 204–5, 208, 216, 219, 222, 224, 230–1, 241, 244, 253, 254, 255, 264; Imperial War Museum (Dept of Documents), 71, 162, 163, 201, 202 *top*; Mrs M. Leeke, 133; Mr J. A. Linsley, 28 *centre*, 34 *centre & bottom*, 141; Mrs Lucas 20; Mansell Collection, dust cover, 18 *right*, 249; Mr J. H. Marsden, 35; Mr C. W. Mason, 37 *bottom left & right*, 195, 221; Rev. Thomas Nevill, 170; Mr C. Nicholson, 220; Mr C. E. Owen, 119 *top*; Mr John Robson, 130; Miss S. Seaton, 60 *bottom*, 202 *bottom*, 266 *bottom*; Mr Brian Seekins, 19, 36, 194 *top*; Mr Ralph Silk, 230; Mrs Catherine Thackray, 153; F. W. Doyle, 132.
Author's photographs, 181 *bottom*, 194 *bottom*, 206 *right*, 268.
The author and publishers also wish to acknowledge permission to quote from copyright material as follows: Chatto & Windus Ltd (the writings of Wilfred Owen), Victor Gollancz Ltd (*Testament of Youth* by Vera Brittain), the Hamlyn Publishing Group Ltd (*World Crisis* by Winston Churchill), MacGibbon and Kee Ltd/Granada Publishing Ltd (*Disenchantment* by C. E. Montague), the Rainbird Publishing Group Ltd (*The First World War* by A. J. P. Taylor), Souvenir Press Ltd (*The Ironclads of Cambrai* by Bryan Cooper), Mr G. T. Sassoon (the writings of Siegfried Sassoon) and Mr H. E. L. Mellersh for quotations from his Imperial War Museum manuscript *Schoolboy into War*, now published by William Kimber Ltd.

LIST OF SOLDIERS QUOTED

Introduction:
The Unknown Soldier

In the Preface to his much praised illustrated history of the Great War, A. J. P. Taylor makes this typically forthright comment: 'The unknown soldier was the hero of the First World War. He has vanished, except as a cipher, from the written records. He lives again in the photographs.'

There is no quarrel with the last sentence of Mr Taylor's proposition. Mention the Great War to any generation in Britain today above the teenage and the images which immediately strike the mental retina will surely be drawn from those superb photographs which have enriched every book or television programme about the war over the past ten or twenty years. Almost totally anonymous (there should somewhere be a memorial to the unknown war photographer), often producing material of brilliant quality in near impossible conditions, these dedicated craftsmen—together with their colleagues the cinematographers—have fixed the men, the weapons and the landscape of that disturbing conflict firmly in the collective imagination.

It is with the second sentence of Mr Taylor's statement that I would venture, if with great deference, to disagree. The unknown soldier has *not* vanished from the written records: the written records, or many of them, simply haven't been read. Perhaps the Tommy has not found his way enough into the *printed* records (though the publication of a number of individual memoirs and anthologies in recent years makes that a less valid statement than it was), but he can still be found vividly preserved in volume after volume of scarcely opened soldiers' diaries, in collections of letters dustily hoarded in trunks and boxes, and in reminiscences written after the event, often with no thought of publication or claim to literary style but with the searing directness of men trying to communicate unimaginably memorable experiences.

Indeed, though some of the material I am referring to has been available for years (for example in the Department of Documents at the Imperial War Museum, London), waiting for researchers with good eyesight and the necessary enthusiasm, a remarkable amount of it has come to light only recently. Television programmes, newspaper articles and books about the war have kept the subject before the public mind and stimulated people into digging out their fading treasure trove. As the last survivors of the war generation reach their eighties they often find in themselves a determined passion to 'do something' with their elastic-banded packages or suitcases of old papers before their uncaring successors consign them to the waste-bin.

9

In particular it is remarkable what discoveries can ensue when a public appeal is made by a writer or a television producer seeking for new jewels with which to enrich the retelling of a well-known war story. He must be prepared to withstand a kind of siege. He must be prepared to abandon his leisure for the next year. He must be prepared to read through much that is repetitive and routine, but he must also be prepared to be at times astonished, at times very deeply moved. And he will certainly conclude that the soldier of the Great War can no longer be described as 'unknown': here surely are the experiences, attitudes, sometimes the inmost thoughts and fears, of the fighting man of 1914–18, clearly and powerfully revealed.

Such was my experience when in 1976 I attempted to write and produce a BBC television documentary film called *The Battle of the Somme*. I appealed through the *Radio Times* for letters, diaries, reminiscences, photographs, drawings and documents relating to that great four-month battle of 1916. The harvesting and sifting of the resultant crop has been going on ever since. Thanks to that appeal, the writing of this book became a virtually essential ritualistic act. Something had to be done to present to the public, in a medium which would allow considerably more scope than a seventy-minute television programme, material of such obvious historical and human interest. Also thanks to that appeal, some very remarkable material which might otherwise have been lost has been salted away in the archives of the Imperial War Museum. So there is more, much more, where this book came from; and it will be there, all being well, when the Great War has receded as far back into history as the Crimea or the Napoleonic Wars have from our own day.

It is necessary immediately to add that for the purposes of this book I have gone beyond the catchment area of my own appeal. Just as I have made my discoveries available to the War Museum, so they have made their own unpublished material (of which there is enough for any number of volumes) available to me. The making of this book has become, in fact, an increasingly exciting process in which a number of War Museum colleagues have gone far beyond advice and assistance into positively active collaboration. The names of those most intimately concerned, as of others whose work has been crucial to this book, are given honourable mention in my note of acknowledgment. I owe them an incalculable debt.

This book by definition is something of an anthology. But I have chosen to present it first and foremost as a story, which begins on 4 August 1914 and takes the British soldier through the main aspects of his experiences in France or Flanders until November 1918 and beyond. I have provided the narrative line: the colour, the detail and the humanity are all from my fellow writers—the soldiers.

Social history has been defined as history with the politics left out. I have not only ignored the politics but, very largely, the strategy, the campaigns and the generals as well. The focus is on the fighting man, whether officer, NCO or plain Tommy Atkins—what he went through, how he reacted, how he survived—or did not survive—one of the most formidable ordeals in history. And the question which this   10

One of the key images of the Great War. The picture is of a dead German taken outside his dug-out at Beaumont Hamel on the Somme in November 1916. Beaumont Hamel was the scene of particularly heavy fighting on the first day of the Battle of the Somme, 1 July 1916; it was here, for example, that the 1st Newfoundland Battalion lost over 90 per cent casualties in a totally futile advance. It gave the British some satisfaction, therefore, to seize this fortress from the Germans as one of the last acts of the hard-fought Somme campaign.

It was here that the poet Wilfred Owen came to the trenches for the first time just two months later. He wrote: 'We were marooned on a frozen desert. There is not a sign of life on the horizon, and a thousand signs of death. Not a blade of grass, not an insect; once or twice a day, the shadow of a big hawk, scenting carrion.'

Quoted Edmund Blunden, 'Memoir of Wilfred Owen'

book is ceaselessly trying to answer is this: *what was it like to be there?* There is a further question implicit which many men of later generations must have asked themselves. How on earth would *I* react in similar circumstances? This book might provide the evidence from which some sort of an answer could be constructed.

It is perhaps important at this stage to mention the book's limitations. It is far-ranging and, I believe, reasonably comprehensive in its subject-matter, but the war it presents is almost exclusively that of the infantryman in the trenches of the Western Front. There is a certain amount of material relating to the artillery, and the medical corps has an honourable mention, but the cavalry, the engineers, the airmen (apart

from one brief section) and all the other branches of the vast and complicated organization that was the British Expeditionary Force in France and Flanders are scarcely mentioned if at all. (In the same way, there is nothing here about Italy, Salonika, Gallipoli or Palestine.) The reader will have to forgive me. I began the process of research and discovery that has culminated in this book by appealing for material on the Battle of the Somme, and that was mainly an infantryman's—and an artilleryman's—battle. Even if that were not the point of origin the bias, I believe, would be very largely in the direction of the trenches: it is there—inevitably—that the imagination goes instinctively whenever this sixty-year-old war is mentioned. In some ways the bias towards the Somme remains too, simply because I have come into possession of much remarkable material relating to that battle and it cries out to be used.

There is one final point. Any notion that it was only officers who could write eloquently about the war and that the Tommy was an inarticulate automaton interested in little beyond his next Woodbine will not survive these pages. I have taken pains to indicate the rank of the man whom I am quoting and the reader will often find, I believe, that a superlative piece of description or a deeply moving comment has come from the pen—or more likely the grubby indelible pencil—of a Private or a

The classic landscape of the Great War. This is Château Wood, in the Ypres Salient; the picture, by a Canadian photographer, was taken on 29 October 1917, in the late stages of the Third Battle of Ypres, popularly known (from the tiny smudged-out village captured on the last day of the battle) as 'Passchendaele'. Four days after this photograph was taken Lieutenant Albert George of the Royal Field Artillery went through Château Wood to rejoin his battery after returning from leave. He wrote in his diary: 'Terrible wind up while passing through Château Wood as every yard the plank road was blown about and dead horses everywhere.' Soldiers often reserved their harshest comments for this battle. An infantryman, Private Jack Sweeney, wrote in a letter home: 'The Somme was bad enough but this is a thousand times worse.'

Lance Corporal. Death or injury came equally to all fighting soldiers whatever their rank: there was a far greater equality of awareness and response among them than has been realized. Under the impact of bombardment or battle an ill-educated Private could write as movingly, sometimes as brilliantly, as any war reporter, with the added immediacy of having been in the experience and not just having watched it. So of course could many a young officer—and there are many accounts by officers in this book that I am proud to include. But it is my impression that in books and anthologies over the past sixty years the ordinary Tommy has had less than his due: I am anxious to restore the balance.

Here are just two examples of first-hand accounts by ordinary soldiers. This is Private Arthur 'Archie' Surfleet, of the 13th Battalion of the East Yorkshire Regiment, describing his first experience of shell-fire:

> The bombardment lasted about an hour, though it seemed an eternity to me. The feeling was so utterly indescribable that I cannot hope to portray it; God alone knows how awfully afraid I was and what a prayer of thankfulness I breathed when quiet was restored. The gradual decrease in noise seemed to give added security to the now badly battered trench and I can remember now, as the last shell shrieked down and flung the earth skywards, an almost awful peacefulness seemed to come over the place and a few birds fluttered and twittered above the trench. I shall not forget too the wonderfully homelike sound of those twittering birds and I could not, even then, help wondering where they had been during that hell through which we had just passed.

Private D. J. 'Jack' Sweeney, of the 1st Battalion of the Lincolnshire Regiment, a Regular who had been in the Army since 1907, wrote in a letter to his fiancée after one of the minor actions of the Battle of the Somme:

> I will tell you just one little thing that happened to me on the Somme in the early hours of 14th Septr—I was wet to the skin, no overcoat, no water sheet, I had about 3 inches of clay clinging to my clothes and it was cold, I was in an open dug-out and do you know what I did—I sat down in the mud and cried. I do not think I have cried like that since I was a child.

These are recognizable human beings, as sensitive and vulnerable as we are, not of some remote, special generation uniquely forged to undergo the horrors and stresses of war. And if this book has any further aim beyond those already stated it is to assert that common bond which connects us with those who fought, lived and died on the Western Front in the century's teens.

A Sergeant, Leslie Coulson, killed in France in October 1916, wrote:

> Who made the law that men should die in meadows?
> Who spake the word that blood should splash in lanes?
> Who gave it forth that gardens should be boneyards?
> Who spread the hill with flesh, and blood and brains?

These are not the words of an unknown soldier going ritualistically into battle with schoolboy clichés on his lips. This poem could have been written in Vietnam or Vimy, Sinai or the Somme, any time in this century. They are the instinctive protest of any vital young man of any age when facing the possibility of his own brutal extinction. The raw material of this book has come from many young men similarly placed and reacting vigorously, intensely, though by no means identically, to the circumstances in which they found themselves. Such situations will be with us in various forms for centuries yet. Only when that is no longer so will a book of this kind have no value.

Explanatory note

In ascribing quotations to their authors, I have usually (though not exclusively, since this would entail much tedious repetition) followed the practice of giving the name, rank and unit of the officer or man concerned at the time of writing—or, in the case of reminiscence, at the period of the war to which the quotation refers. One consequence of this is that, for example, Corporal F. W. Billman, 9th Battalion East Surrey Regiment (or, in the formula used here, 9th Bn East Surrey Regt), appears elsewhere in the book as a Sergeant and may well quite possibly appear at another point as a Corporal again. This is not an indication of demotion, simply that I have gone back for my material to an earlier stage of the war. One other consequence is that someone who was later commissioned or rose to higher rank after the war may well be referred to throughout as a Private. Every effort has been made to be as scrupulous as possible in these ascriptions; it is hoped that any unintentional errors will be forgiven.

It will perhaps be useful for the reader to know that an infantry battalion consisted of approximately a thousand men, of whom thirty were officers. Battalions were subdivided into four companies; each company into four platoons; each platoon into four sections. Four battalions usually, though not exclusively, made one brigade, and three brigades made one division. Division was perhaps as high as any ordinary soldier thought; beyond that were the corps, and beyond them the individually numbered armies—all subsumed, ultimately, into the British Expeditionary Force, known to everybody as the BEF. It was as the BEF that Britain's small professional army hurried to France in 1914; it was still the BEF when, an army of two million men, it marched to victory in 1918.

1

'A Call to Arms'

Recruits waiting for their pay in St Martin's churchyard, London. The style of headgear alone is indication enough of the social mix of these newly joined volunteers. It is perhaps worth adding that not all recruits of birth and education instantly became officers. Many spent months as ordinary Privates before being picked out for commissions. They were not ashamed of this either. For example, W. T. Colyer: 'No man can really call himself a soldier until he has had a good taste of all the dirty work the ordinary private has to do.'

As the war began which was to last four-and-a-quarter years and claim an average of fifteen hundred British casualties per day, the Kaiser told his troops: 'You will be home before the leaves have fallen from the trees.' Almost everybody in Britain, except a few hard-headed realists like Kitchener who was prophesying a long struggle that would only be won with the aid of 'the last million men', appeared to anticipate a brisk, spectacular and triumphant campaign. The worry of the would-be volunteer was that the war might be won before he got to it.

Britain went to war at 11 p.m. on 4 August 1914. On the morning of 5th August W. T. Colyer, ex-public schoolboy of Merchant Taylors', sat at his office desk in London, bitterly regretting that he had no military connections and thinking angrily of the Germans.

> Would they invade us, I wondered. By George! If they should they'd find us a tougher nut to crack than they expected. My bosom swelled and I clenched my fist. I wished to goodness I were in the Army. I felt restless, excited, eager to do something desperate for the cause of England.
>
> And then the impulse came, sending the blood tingling all over my body: why not join the Army now? A great and glorious suggestion. It might not be too late.

Colyer reported that same day to the HQ of the Artists' Rifles at Duke Street, Euston, where he found 'a roomful of fellows obviously bound on the same mission as myself. I say obviously, for although they were chatting in a blasé way, there was an eager light in their eyes, which betokened the ardent impelling force within.'

He swore his oath and signed on.

> So the great deed was done; the contract with HM the King was signed and I went home throbbing with a new vitality, as (I imagine) a man might who has just plighted his troth to the girl he had loved at first sight.

The same day over two hundred miles to the north a young member of the Liverpool Cotton Exchange, Lionel Ferguson, also took the oath. His first war memory was of the clack-clack of door-knockers in Liverpool the previous evening as the police went from house to house, delivering call-up wires to reservists. The next day he went to the Cotton Exchange as usual, found virtually no business being transacted and then made his own impulsive decision.

16

That afternoon I decided to join the Liverpool Scottish. What sights I saw on my way up to Frazer Street; a queue of men over two miles long in the Haymarket; the recruiting office took over a week to pass in all those thousands. At the Liverpool Scottish HQ things seemed hopeless; in fact I was giving up hopes of ever getting in, when I saw Rennison, an officer of the battalion, and he invited me into the mess, getting me in front of hundreds of others. I counted myself in luck to secure the last kilt, which although very old and dirty, I carried away to tog myself in.

Colyer and Ferguson were two of the very first to respond to the joyous, crusading mood which swept Britain the moment that war was declared. A few weeks earlier there had not been a storm cloud on the European horizon; now people seemed to accept the idea of war with Germany as inevitable, even ordained.*

There were no doubts as to the justice of the British cause. On 7th August the newspapers reported the speech made by the Prime Minister, Asquith, to an enthusiastic House of Commons, in which he enunciated what was to become the classic justification for going to war.

I do not think any nation ever entered into a great conflict—and this is one of the greatest that history will ever know—with a clearer conscience or stronger conviction that it is fighting not for aggression, not for the maintenance of its own selfish ends, but in defence of principles the maintenance of which is vital to the civilization of the world.   *Cheers*

We have got a great duty to perform; we have got a great truth to fulfil; and I am confident Parliament and the country will enable us to do it.
Loud cheers

In this euphoric climate Kitchener's 'Call to Arms', in which he asked for 100,000 men between nineteen and thirty, was soon fully answered. Before the end of August, he had appealed for 100,000 more and raised the recruiting age to thirty-five. By mid September half a million men had been enlisted and the recruitment of another half a million was beginning. And the high tide of volunteering fervour continued to flow through the winter and into 1915, so that by the time conscription was introduced in early 1916 some two million men had taken the King's shilling. A. J. P. Taylor has described it as 'the greatest surge of willing patriotism ever recorded'. In Churchill's phrase, this was the rallying of 'the ardent ones'. It is the particular tragedy of this story that so many of these men were to be savaged by the brutal, highly unromantic mode of warfare which was so soon to develop in France and Flanders,

---

* My father, a volunteer of 1915, met a friend in the street within hours of the outbreak of war, who said to him: 'Well, it's come at last!' (The friend, incidentally, was to become one of the war's fatalities.) A great war with Britain and Germany in opposite camps had been, if nowhere else, in the fictional air for years. W. T. Colyer, quoted several times in this chapter, was one of many much affected by an apparently prophetic novel by William Le Queux (*The Invasion of 1910*, published 1906) in which the greatest of all wars was to begin with the invasion of England. When no war came Colyer felt, he writes, 'a distinct sense of disappointment. I felt I had had my leg pulled by Mr Le Queux.' Now, four years later, Le Queux was, to some extent at least, vindicated.

Army Form D 463A: notice to a soldier in the reserve to return to the colours. It is dated 4 August 1914, the day war was declared.

    In 1914 Britain had a small Regular Army and a Territorial Force primarily intended for home defence. To this was now to be added a vast new Citizens' Army. Britain, primarily a maritime power, had to face the challenge of becoming an effective land power overnight.

Kitchener's first appeal, as it appeared in the newspapers of 1914.

THE FIRST ADVERTISEMENT

Army Form B 2505A—the form which committed men to the soldier's life.

Army Form B. 2505A.

(T8148). W9669—1073. 500,000. 12/14. Sir J. C. & S.

SHORT SERVICE.

(For the Duration of the War.)

NOTICE to be given to a MAN at the time of hi⋯⋯ to
join the Army

Date⋯⋯⋯⋯

You (name)⋯⋯⋯⋯

are required to attend* forthwith, or

at⋯⋯⋯o'clock⋯⋯on the⋯⋯⋯⋯day of⋯⋯

at⋯⋯⋯⋯⋯⋯

for the purpose of appearing before a Justice to be att⋯⋯

Army, in which you have expressed your willingness to g⋯⋯

The General Conditions of the Contract of Enlistm⋯⋯

enter into with the Crown are as follows :—

1. You will engage to serve His Majesty as a Soldier in t⋯
   of the war, at the end of which you will be discharged wit⋯
   with Hospitals, Depots or Mounted Units, and as Cler⋯
   the termination of hostilities until your services can be s⋯
   exceed six months.

2. Your term of Service will be reckoned thus :—
   1. The Service shall begin to reckon from the date ⋯
   2. If guilty of any of the following offences :—
      (a) Desertion from His Majesty's Service
      (b) Fraudulent Enlistment,
      the whole period of Service prior thereto sha⋯

3. You will be enlisted for General Service, and app⋯

4. If serving beyond the seas at the time you ar⋯
   to the United Kingdom free of expense.

5. When attested by the Justice you will be lia⋯
   time being in force.

6. You will be required by the Justice to a⋯
   and you are warned that if you make at the time⋯
   will thereby render yourself liable to punishment.

Signature of the Non-Commissioned }⋯⋯
Officer serving the Notice

*The Recruit is to have the option of being attested ei⋯
forthwith, the words "or at⋯⋯o'clock on the⋯
wish to be attested forthwith, the hour (with the⋯
will be inserted, and the words " forthwith, or "⋯

CERTIFIED COPY OF ATTESTATION.

No.⋯⋯⋯⋯ Name⋯⋯⋯⋯

Corps⋯⋯⋯⋯

Questions to be put to the Recruit before enlistment.

1. What is your Name? ⋯⋯⋯⋯ *Harry Clifford King.*
2. What is your full Address? *Kings Cross* ⋯ 2. *25 Vernum Bdgs Grays Inns Rd*
3. Are you a British Subject? ⋯⋯ 3. *Yes*
4. What is your Age? ⋯⋯⋯⋯ 4. *27* Years, ⋯ Months.
5. What is your Trade or Calling? ⋯⋯ 5. *Drapers Clerk*
6. Are you Married? ⋯⋯⋯ 6. *No*
7. Have you ever served in any branch of His Majesty's Forces, naval or military, if so, *which? ⋯ 7. *Yes J Vols*
8. Are you willing to be vaccinated or re-vaccinated? ⋯ 8. *Yes*
9. Are you willing to be enlisted for General Service? ⋯ 9. *R.F.A.*
10. Did you receive a Notice and do you understand its meaning, and who gave it to you? ⋯⋯ 10. *Yes Offic* (Name⋯⋯ (Corps⋯⋯
11. Are you willing to serve upon the following conditions provided His Majesty should so long require your services?
    For the duration of the War, at the end of which you will be discharged with all convenient speed. If employed with Hospitals, depots of Mounted Units, and as Clerks, etc., you may be retained after the termination of hostilities until your services can be spared, but such retention shall in no case exceed six months. ⋯ 11. *Yes*

I,⋯⋯⋯⋯⋯⋯⋯do solemnly declare that the above
answers made by me to the above questions are true, and that I am willing to fulfil the engagements made.

ATTESTED.

SIGNATURE OF RECRUIT.
Signature of Witness.

OATH TO BE TAKEN BY RECRUIT ON ATTESTATION.

I,⋯⋯⋯⋯⋯⋯swear by Almighty God, that I will be
faithful and bear true Allegiance to His Majesty King George the Fifth, His Heirs and Successors, and that I will, as
in duty bound, honestly and faithfully defend His Majesty, His Heirs and Successors, in Person, Crown, and dignity
against all enemies, and will observe and obey all orders of His Majesty, His Heirs and Successors, and of the Generals
and Officers set over me. So help me God.

CERTIFICATE OF MAGISTRATE OR ATTESTING OFFICER.

The Recruit above named was cautioned by me that if he made any false answer to any of the above questions he
would be liable to be punished as provided in the Army Act.

The above questions were then read to the Recruit in my presence.

I have taken care that he understands each question, and that his answer to each question has been duly
entered as replied to, and the said Recruit has made and signed the declaration and taken the oath ⋯⋯

⋯⋯on this⋯⋯⋯day of⋯⋯

Signature of the Justice⋯⋯

I certify that the above is a true copy of the Attestation of the above named Recruit

Approving Officer⋯⋯

* If so, the Recruit is to be asked the particulars of his former service, and to produce, if possible, his Certificate of Discharge, and Certificate
of Character, which must be returned to him conspicuously endorsed in red ink, as follows, viz. :—(Name)
re-enlisted in the (Regiment)⋯⋯⋯⋯on the (Date)

19

and which Churchill in an even more memorable phrase was to describe as 'fighting machine-gun bullets with the breasts of gallant men'. But all that was hidden in the future in the buoyant summer weeks of 1914.

There were, inevitably, other motives mixed with the patriotic one among those who volunteered. For some it was a chance to exchange the dull routine of their lives for the possibility of travel and excitement.

> I had just signed articles of clerkship in my father's office, to become a solicitor, and had to face the prospect of going down to the office every morning and coming back from the office every evening for the next five solid years. And here was a glorious opportunity to break away and look for adventure—and of course everybody said 'good lad!' and 'how brave you are!'
>
> *Lieutenant Philip Howe, 10th Bn West Yorkshire Regt*

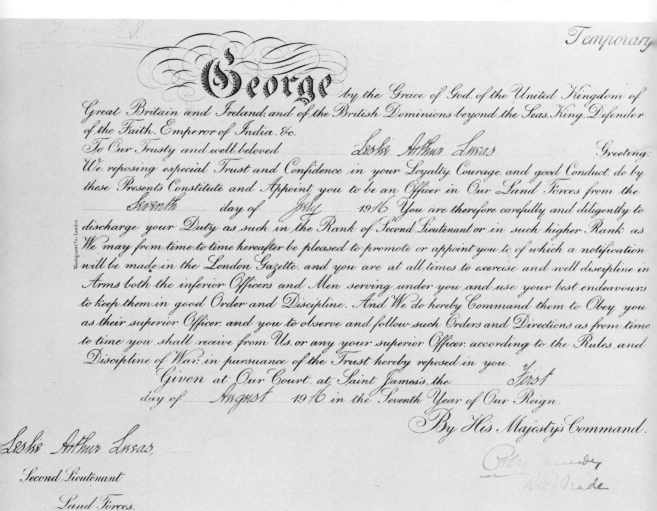

For young men of profound Christian conviction there was an inevitable crisis to be faced. Could the followers of the Man of Nazareth, the author of the solemn command to 'love your enemies', enlist as a soldier and kill Germans? This is how a young missionary, George Buxton, a Christian of the utmost fervour, who was later to become a pilot in the Royal Flying Corps and to be shot down and killed near Passchendaele in 1917, argued the case in a letter to his brother in January 1915.

> There is no sin in volunteering, God means us to stand up for everything that's right, and if every Christian is going to stand out of the firing line because he thinks it's not for him, then what is left? . . . It's a great mistake to say Christians shouldn't carry a rifle. I should hate to kill anybody, but then those who are carrying rifles are not murderers, they equally are human and don't love killing others, they do it because it's their duty. Then if it's their duty, it's ours equally in a right cause. . . . We have a 'hope of Eternal Life', then on what grounds can we leave the 'dangerous killing work' to those 'without hope and without God'. If we do, won't we rather be held responsible for the blood of those men who are left to go their way without a warning or a Christian example? Especially in this war, where our cause is right, we didn't make the war, the blame doesn't rest on us, Germany forced it and will undoubtedly be punished by God. Such are my views on the great question of the day—'VOLUNTEERING—SHOULD CHRISTIANS CARRY A RIFLE?'

'The Lord is with our armies,' he writes, towards the end of the same letter, and in another letter some time later he returns to the same subject: 'We could not go on doing the common task while others sacrifice all for our freedom. We Christians must take up the sword also.'

For most, however, the motives for volunteering were extraordinarily simple: the national mood, the national conditioning over the long decades of Britain's imperial prime, made it inevitable.

> We had been brought up to believe that Britain was the best country in the world and we wanted to defend her. The history taught us at school showed that we were better than other people (didn't we always win the last war?) and now all the news was that Germany was the aggressors and we wanted to show the Germans what we could do.
> *Private George Morgan, 16th Bn West Yorks Regt, 1st Bradford Pals*

The desperate anxiety of the volunteer was that he would not be accepted. Sixteen-year-olds swore they were nineteen and heaved sighs of relief when winking recruiting sergeants pretended to believe them. The medical examination was another formidable barrier that had to be crossed.

Left: The soldier was bound by his King's Shilling and his oath; the officer was bound by his King's Commission. Every officer had his own copy of this splendid document. Soldiers commissioned from the ranks were officially discharged from the army and then re-joined as officers

Official photograph captioned: 'Recruits giving particulars at a recruiting office.'

Volunteers came from all classes and were inspired by strong simple motives. C. E. Montague, in his famous book *Disenchantment* (published in 1922, well before the high tide of anti-war books), wrote:

> Each of them [the volunteers] quite seriously thought of himself as a molecule in the body of a nation that was really, and not just figuratively, 'straining every nerve' to discharge an obligation of honour.... All the air was ringing with rousing reassurances. France to be saved, Belgium righted, freedom and civilization rewon, a sour, soiled, crooked world to be rid of bullies and crooks and reclaimed for straightness, decency, good-nature, the ways of common men dealing with common men.

The same basic assumptions underlay this simple statement by an infantryman: 'I felt that what we were going to do was something that had just got to be done. Had not the Kaiser invaded Belgium and were not the Germans a bad crowd? Our intention was to defeat them and put them back in their proper place.'

Private Thomas Bickerton, 3rd Bn Royal Sussex Regt

I thought it would be the end of the world if I didn't pass. People were being failed for all sorts of reasons: if they hadn't got sufficient teeth, for example: they were glad enough to get them later! When I came to have my chest measured (I was only sixteen and rather small) I took a deep breath and puffed out my chest as far as I could and the doctor said 'You've just scraped through'. It was marvellous being accepted.

When I went back home and told my mother she said I was a fool and she'd give me a good hiding: but I told her, 'I'm a man now, you can't hit a man.'
Private George Morgan

There has been no time like it in Britain's history. Bands pounding down the streets, patriotic songs endlessly sung in music-halls, a stream of often brilliantly conceived posters, the poetry of poets like Rupert Brooke, the speeches of politicians and other, self-appointed, tribunes of the people, not to mention women with white feathers lurking on street corners—all these and much more produced a heady atmosphere in which amazing acts of personal and communal patriotism became possible. To give one small example. In September 1914 the Northern Foxes Football Team of Leeds met to discuss the election of officers and the arranging of fixtures for the 1914–15 season. One of the members suggested that the whole club should enlist, which after some discussion was put to the vote and passed; the only member allowed to exempt himself was a Quaker. They joined the Leeds Pals Battalion (15th Bn West Yorkshire Regt), one of the battalions which suffered most heavily on the first day on the Somme.*

Vera Brittain, in *Testament of Youth*, has written movingly of the bitter reaction, later, of thoughtful young men 'who found [themselves] committed to months of cold and fear and discomfort by the quick warmth of a moment's elusive impulse'. And it is inevitably moving to reflect that among those who strutted proudly through the 1914 streets were many destined to lie in the war cemeteries of France or to become the pitiful wrecks selling matches on the street corners of the twenties and thirties. But for the moment the mood was one of high excitement and enthusiasm. The shortage was not of men but of accommodation and *matériel*. W. T. Colyer, who had joined the Artists' Rifles on 5th August, hoping it might not be too late, found himself with no barracks to sleep in but equipped with the most easily recognizable symbol of his new status: a rifle. It was enough to mark him out as a hero of the hour.

So home I went each evening, with my rifle on my shoulder. As I walked through the streets people looked admiringly at me, and I felt more than ever pleased with myself. Girls smiled at me, men looked at me with respect, the bus-drivers wished me luck and refused to take money for my fare, and everybody made way for me, as being on the King's business.

* I am indebted to Mr A. Ibbotson, former Leeds Pal, for this story. He in fact was the proposer of the motion in question.

Recruits taking the oath. For what they are saying see Army Form B 2505A: 'OATH TO BE TAKEN BY RECRUIT ON ATTESTA-TION'.

2 'The Tents are Astir in the Valley'

'Kitchener's Army', Frensham Common, October 1914.

> 'Kitchener's Army!'—a phrase which may well stand for a hundred years,
> and, indeed, may stand for all time as a sign and symbol of British determina-
> tion to rise to a great occasion and to supply the needs of a great emergency.

So wrote Edgar Wallace, in one of the earliest accounts to be published of the raising
of Britain's Great War army of volunteers. Already famous for his thrillers and with
the added qualification of having been a war correspondent in South Africa, he was
a natural choice for a rousing, propagandist piece of instant history. His book,* which
appeared in 1915, gave a vivid if inevitably uncritical picture of a nation suddenly
transformed by the call of duty.

> Playgrounds and open spaces, in which the voices of children had predomi-
> nated, now resounded to the sharp, staccato words of command issued by
> drill-instructors. The patter of children's feet was gone, and in its place the
> tramp of marching men. Healthy young Britons in their shirt-sleeves
> wheeled and formed, advanced and retired . . . and with head erect and
> chest expanded, went seriously to the business of preparing themselves for
> national defence. . . . All over England, in every private park, on every com-
> mon, on every recognized camping-ground, were to be seen . . . the white
> tents of this new force.

The months of training in Britain of the men destined for the Western Front have
usually been described as a time of innocent and happy euphoria. For C. E. Mon-
tague† this period was 'a second boyhood. . . . Except in the matter of separation
from civilian friends, [our] daily life was pretty well that of the happiest children.'
'Some of us grumble, and go sick to escape parades,' wrote Donald Hankey,§ 'but
for the most part we are aggressively cheerful and were never fitter in our lives. . . .
We're Kitchener's Army, and we don't care if it snows ink!' Even Siegfried Sassoon
could write at this time, in his poem 'Absolution': 'We are the happy legion.'

It would be untrue to suggest that the unpublished records—the diaries, letters
and comments of the ordinary soldier—conflict in any major way with this generally

* *Kitchener's Army and the Territorial Forces* (sub-titled 'The Full Story of a Great Achievement'), pubd George Newnes,
London.
† *Disenchantment*, pubd 1922.
§ *A Student in Arms*, pubd 1918.

accepted view, but they certainly give it a much more down-to-earth interpretation. In a gigantic national upheaval of the kind that these men were experiencing, there was bound to be muddle, incompetence and thousands of unsolvable problems. High hopes and martial ardour might carry the volunteer through the doors of the recruiting office, but thereafter he had to be housed and fed—even a crusading army has to march on its stomach. The enthusiasm of the most patriotic could easily be strained by poor conditions.

Four days after the outbreak of war, Lionel Ferguson, who had joined the Liverpool Scottish as a Private on 5th August, was marched off with his fellow recruits to their first quarters—a local stadium.

> This spot proved to be our prison for nearly a week. We made the best of very bad and dirty accommodation, and our only leave was for $\frac{3}{4}$ of an hour during that evening, then only within half a mile radius, as orders were then expected for a move at the shortest notice. We laid down to rest at 11 p.m. all tired and cross.

> *Sunday, 9th August*
> I got out for half an hour before dinner and had a hot bath at the L. & N.W. Hotel, and not before it was needed, as the dirt and dust was awful, also our company had only one tap to wash under, situated about 2 ft from the floor in a very dirty urinal. . . . How bored I was with life for we had nothing to do but sit on a hard and dirty floor.*

A few days later Ferguson and the other members of his company returned to their stadium after drilling for hours in the August sun in a nearby park. 'Hot, dusty and tired, we returned for a late tea to be informed no leave for "A" Coy—just the "Ruddy limit", we thought, but were learning to obey and know that orders is orders.'

The following morning they entrained before dawn for Edinburgh. It was a long tedious journey, for which the only food supplied was bully beef. They tried to get extra food at Preston, but the previous troop train had taken it all. They did get some at Carlisle, and it was here too that boy scouts came along the train to refill their water bottles. In fact it was the attitude of the civilian population which provided the one heartening aspect of the journey. 'The kindness of everybody to troops is wonderful, even the cottage folk all the way up turned out and waved hands and handkerchiefs, which was encouraging to us tired men.'

Next day there was a similar experience for them, this time in the centre of Edinburgh. 'We looked just "It" marching down Princes Street, getting a fine reception from the natives.' But once under canvas, bad conditions again become a constant theme in Ferguson's diary.

---

* It is perhaps fair to Private, later Captain Ferguson, to add that on that same Sunday he had been much moved at a service in the stadium at which such hymns as 'Oh God our help in ages past' and 'Eternal Father strong to save' had been sung. He wrote, 'The words seemed more impressive this morning than ever before, for we knew not ... what was going to happen to England & ourselves.' But for him high patriotic ideals didn't mean forgiving army incompetence.

Sunday 16th August
The food in camp is very bad, quite unfit to live on; in fact we have to buy porridge etc. from the local women, who sell it at 3d a bowl over the park wall.

Wednesday 19th August
I loathe all this diet and however hungry cannot look forward to the camp food. With all this 'life' one has to eat however and it is no use growsing.

But a few days later he is protesting again:

Thursday 27th August
We had a rotten dinner which everybody refused to eat so we foraged on our own.

Supplying adequate food to such a vast influx of men was inevitably a major problem, particularly in the early days. Clifford Carter, a Private in the 10th Bn East Yorkshire Regt, a locally raised battalion generally known as the Hull Commercials, wrote in his diary on 18 November 1914:

Breakfast	dry bread and cheese
Dinner	dry bread and cheese
Tea	cheese and dry bread

However, by June 1915 Private Peter McGregor, 14th Bn Argyll and Sutherland Highlanders, was writing enthusiastically to his wife:

Dinner today was very good—stew, potatoes, cabbage. . . . The officers come round at meal times and ask if we are satisfied—any complaints. Today I finished my dinner and was sitting waiting to get up, when the officer commanding came round and saw me sitting and said: 'Have you had your dinner?' I answered: 'Yes, sir.' He said: 'And all right?' 'Yes, sir.' 'Will you have more?' 'No, thank you, sir.'

But there were other inadequacies more significant than lack of food. Private Henry Bolton, 1st Bn East Surrey Regt, who joined immediately on the outbreak of war, wrote in the diary which he kept for most of his two-and-a-half years as an infantryman:*

We were generally handicapped by shortage of rifles and equipment, for I was doing my first two months training in the clothes I enlisted in. [He had in fact joined up in best suit and boater!] I received my first suit of khaki (and that a second hand one) the last week in November, my rifle about three weeks after and then another suit the week before Christmas, this time I had a new tunic and old trousers.

* He was killed on 1 January 1917.

Feeding Britain's armies. The cook house of the 6th Bn South Staffordshire Regt at Wolverhampton in the early days of the war.

As was to happen later on the Western Front, weather could play havoc with the boy-scout open-air life of Kitchener's new recruits 'Rain! Rain!! Rain!!! Boats would have been more useful than boots.'

Private Clifford Carter
Hull Commercial

Our next move was to Killinghall Camp on the outskirts of Harrogate. Conditions here were very bad. The weather was wet and there were no duck boards to walk on and no tent boards for the tents, and we just seethed in mud. Conditions were so appalling that complaints were made and Horatio Bottomley, the Editor of *John Bull*, got to hear about them and came up to visit the camp. I believe he had dinner in our Officers' Mess that night. Anyway, we eventually received duck boards and life became a little more bearable.

Private Thomas Bickerton
3rd Bn Royal Sussex Reg

Men of the Sheffield City Battalion (12th Bn York & Lancaster Regt) at 'spud fatigue'.

Men of the 10th Bn Royal Fusiliers washing up. The army's code of practice in this matter was not to everyone's taste. 'The washing up arrangements are very bad, as the small quantity of water we get is put in a few flat bath tubs for the use of the whole battalion; before long the water is an excellent soup.'

Lionel Ferguson
Liverpool Scottish

W. Carson Catron, like Clifford Carter, a Private in the Hull Commercials, wrote of the early days of his battalion: 'Before we got uniforms we learnt to become soldiers in civilian attire with arm-bands. On a route-march one day it commenced to rain and a new recruit put up the umbrella he had brought with him.' Significantly, he added the further detail: 'Our then CO even addressed us as "Gentlemen!"'

It was in fact the high period of the amateur soldier. The most unlikely companions in civilian life found themselves comrades in the tents and hutted camps that sprang up all over the country. Chauffeur-driven limousines waited at camp-gates to pick up well-connected Private soldiers at evenings or week-ends. Businessmen rubbed shoulders with bus-drivers, clerks with coal miners, professors with factory workers. This new mix produced one very important change in the traditional make-up of the British army: it introduced into the ranks a large number of questioning men who did not take the arbitrary decisions of military officialdom too kindly and were, in particular, likely to react angrily against what they considered to be a lack of fair play.

Roland Mountfort, a former head-boy of King Henry VIII School, Coventry, who spent four years in the ranks before reluctantly accepting a commission, described in a letter home from Salisbury Plain a minor if genuine case of disaffection in early 1915. His battalion was the 10th Royal Fusiliers, which largely consisted of men recruited from the business houses of the City of London.

Mountfort's company was due for shooting practice at what he describes as 'the rottenest butts I ever saw': reveille was to be 3.30 a.m. the next morning, parade 4.15.

> The Sgt-Major was due to wake the Coy, but the night before he had got 'beastly drunk' and when aroused by the sentry promptly went to sleep again. He didn't get up till 4 when he was called by the Cook Sgt who had got the men's breakfast ready. But that gave us only 15 mins to dress, have breakfast, see to our rifles and get on parade. The result was of course that before we were dressed they served our breakfast and before we could touch that they were yelling 'come on parade'. Some stopped to snatch a mouthful of bread and butter, some didn't have time to do that, but anyway at 4.15 the only men out were the 4 officers and the Sgt-Major and the whole Coy was reported as being late on parade.

After ten hours of firing in 'a heavy and bitterly cold rain', the CO and the Company Commander turned up to visit them at the butts; the latter addressed the men.

> He said the Company had disgraced itself; he was once proud to command us, now he wasn't. Leave for the whole company was stopped; fourteen men who went to a portable coffee stall without permission had their names taken and were subsequently given 3 days CB [Confinement to Barracks].

29 'This rotten Company' was their officer's ultimate insult to them. Stung by this

The members of 'D' Company, 10th Bn Royal Fusiliers, in happy mood at Colchester in 1914. Roland Mountfort's Company was 'C', but 'D' Company was also involved in the incident described in this chapter.

description, with everything soaked through and the water squelching in their boots, they arrived at their tents.

The next morning matters got worse.

> The men on the CB charge insisted on being taken to the CO to protest. The NCOs of the Company consulted together and decided to make the Company Commander apologize for the way he had addressed us or they would resign in a body. All afternoon knots of men stood about in the camp in the way men will when things are fermenting & I'm sure it only wanted one spark of insult from anyone in authority to set the whole situation ablaze.

In the end the matter was resolved by an unspoken decision to take no action and let the matter drop, a negative reaction which was the equivalent of a climb-down by the battalion command in the face of the quite obvious anger of the men. The Company Commander, when the NCOs went to look for him, was suddenly found to have gone off on leave, and the CO promised to go into the case on the following Monday. 'So everything is standing over; and to stand over in a case of this description is to simmer down and generally settle.'

Mountfort then comments somewhat bitterly.

In any other Battn the men would never have put up with the mismanagement and annoyances as we have done. The Gordon Highlanders at Tidworth refused to come out on parade when they had had no breakfast.... Similar things have happened in the Gloucesters and other regiments. But we, being clerks & not miners or dockers have no idea of union or concerted action.

There were worse incidents than that, in which men died. On a January day in 1915, 12,000 men were marched to a parade ground near Woking to be reviewed

Men of the 10th Bn Royal Fusiliers ready for foot inspection after a twenty-mile march in November 1914. Care of the feet was an important military duty. The following instructions are taken from the 'small-book' issued to regular soldiers:

To prevent sore feet, cleanliness and strict attention to the fitting of boots and socks are necessary. Before marching the feet should be washed with soap and water and carefully dried. The inside of the socks should be well rubbed with soft or yellow soap. After the march the feet must again be washed and clean dry socks put on. Soaking the feet in salt or alum and water hardens the skin. The nails should be cut straight across and not too close.... Men are cautioned against getting boots too small for them.

by Lord Kitchener and the French Minister of War. Second Lieutenant Ian Melhuish, 7th Bn Somerset Light Infantry, described what happened in a letter home to his mother.

All Friday morning it snowed and in the afternoon it rained. We left Barracks at 11 a.m. for the Review Ground. Of course the roads were awful, thick slush and mud, and naturally everyone had their boots full of water. Long before we had completed the 7 miles to the ground most of us were wet to the skin.

Well, we got to the ground at 1.30 p.m. Kitchener did not turn up till 4 p.m. and then only went by in a closed car and we did not see him.

Those 2½ hours standing in water and slush over our ankles, wet through with a biting wind driving sleet and heavy rain against you all the time, was about the nearest attempt at hell I have so far experienced.

The only recreation and amusement was to count the people who fainted and had to be carried out. The engineers won with 32, our company had 8 only.

The scandal was that 12,000 men had been brought out 7 miles from home with one ambulance wagon to hold 6. The remainder had to lie in the slush, some almost covered, until help arrived.

Of course, some suffered from exposure, fortunately only two died.

However, Melhuish could see a good side even to this unhappy episode.

Fortunately 'it's an ill wind etc.' and it has been shown that the men are splendid. They held the most splendid discipline worthy of the best trained soldiers, laughing and singing though they were too cold to move their hands. I don't think Germany will win.

It would, however, be historically inaccurate not to state that though there were grievances there was much cheerfulness and gusto as well.

The men were entirely ignorant of discipline and often uncouth; but they worked splendidly together and seemed to enjoy the novel life. Laughter in the ranks was a very common occurrence. I remember on route marches having to stop my men making excessively rude remarks to people who passed on bicycles.
Captain R. S. Cockburn 10th Bn King's Royal Rifle Corps

We used to march to and from Lords Cricket Ground and Hampstead Heath singing our marching songs: and thoroughly enjoying the whole business. Our favourite song was 'Mary had a little lamb' and was remarkable for having eleven verses, only one of which was respectable, and that one was usually left out. *Private W. T. Colyer, 1st Bn Artists' Rifles* 32

The awareness of the ultimate purpose of all this was not forgotten. For many there was an intense excitement in assimilating the soldier's craft. A newly commissioned young officer in the Welsh Guards, Arthur Gibbs, expressed his enthusiasm in the letters which he wrote home in the late months of 1914, though he was also quite clear that this was shadow-play for a very dangerous reality.

> I am fairly bitten with the military fever and am learning all I can.... I spent yesterday morning shooting on the big range. I had never shot before, so I didn't do it very brilliantly: there is quite a lot of kick and the noise is considerable. There were only four firing at once and it was quite loud enough to make one's ears ring. What it must be like in the firing line with thousands going on, besides shrapnel and explosive shell, passes comprehension.

For the present, however, the actual fighting was for most of them weeks or months away. Men peeled potatoes, route-marched, dug trenches, fired rifles (when they had them), stuck bayonets into sacks to the accompaniment of blood-curdling yells, fought mock-battles and generally played at war. Meanwhile countless thousands of cheerful postcards were posted hither and thither about the country, depicting grinning Tommies in every conceivable variety of military activity—or simply as themselves. Pictures appeared on mantelpieces, beside the beds of doting mothers or fond sweethearts, in albums lovingly compiled. The Somme, Arras and Passchendaele were far off.

> These were the happy days when you could capture a village by merely marching into it; when you could hold up a Battalion by merely pointing a dummy machine-gun and refusing to budge; when you usually had lunch with the enemy, each side claiming a victory, over cheese, sandwiches, chocolate, apples and water. *Captain R. S. Cockburn*

Side by Side to War — The 'Pals' Battalions

MILLS 21330 3RD (CITY) BATTN AT KNOWSLEY. CARBONORA LPOOL. (Copyright)

The 19th Bn the King's Liverpool Regt—the 3rd Liverpool 'Pals'—a 'Pals' battalion from the city where the idea began. This is a remarkable picture of a whole battalion drawn up in parade: the date is late 1914.

This card was sent by a young Pal, Will Home, to his fiancée. The message on this card reads 'Puzzle find Will. Directions. Take left half Batt (facing front). Take 5th Platoon. Count 9 people from side nearest wood. That's him!! *Quite Easily Done.*'

PLEASE BRING THIS CARD WITH YOU

University and City Special Battalion.

Town Hall,
Sheffield, 9th Sept., 1914.

You are requested to attend at the Corn Exchange, on Friday, the 11th inst., between the hours of 8 a.m. and 1 p.m., for Medical Inspection and Attestation.

The pressure at Regimental Depots being very great, it is unlikely that the Battalion will leave Sheffield for some weeks. Training will begin in Sheffield, and meanwhile you will continue to live at your present residence.

By Order,

E. A. MARPLES,

Captn. and Acting Adjutant.

The Early Days of a Local Battalion
A Sheffield volunteer is summoned for attestation (left); and urged to spread the good news amongst his friends (below).

SHEFFIELD UNIVERSITY AND CITY SPECIAL BATTALION.

It is most important that I should be enabled to report the Battalion 1,200 strong without delay.

Probably 250 will be required next week to complete establishment.

If possible, send one or two of your friends to enrol on Monday.

G. E. BRANSON.

Lord Mayor.

The 'Pals' Battalions were a unique phenomenon of the Great War. It was official policy to afford 'special facilities to men wishing to enlist in bodies; such bodies of men will, if possible, be drafted to regiments so that they may serve together'. It was therefore entirely natural that local communities should sponsor the founding of locally based battalions precisely intended to preserve the companionship of peace in the circumstances of war. As the *Bradford Daily Telegraph* put it (Bradford raised two 'Pals' battalions): 'The special inducement of the new Battalions is that young men shall be enlisted to serve shoulder to shoulder with their friends and colleagues in civil life.'

The idea took root in Liverpool and spread rapidly through the industrial areas of England and Scotland. The battalions acquired their local names first and their official ones afterwards. To their members it was the local names by which they were always known. Thus the 15th West Yorks was always the 'Leeds Pals'; the 12th King's Own Yorkshire Light Infantry was the 'Halifax Pals'; the 18th Durham Light Infantry was the 'Durham Pals'. A combination of local pride, national patriotism and sheer gusto (not unlike the fervour of football supporters today) produced, among other miracles, two 'Pals' battalions from a relatively small town such as Barnsley, two from Salford, four from Liverpool, four from Hull, seven from Manchester. Glasgow's three battalions included one almost entirely consisting of former members of the Boys' Brigade. Newcastle produced a Commercial battalion and a battalion of 'Railway Pals' (and as if this were not enough the Newcastle area raised four battalions of Tyneside Scottish and four of Tyneside Irish). Sheffield produced its famous City Battalion; Accrington and district raised the 'Accrington Pals'; Grimsby had its own variant, the 'Grimsby Chums'.

But men who served together could die together as well. The effect on a local community of a battle like the Somme was appalling. In fact the Somme put paid to the whole concept of the 'Pals' battalions. There was nothing like them ever again.

An early parade of the Sheffield men at Bramall Lane Cricket Ground, 1 October 1914.

The Bradford Pals

Scenes from their early days of training. The *Bradford Argus* commented: 'The Pals—happy name for men who have entered into so significant a comradeship...'

The Spirit of the Pals

The following poem, written in France by a member of the Bradford 'Pals', was published in the *Bradford Daily Telegraph* in July 1916— ironically just as the news of the tragic losses incurred by Bradford's two 'Pals' battalions was beginning to come through.

We gets our rum and lime juice
   We gets our bully beef
Half a dozen biscuits
   That break your bally teeth;
We gets no eggs for breakfast
   But they send us over shells,
And you dive into your dug-out
   And get laughed at by your pals...

The dust blows in our dixies
   And there's dirt upon our 'mit'
So can you really wonder
   Why the Pals are full of grit?
So still we mustn't grumble
   For we're feeling well and fit
And our greatest consolation is
   WE ARE HERE TO DO OUR BIT.

O. H. M. S.

s been suggested to me that there are many
, such as Clerks and others, engaged in com-
l business, who wish to serve their KING and
TRY, and would be willing to enlist in the New
if they felt assured that they would be serving
heir own friends, and not put into Battalions
unknown men as their companions.

KITCHENER has sanctioned the raising of a Hull Battalion which
composed of the classes mentioned, and in which a man could be
hat he would be among his own friends.

**:ONDITIONS OF SERVICE WILL BE THE SAME
OTHER BATTALIONS IN THE REGULAR ARMY.**

The New Battalion will be 1000 strong, and will be named the

(HULL) BATTALION EAST
YORKSHIRE REGIMENT.

wish to serve in it will be enrolled, enlisted and clothed at the **WENLOCK**
ACKS, HULL. Recruiting will commence from **10 a.m.** on
DAY, 1st SEPTEMBER. For the present, Recruits joining will be
their own homes.

ll be glad to receive the names of ex-Officers who will help in the
ork until the Officers have been appointed to the Battalion.
r W. H. CARVER has been temporarily appointed Acting Adjutant
Battalion at Wenlock Barracks.

OD SAVE THE KING.

NUNBURNHOLME
LORD LIEUTENANT, E. YORKS.

◄ **The Hull Commercials**
The 1914 poster which launched the battalion which became
known as the 'Hull Commercials': it became the 10th not the
7th Battalion, East Yorkshire Regiment. Hull also produced a
'Tradesmen's Battalion', a 'Sportsmen's Battalion', and a
fourth battalion, into which all the rest of the local volunteers
were put, aptly named 'T' Others'.

The early days of the Hull Commercials: bowlers, straw
boaters, trilbies, cloth caps suggest a fair social range among
the recruits

The Grimsby Chums
The Sergeant-Major in reality as opposed
to an artist's impression: Company
Sergeant-Major Stebbins of the 'Grimsby
Chums'. Known to the young raw
soldiers whom he trained as a typical
old-time NCO.

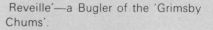 Reveille'—a Bugler of the 'Grimsby
Chums'.

3

'Tickled
to
Death
to Go'

19th Liverpools. Kit inspection before leaving Grantham for 'Somewhere'.

Mock-battles in England were all very well, but the real battles were taking place in France. Men had not taken the King's shilling to wage war on Salisbury Plain. Suppose it were all over before they had the chance to show the Kaiser what they could do.

> We felt that time was slipping away. At any moment there might be a decisive battle on land or sea, the war would end and we would be too late for the hunt.

So wrote W. T. Colyer, recalling the sense of deep frustration felt by himself and his fellow soldiers of the 1st Battalion of the Artists' Rifles when, in September 1914, they were despatched, not to France, but to garrison the Tower of London. Now their desire to get to the front dominated their thoughts.

> It was the chief topic of conversation: should we get there in time to be any good—should we ever get there at all? We very much resented what seemed to be the popular estimate of us, viz., that we were a sort of mobilized gentlemen's club, quasi-military in character, officially recognized but not likely to be used for any serious military purpose.
> And then suddenly, one afternoon, the magic order came. Battalion to make immediate preparedness to entrain the next morning.
> And our destination?—No official information given on this point.
> Any unofficial information?
> Yes—France!

Colyer's almost boyish enthusiasm was, however, by no means universally shared. For Lance Sergeant Elmer Cotton, 5th Bn Northumberland Fusiliers, leaving England for the front was a sad and disturbing experience.

> I was leaving a wife, home and friends and all I held dear to me behind and departing for an unknown destination with all the apprehension of death, wounds and hardships ahead. Packed together 8 per carriage and including full equipment, with blackened railway windows and hard seats, we journeyed south to Folkestone via York, Cambridge, Liverpool St, London and Tunbridge Wells . . .

Before their departure for France, the 9th Battalion of the Royal Sussex Regiment had a final march through their home county, as one of their number, Private Tom Macdonald, later recalled:

> All the villages en route were out to welcome us and say farewell. Many relations of the men were crying. We happened to halt for ten minutes at cross-roads near Bolney and a lot of villagers were collected there and among them was an old Aunt of mine, my Aunt Eliza, who I was very pleased to see. When the time came to march off I threw my arms around her and said 'Good-bye Aunt Eliza'. This was heard by my pals and they all took up the cry: 'Good-bye Aunt Eliza, good old Aunt Eliza.' This was carried back by the rest of the Battalion who took it up. The old lady was laughing and crying. She never forgot that farewell and always in her letters she referred to it later.

Sometimes a departure was turned into a major official occasion.

> I left Devonport on 17 February 1915 by special train to Southampton via Exeter and here we were met with a great reception & were all given tea, also a bag containing a sandwich, orange, apple & cigarettes with the Card of the Mayoress & Committee of Exeter with the words 'Wishing you good luck'. *Private Henry Bolton, 1st Bn East Surrey Regt*

So at last the long-awaited moment came when the soldier was poised to leave the shores of England for who-knew-what fate in a foreign land. Second Lieutenant Cyril Rawlins, 1st Bn Welch Regt, waiting to go aboard at Southampton, wrote home to his mother:

> Now, dearest muv, keep your heart up, and trust in Providence: I am sure I shall come through all right. It is a great and glorious thing to be going to fight for England in her hour of desperate need and, remember, I am going to fight for you, to keep you safe: the greatest thing you can do for me is to keep cheerful and don't forget to write often and tell me all the scraps of news.

For Captain R. S. Cockburn, 10th Bn King's Royal Rifle Corps, also waiting in Southampton, the eve of his departure was marked by a strangely harrowing experience.

> At the beginning of the war there was an idea, very widely accepted, that men who had been to France, who had fought there and who had then returned to England, were mysteriously altered in appearance. Their eyes were said to indicate that they had been at the front and had 'seen things'.

And there in his Southampton hotel was just such a man, not a British but a Belgian officer.

> I almost started with fright when I first looked at him. He had the face of

a ghost. His face was as near being yellow as it could be, without being painted. His cheeks hung down like two heavy bags. His eyes were large and grey-green in colour and in them was a kind of haunted, nervous stare, fascinating in its horror. Surely, I thought, this man has been down into hell, and has only escaped by the skin of his teeth! And I fell to wondering whether we should all come to look like that after we had been through a few battles.

Private C. W. Mason, 10th Bn Lincolnshire Regt, the Grimsby Chums, also found his enthusiasm somewhat chastened at Southampton.

Whilst waiting on the quayside to embark a huge Hospital ship came in filled with wounded. From the upper deck a voice shouted, 'Are you down-hearted?' to which we replied to a man, 'No-o-o!' Back came the voice, 'Then you bloody soon will be!'

For Private Colyer, relieved of the irrelevant tedium of guarding the Tower of London, embarking for France was exactly the uplifting experience he had hoped it would

'Everyone had within him the hope of approaching that far-off, longed-for ideal ... the passport to France.' So wrote C. E. Montague in *Disenchantment* and certainly there were many who echoed that ardent attitude. 'This was indeed a noble adventure, an adventure such as I had never dreamt of in my humdrum life before the war. I felt immediately elevated and inspired, and thanked Heaven for being where I was' (Private W. T. Colyer). One of the paradoxes of the First World War is that there were many who retained this heroic view throughout in spite of the disillusion experienced by many of their colleagues.

On board a troopship bound for France. The ship is SS *Rowanmore* and the date is 21 September 1914. A private photograph taken by a young artillery officer.

The other side of the Channel—troops newly disembarked on the quay at Le Havre. Le Havre and Boulogne were the usual ports of entry for the British soldiers bound for the front. For the vast majority of Tommies this was their first experience of being 'abroad'. It could be disappointing, as it was for Private Colyer, who had left for foreign shores with such high expectations and who found himself surrounded on all sides by—Englishness: 'The hotels could be forgiven for their English names, but I felt I simply could not excuse an inscription which, after I had crossed a wide road to get nearer and try and translate it, read as plainly as possible "Fish and Chips sold here"! Romance was brutally killed forthwith.'

'As we marched through Boulogne, little French boys ran alongside asking for chocolate and cigarettes, and also suggesting that they could fix up an appointment with their sisters for 5 francs!'

Private Thomas Bickerton, 11th Bn Royal Sussex Regt

be, in spite of the fact that the boat had no accommodation for the soldiers and stank abominably of stables and engine oil.

> The romance of it . . . the mystery and uncertainty of it . . . the glowing enthusiasm and lofty idealism of it: of our own free will we were embarked on this glorious enterprise, ready to endure any hardship and make any sacrifice, inspired by a patriotism newly awakened by the challenge to our country's honour.
> Nothing could have been more romantic than our passing out into the open sea. As I looked back on the receding coast the sun was sinking slowly behind it, forming an ever-changing colour scheme such as an artist might travel miles to feast upon. The moving boat left a visible track on the calm water, which seemed to stretch right back to the shore, as though to remind us that we could never be entirely cut off from the dear land of our birth.
> Good-bye, good old England, good-bye!

Second Lieutenant Kenneth Macardle, 17th Bn Manchester Regt, crossed to France on a similarly gracious day. 'So England bade me God speed with her sweetest, tenderest smile.' But his first sight of France was less agreeable, and ominous too.

> Boulogne was hot and dark and sultry. Boulogne was tiresome. While we were waiting at the station a hospital train came in and trench-stained men, badly hurt, some of them looking quite dead, were hurried out of it and away on stretchers.

The war was getting very close.

For most men, however, there was one essential experience of British army life in France to be undergone before they could be pronounced ready for despatch eastwards towards the front line: a period of intensive training at the Base Camp at Étaples. 'Eat-apples', or 'E-taps', as it was variously known to the Tommy, had enough facilities to cope with 100,000 men: here too in the sand dunes near the railway was the notorious 'Bullring' training ground.*

> The camp was well supplied with Canteens, Cinemas and Concert Parties, but for all that no one ever heard a Tommy say he would like to stay there. The daily march to the 'Bull Ring' and the long tiring hours of training were torture, and men were glad to get away even if it meant trenches again.
> *Private Clifford Carter, Hull Commercials*

---

* It is perhaps worth adding that Rouen had its base camp and its 'Bullring' too, but Etaples outstripped it both for size and unpopularity.

A scene at the enormous 'Bullring' training ground near the base camp at Étaples. Conditions here were arduous and the discipline severe: Étaples was not a popular place with the Tommy—or his officers for that matter. It was also very exposed to the weather. 'Étaples appears to be one of the coldest spots in France. A vast camp with a great concentration of military policemen to the square yard.'

Captain J. H. Dible, RAMC

'On a fine morning [the Bullring] is beautiful (it overlooks the river mouth with the picturesque woods of Le Touquet and Paris-Plage on the opposite bank) but it is a windy spot.... We arrive back in camp white as millers from the dust, a sight never to be forgotten by those who witnessed it.'

Captain Lionel Ferguson, 13th Bn Cheshire Regt

The photograph, taken on a wintry morning, gives some indication of the size of this training ground and of the huge numbers of men involved. Captain Ferguson wrote: 'It is a wonderful sight to see so many men leaving and returning to camp, quite 100,000 ...'

I think this was about the most detested base camp ever. It was known to all and sundry as the Base Wallah's Paradise, because the people running it seemed to be happily ensconced there for the duration. The various drafts were put through a few days' rigorous training, bayonet fighting, formation drills, etc. Included in the training was passing through a chamber in which Gas had been released (the Instructors used to say, 'just to get you used to the real thing, *when you get there*'). At the camp one also saw the spectacle of the compounds housing, under military guard, some of our own boys waiting Court Martial for such offences as deserting, etc.

Private Clifford W. Saunders, 7th Bn Northamptonshire Regt

It was at the Bullring at Étaples in the spring of 1916 that Lionel Ferguson, formerly a Private of the Liverpool Scottish but now a Lieutenant in the Cheshire Regiment, noted in his diary the following extract from daily orders:

DISCIPLINE, Courts Martial. No. 1105
No. 15873 Private A∗∗∗ B∗∗∗∗∗∗∗, 10th (S) Bn Cheshire Regt.
Was tried by F.G.C.M. on the following charge
'Cowardice in the face of the enemy'
The sentence of the court was to suffer death by being shot.
The sentence was duly carried out at 3.38 a.m. on 30 May 1916.*

Private Frank Bass, 1st Bn Cambridgeshire Regt, spent ten days at Étaples in September 1916 and kept a detailed diary. It is a cool, unprejudiced account, including the good ('best dinner we have had in the Army') as well as the things he dislikes—the occasional 'army absurdity' or, most disturbing of all, the 'callousness' of their instructors. It was, it should be remembered, a gloomy period of the war: the Battle of the Somme was well into its third month, with disappointingly small gains and staggering losses. It is very much in Private Bass's mind as he writes.

Saturday, September 16th
Parade at 9 a.m. and march to Boulogne Station to entrain for Base. We start for Étaples at 11 a.m. On arrival at Base, draw rifle, oil bottle and pull through, gas helmet, etc. Base very depressing. Reports that we may not be here for more than three days before going 'up the line': but could be anything from 3 days to 3 weeks. War of 12 months ago was nothing to what it is now. Only 78 men remain from one Battn. . . . Went to service at Church Army hut tonight—very nice. After service, went round fruit stalls in the Camp. Every day, villagers from Étaples come with stalls into the Camp and hold a sort of mart with chocolates, fruit, postcards and the

* According to official figures 332 British soldiers were executed in France and Belgium during the war: on average one soldier every five days. Desertion was the leading cause, followed by cowardice and murder. Nine out of ten death sentences were commuted. Early in the war relatives were informed of executions but later the practice grew up of softening the blow by saying that executed men were 'killed in action'. The name has been suppressed and the number falsified in the extract given above. This is a legal requirement: there is a hundred-year embargo on this type of information.

eternal 'Spearmint'. They seem to think we can't exist without the latter and that it is the staple article of sweet in the English Army.

Sunday, September 17th
Apparently same as any other day. Reveille 5.30. Breakfast 6. Parade 8.00 for 'Bullring' or No. 2 Training Camp. Bayonet fighting with the Royal Scots. 8 of us, including Adams, Coulson and myself, went over final assault and went over all right, I think. After this, rapid loading and firing and then bayonet fighting again. Marched back to best dinner we have had in the Army.

Wednesday, September 20th
Parade 7.45 for Bullring. Lecture on gas. Officer lecturing had been two years here and through two gas attacks. Callousness of lecturers shocks us. . . . Night ops. at night. Didn't know what we were supposed to be doing or whereabouts we were. Strolled aimlessly about. Never been on night ops. which were any good—always a washout. Nobody knows what to do. Officers all swearing and general confusion.

Thursday, September 21st
Uncomfortable night—15 men in our tent. Plenty of empty tents about but they must cram 15 in one and leave others empty. Another Army absurdity.

Sunday, September 24th
Reveille at 5.30 again and parade to Bullring. Lectures all morning, all our instructors giving us their experiences at the front. All these men seem particularly callous and talk of killing as nothing at all. 'Remember, boys,' one of them said, 'every prisoner means a day's rations gone.'

Then Bass and his colleagues get the 'bad news' that they are to be transferred from their own battalion to the 9th Norfolks and sent at once to the front. He comments that Government is making a great mistake in transferring men from one regiment to another. Thanks to this system, 'lots of men have left their friends and are very discontented'. He concludes wryly: 'Good way to encourage "esprit de corps".'

The change leads to a scene of great confusion on their last day, as badges, shoulder titles, even identity discs have to be handed in.

They allow us to keep nothing. Two men deficient of hat badges and beast of a row about it. CSM of Stores threatens to bring them up on charge of confiscating HM property. Eventually they got fresh ones and had a debit posted to them, in their paybooks, of 2d. Adams lost his pull through and went to get another, quite willing to pay, and QM Sgt. treated him like a criminal—debited him with 1d.

Drew second gas helmet, goggles and 120 rounds of ammunition. We are absolutely full up now with equipment, etc., and I sincerely hope we get no more.

We go up the line tomorrow.

46

Sketches of Tommy's Life

It says something for the national character that, at any rate in the earlier years, it was taken for granted that the war could not be taken entirely seriously; that this was a crusade mixed with generous amounts of farce. The famous cartoons of Bruce Bairnsfather published in *The Bystander* (and enjoyed, for their accuracy as much as their wit, by the men at the front) are the classic case (see pages 126 and 127). These sketches, sold in sets in France, are another example. In fact, soldierly humour was a tremendous safety valve, existing as a kind of comic descant to the horrifying realities of Western Front warfare.

There were four sets in all, 'In Training', 'At the Base', 'Up the Line' and 'Out on Rest'. Each set consisted of eight cards and bore, on its wrapper, the following message: 'There will come a time when you may be glad to have something of this sort to remind you of the bright or funny side of the war.'

Historically, their most interesting feature, as with Bairnsfather's cartoons, is their closeness to reality.

Sketches of Tommy's life
In Training. No 1

"That seems to mean me all right"

Sketches of Tommy's life
In Training. — No 6

You are a Trained Soldier as soon as you finish your firing course. It's hard tho shoot well at this time, on account of having so many to help you hit the bulls eye.

Sketches
of Tommy's life
In Training. — N° 7

It was a thrilling moment that day, at tea time, when our lot were told off
for the Overseas draft.

Sketches
of Tommy's life
At the Base. — N° 4

The new soldier at the Base soon learns that the most important weapon he
possesses is his jack knife. He'll have to do most of his overcoming
of difficulties with it !

BOO-LEE BEE-E-E-F ?
BIS-KWEET ?

We left the Base in great style and in cattle trucks. We must have averaged
a good mile an hour. The juvenile population along the way make
earnest enquiries concerning our « iron rations ».

Sketches
of Tommy's life
At the Base. — N° 8

Sketches
of Tommy's life
the line — N° 3

We marched into the Trenches, late in the evening, going across fields
on « duck boards ». There is nothing to be seen but shell-holes, and
wintry looking tres.

Sketches
of Tommy's life
Up the line — N° 5

The main duties in the Front Line in the daytime are watching the periscope, and looking up in the air for « trench mortars », with a whistle
ready to blow for a warning.

*Sketches
of Tommy's life*
Up the line — **N° 6**

Waiting for the barrage to lift. It makes you feel small and sort of lost !

Visé Paris 765

*Sketches
of Tommy's life*
Out on rest — **N° 1**

A wash up in the rest trenches

Visé Paris 800

*Sketches
of Tommy's life*
Out on rest — **N° 4**

A regular carouse of coffee and fried eggs is one of the things we always
have when we get to one of these villages.

Visé Paris 800

*Sketches
of Tommy's life*
Out on rest — **N° 7**

" Dear Dolly : I am at present staying at a farm, and am in the pink... "

Visé Paris 800

4

'Up the Line'

The twilight world of the Western Front. This photograph is of an Australian sentry at Fleurbaix, June 1916. It was obviously taken some way behind the front-line trenches: such a perfect photographer's target would also be perfect for a sniper.

Thursday, September 26th, 1916
Up at 5.30 to depart for Front at 6.30. Breakfast supposed to be at 5.30
but had a job to get it and when we did, only jam. Paraded at 6.30 and
marched to sidings . . .

So Private Bass described in his diary the beginning of his journey to the front, a
journey which was to consist of hours in a crowded, slowly moving train, followed
by even more agonizing hours of marching. This in fact was the classic progress 'up
the line': train to the railhead, after which the Tommy had to fall back on the standard
means of troop-transportation in the Great War—his own feet.

Travelling in the troop trains of French railways was, for the British soldier, one
of the war's unforgettable ordeals. It was bad enough covering the fifty to sixty miles
from the base at Étaples: those who came via Le Havre and Rouen had to put up
with the irritations and discomforts of a journey of almost Russian proportions.

Private Jack Sweeney, a Regular of the Lincolnshire Regiment, gave the bald out-
line of such a journey in a letter home in July 1915:

I received your parcel on the same afternoon as I left Rouen. It could not
have come at a better time as we were in the train from 12 o'c p.m. on Friday
night until 9.15 o'c a.m. on Sunday, and all we had in the way of food was
six hard biscuits and a pound of bully beef and that was all we got until
10 o'c on Sunday morning, so you can see how nice that box of chocolates
was to me and my chums.

The standard accommodation provided for the Tommy on these troop trains was
hardly calculated to impress him with the importance of his contribution to the war.

We were not expecting to travel first or even second class on the train, but
we thought we might have a reasonable chance of 3rd. It turned out we
were to go about 7th class; i.e. in plain cattle-trucks with a little straw on
the floor of them.   *Private W. T. Colyer, 1st Bn Artists' Rifles*

Each truck bore the legend:

HOMMES   40
CHEVAUX   8

51

'We were not expecting to travel first or even second class on the train. . . . It turned out we were to go about 7th class.' A French troop train from the early days of the war. The picture, from a private collection now in the Imperial War Museum, shows the train in which the 1st Cameronians travelled on 20 August 1914. The station is at Busigny.

which, Colyer continues,

> produced an uncomfortable feeling of suspense as to whether it meant '40 men or 8 horses' or '40 men *and* 8 horses'. After 39 other people were duly packed into my truck I was more than ever anxious about the 'chevaux 8' business.

Even without the horses, forty men in one truck meant no freedom to relax or to stretch tired limbs. Tom Macdonald, 9th Bn Royal Sussex Regt, put it pithily in his memoir: 'We were transported in cattle trucks. Jammed in, no room to move. Many, many hours of discomfort and ended up heads and legs everywhere.' That was in 1915. Three years later it was just the same. On New Year's Day 1918 Private Harry Rossall, 73rd Field Ambulance, 24th Division, travelled on a similar train with the added discomfort of bitterly cold weather.

> Arrived at Rouen station. Trucks packed and men lying partly on one another. Someone saw an apology for a brazier by the side of the railway and got it into the truck. Anything burnable was collected and eventually the fire was burning merrily. Then it set fire to the truck floor. The doors were jammed with the gear, packs etc., the smoke was terrific. Eventually someone nearest one door made an exit and shouted to the next van to stop

the train. We all had to get out and get in where we could. It was a slow job getting the burning truck shunted away. Nobody bothered and it was left with smoke pouring from it and a nice hole in the floor. They should have had central heating.

If these trains had gone steadily and purposefully on their way they would have been more tolerable, but that was something the transport authorities never seemed to achieve. Private Henry Bolton, 1st Bn East Surrey Regt, described in his diary a journey of 1915 on the same route, eastwards from Rouen.

Instruction issued to a Private of the Army Ordnance Corps at Le Havre in 1916, before travelling up to the Somme battle area in charge of a truck of an ordnance train. Instructions 5 (a) and (b) make particularly interesting reading in the light of the accounts by Privates Harry Rossall and Henry Bolton in this chapter.

Instructions to Convoymen.

010898 Pte Ingham H.

........68....Coy., Army Ordnance Corps.

(1).   You will proceed to-night to _14 CT._. Railhead as Convoyman in charge of truck Nos _39045_

(2).   You will report to the Railhead Ordnance Officer immediately on arrival at railhead, handing to him the way bills and vouchers annexed hereto. In the absence of a Railhead Ordnance Officer, you will report to the R.T.O. of the Station.

(3).   You will obtain the receipt of the Railhead Ordnance Officer, or of his representative, to one copy of the way bill, and subject to the orders of the Railhead Ordnance Officer, or in his absence of the R.T.O., you will return to Havre by next available train. _reporting immediately to your Sect Sgt Major after having handed your papers and documents to me_

(4)   You will report to nearest R.T.O. if delayed and the reason is not apparent.

(5).   You are warned:-
       (a) That no fires are to be permitted in trucks.
       (B) That you are not to leave your trucks en route, or to leave confines of railhead station except under the orders of an Officer.
       (c) That you are responsible that all guns, vehicles or loose stores are properly secured. You will, at the first opportunity, call the attention of an R.T.O. or of a T.C.O. to any loose stores --- and see that they are secured.

                        Sgd. A.M. Hidden, Captain,
                             O.i/c. Issues,
Havre.   for Ordnance Officer, Base.
14/8/16

We started on our journey after 5.30, having left for the station about 2.30, and a very trying one it was for we had a terrible lot of stops. Some of the stops were long enough for us to get out and make tea while other men would be frying a piece of bacon but more than once did we have to get back into the train with our water half boiled and our bacon half cooked.

Also in 1915, Second Lieutenant Cyril Rawlins, 1st Bn Welch Regt, did the same journey in what he described in a letter to his mother as

One of the largest trains I ever saw: 38 coaches of all sizes and shapes: we had two smashes on the way up: couplings pulled out, with a fearful jerk and consequent delays of half an hour, whilst we all got out to stretch our legs and the men made fires and cooked food in their billy cans.

These trains seemed to need to stop 'simply to breathe', wrote Captain R. S. Cockburn, 10th Bn King's Royal Rifle Corps, in his reminiscences, adding that the only relief from the tediousness of one 'lamentably slow journey' which he experienced was

the amusing though still rather irritating sight, whenever the train halted, of numbers of small French boys giving vent to everlasting cries of 'Souvenir!' 'Bullee-beef!' 'Beesket'.

But such details apart, Cockburn saw little humour in this ludicrously inadequate mode of transport. Even officers had to put up with desperately uncomfortable conditions: on one winter journey, he noted, the officers' carriage had not been repaired for a long time and one door was completely broken off, so that the officers had to get out and jog along the line by the side of the train to avoid being frozen in the night. His final verdict on this phase of the transportation of the British Army to war was uncompromisingly severe:

There was nothing worse for the morale of an officer or man crossing to France for the first time or coming back off leave to take part in some important fight than his railway journey up to the front.

And then there was the inevitable march onwards from the railhead. This is Private Frank Bass's description of the second stage of his progress 'up the line':

We alighted at Corbie and had rations served out to us. Our packs were put on an ASC* lorry and we started the march up to Brigade HQ with equipment and rifles. Rottenest march I have ever been on—rotten roads and we had to march about 15 miles. When we got there, found we had to sleep in the open. No one knew we were coming and we might just as well have stayed at the Rail Head for the night. Army have no consideration for the men at all.

* Army Service Corps; jocularly known as Aly Sloper's Cavalry.

The misery of long marches along the uneven roads of France or Flanders is a constant theme in the letters and diaries of the British soldier. It is one of the curiosities of that war, in which the massed industries of the combatant nations were harnessed to produce guns and munitions on a massive and ever-increasing scale, that the idea of increasing the mobility and sparing the energies of the fighting man by providing regularly available transport for him never lodged itself in the minds of the military hierarchies. Feet had carried the armies of Wellington and Napoleon about Europe; feet could carry the armies of Joffre, Haig, Falkenhayn or Ludendorff. The Tommy was not unaware that there were alternatives to the constant reliance on his own army boots, but he was also aware that such alternatives were rarely seen and even more rarely on hand. Sergeant F. W. Billman, 9th Bn East Surrey Regt, confided to his diary in September 1916:

> Again we are marching. All this marching is done to save wearing out the tyres of motor-lorries and buses that one sees pictures of, carrying the Tommies about France. At least, so I think.

There are indeed many familiar pictures of Tommies in London buses waving cheerfully at the camera as they proceeded up or down the line,* but for the vast majority of men it was the long exhausting march, hour after hour, sometimes in rain or snow, sometimes in the equally pitiless sun, that was the norm. They found the going hard and said so.

> It was most most depressing, plod, plod, legs and boots going on and on and when a halt came we would just fall down, after having a leak, and the pack was getting heavier and heavier. When you took it off you seemed to rise in the air. We had 120 rounds in the pouches and Iron Rations, Full Pack and Rifle. The whole lot certainly weighed one down. In the finish one would be kind of sleeping whilst marching and when a Halt came they would have to kick the chaps to wake them to continue.
> *Private Tom Macdonald, 9th Bn Royal Sussex Regt*

> We left Gorre for La Beauvrière. This was one of the worst marches we ever had; it was a blazing hot day, and the men had had no rest for a long time, and we marched nearly three hours without a halt. Several men fell out on the way, and one or two NCOs who also fell out were afterwards reduced to the ranks for this.
> *Rifleman A. H. Young, 1/18th Bn London Regt, London Irish Rifles*

> We marched fifteen miles on Wednesday. It doesn't sound much, but when you think of the heat of the day, the weight of the packs and the state of the French roads you will understand it was an amazing strain on our

---

* Transport by bus was not always an unalloyed pleasure. My father recalls how on one occasion in 1918 he and his colleagues climbed delightedly aboard a fleet of buses, decided in spite of threatening weather to make for the open upper deck as opposed to the boarded-up lower deck and found themselves sitting through three hours of solid rain while the buses moved not an inch.

endurance. The French roads are horrible. Through every village and for a mile or two each side they are composed of great rough cobble stones, about 8 inches square and not over carefully laid. Apart from the unevenness there is the difficulty that the nails of our boots step on them as on ice. If two villages are only a few miles apart the cobble stones carry on and join up the two, so that they stretch for miles. Our packs I cannot find words to describe. It is a cruel, unnatural weight that no man should be called upon to carry.

Lance Corporal Roland Mountfort, 10th Bn Royal Fusiliers

Junior officers often marched with the men: they were spared the weight of rifle and pack, but for young Second Lieutenant Cyril Rawlins, there was the formidable responsibility of not showing any hint of fatigue or weakness.

Marching: the sun beats down pitilessly. The men have discarded their tunics and tucked their handkerchiefs under their hat brims behind. No one speaks, it is too hot; the sweat is dripping off my eyelashes, my clothes are drenched, my feet burn; ahead the white dusty glaring road; cars race past and we march in a fog of dust. We fix our eyes on a distant church spire: oh how slowly it grows nearer. We can halt there. Passing an esta-minet, the heat reflected from its walls seems to strike us in solid waves: the green shutters are closed and thro' the open door a glimpse of men at a table and glasses: a cool interior! A young fellow falters: I take his pack and rifle. 'Stick to it, lad,' as though I was not fagged myself! But I must show no sign: must make a joke now and then to cheer them up. I repeat to myself, 'you must stick it, you must show them how.' I would give any-thing to fall out: the grassy banks draw like magnets. Oh! to fling myself down there. A little cloud creeps across the sun: we breathe a prayer of thankfulness: the fiery eye is dull for a few blessed moments, then glows again.

Thinking of water: the river at home, the aqueduct, the slow black water beneath. There are men at home this very moment lying in punts in quiet backwaters, under the willows.

Standing naked in a tub: my man Bobbet slings buckets of cold water at me. Some men have never known thirst, or fatigue: have never known the trial of the long march, have never known the blessed relief of rest.

Senior officers could make or break their men on such marches.* Tom Macdonald's 9th Battalion Royal Sussex Regt were fortunate not so much in their Commanding

* There are authentic cases of men dying on the march. In 1916 during the Somme the Post Office Rifles and the other battalions of 47th Division marched down from the north in paralysing heat, weak from months of trench war and in full marching order at a rate of twenty miles a day, causing several deaths from heat stroke and fatigue—for no purpose as weeks elapsed after reaching the Somme before the division was thrown into the fighting.

During this march a General rode up on his charger to the Post Office Rifles column and told them some glorious news about a Russian victory—to which a great shout went up: 'F—— the Russians'. The General was so enraged that he ordered the CO to make the men march to attention for the rest of the day—but his order was soon forgotten. (I am indebted to the late Wing Cmdr Shewry, Post Office Rifles Association, for this story.)

Though frequently, for the Tommy, conspicuous for their absence, buses were in fact used to transport men to or from the front throughout the war. (The picture above, taken in April 1917, is actually of men going *from* the front: they are embussing in Arras to withdraw to a rest area.) The Admiralty introduced them first, during the operations that culminated in the fall of Antwerp in October 1914. The Army took up the idea almost immediately and 150 buses were on hand in time to participate in the First Battle of Ypres in October–November 1914. By late 1916 each of the five armies on the Western Front had its own Auxiliary Bus Company. Later two other companies were added and a system arrived at whereby the seven bus companies, comprising 1800 officers and men and 650 vehicles, were placed at intervals behind the line along the trunk road from Amiens to Ypres.

The first buses arrived in their civilian colours; soon, however, they were painted khaki and had their lower decks boarded up. A full bus load was twenty-five fully equipped men. Unfortunately for the men, buses were not always available at the time when they would most have appreciated them.

Officer as in their Second in Command, Major Langdon, who later became their CO and was, according to Macdonald, 'loved by all'.

> Major Langdon only rode his horse on ceremonials. When on the march he marched with the men, and let any sick soldier ride on his horse. He was at the last of the column and at every halt, which was every one hour's march for 10 minutes, he would go forward to the CO and report if any men had fallen out. Once on our march to the front the CO and he had words. The CO had gone well past the hour for the usual halt. I think he was trying to get to the top of a big hill. Well, Major Langdon, whose nickname among the boys was 'Cushy' (meaning easy), told the CO he had gone past the hour. Cushy said he marched with the men and realized what it meant, whereas the big fat CO rode his horse. This pleased the boys when they heard.

But even the longest and most tedious of marches had an ending, bringing the Tommy, at last, to the borders of that unique zone around which his imagination had inevitably played through all the long months of training and preparation: the Western Front. It announced its presence from some distance away, as Private Frank Bass, who arrived at the Somme front during the great battle in September 1916, recorded in his diary:

> We are now within sound of the guns—one big gun keeping us awake all night. Like a thunderstorm all night. Crowds of Indian Lancers about here. As I write this a large observation balloon is floating above us and another has just descended about a hundred yards away. Very large thing, 20′ or 30′ long.

For Second Lieutenant Cyril Rawlins the approach to the front led him, once again with his column of marching men, through a known danger zone of about five hundred yards that was under constant shell-fire. He attempted to describe the scene, sounds included, for his mother.

> Yesterday as we were jingling over the cobbles past the danger zone, sure enough, away to the right came Ponk! Ze-e-e-e-e-ee-E-Bang! right over our heads. Again: Ponk! Ze-e-e-e-ee-E-Bang! A little nearer. The road just there is bare of cover, but a little way along on the right was a large barn, shell-holed. I would have given quids and quids just to run to that barn: but I am in front of my column, so I merely glance up in a casual way (what an effort) as if I'd been reared on shrapnel, whereas it's my baptism!

'The French roads are horrible. Through every village and for a mile or two each side they are composed of great rough cobble stones ...'

British infantrymen on the march through the village of Vieux Berquin after the battle of Loos, 1915.

Marching through France or Flanders left many men with vivid if agonizing memories. There were, however, occasional and much welcome compensations:

> Very hot day, marched at 7 a.m., 15 miles, halted about mid-day by the roadside for 3 hours and had the luck to be right on top of a vineyard loaded with sweet ripe grapes. The temptation was too great & despite the stringent order against looting, the troops could not resist helping themselves. The Sergeant-Major turned us away once but the men soon went back in ones and twos & the officer seeing the crop was abandoned gave way to us & we fell to with a vengeance. I don't think I ever enjoyed a feed better.
>
> *Private E. A. Luther, Rifle Brigade, September 1914*

Perhaps the grimmest approach to the front was through the scarred remains of Ypres, that Flanders city crouched behind its infamous Salient which had the most sinister reputation of all among the many towns caught in the coils of the Western Front—its only possible rival being Verdun. Private Jack Sweeney, 1st Bn Lincoln-shire Regt, had no doubts about its awfulness.

59

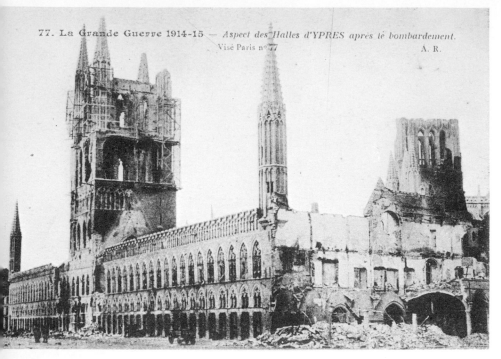

77. La Grande Guerre 1914-15 — *Aspect des Halles d'YPRES après le bombardement.*
Visé Paris n° 77   A. R.

Ypres

Ypres—known to the Tommy as 'Wipers' or 'Eepray': or, in the words of Private Sweeney, as 'Worse than Hell'. (Left) The famous Cloth Hall—a it was after the early bombardments. Later it w reduced to an almost unrecognizable heap of rubble. (Below) As it is today, completely restored

It was Ypres and its notorious Salient which gave rise to one of the most haunting soldier songs of the Great War:

Far, far from Wipers
I long to be,
Where German snipers
Can't get at me.
Damp is my dug-out
Cold are my feet
Waiting for a whizz-bang
To put me to sleep.

At the end of the war the British Military Cross and the French Croix de Guerr were conferred on the town.

It is known to us men as 'Worse than Hell'. It is a terrible place and fighting is always going on there. It was once one of the prettiest towns in France* but now it is only a heap of ruins with dead civilians and soldiers everywhere. Our soldiers dread to hear that they have to go to that place—anywhere except there is the cry.

Sweeney was writing in July 1915. Three months earlier Lance Sergeant Elmer Cotton, 5th Bn Northumberland Fusiliers, had arrived at the front through this same 'terrible place' and found it a sobering introduction to the harshness of war.

By the time we arrived at the outskirts of Ypres the traffic of ammunition and ambulance wagons had ceased and we were alone on the road. The only noise we heard was the echo of our own steps and the occasional roar of a gun or a bursting shell. Suddenly we came across a corpse lying across the pavement and the gutter—it was the body of a peasant—his bundle was lying some yards away having been precipitated forward when he fell. Just over the canal bridge a timber wagon and two shattered horses came into view and we walked through the blood of these noble animals as we passed them on the road. We were now in the town proper—everywhere nothing but ruins could be seen—not a house but was either shattered by shells or gutted with fire. Many walls leaned at dangerous angles into the streets and in the dim light of night each ruin seemed to me to represent the work of some grinning demon who was lurking in hiding behind these ghostly houses. On our way we passed more dead horses, which in many cases were in a state of decomposition and emitted a fearful odour of rottenness.

It was in this setting that Cotton's battalion had their first taste of war—a random German shell.

My back and pack were struck by a shower of debris and flying dirt while quite a number of men fell and bled for their country. Jack Duncan was in front of me and he received a severe wound from this, our first shell. He was carried onto the pavement and left for the attention of the doctor.

Tommy had arrived at his war.

* Ypres is actually in Belgium.

5   'In the Trenches'

The Western Front at night: star shells are being fired to illuminate No Man's Land—each side being anxious to know what the other was doing under the cover of darkness. Many soldiers, like Lieutenant Lillywhite, commented on these 'free firework displays' provided during the night hours. The front had its uncanny beauty at such times. This picture was taken during the second night of the Battle of the Somme, near Beaumont Hamel, in July 1916.

My dear Mother,

I am writing this in the trenches. I came up last night after travelling and messing about Belgium for 12 hours. I am surprised to find how quiet it is here. Except for sniping there is nothing doing.

We are in good trenches and hold a good position. It was a fine sight coming up last night to see all along the line as far as you could star shells going up. It was like a firework display.

I was surprised to find that far from being in a funk as I expected I did not mind coming up at all. It is not at all bad here because there are plenty of funk holes if the Bosche gets really nasty.

So Second Lieutenant Geoffrey Lillywhite, 9th Bn East Surrey Regt, described his introduction to the front line in May 1916, having at last won the right to say that he was 'in the trenches'. Private Jack Sweeney, 1st Bn Lincolnshire Regt, achieved that distinction as early as November 1914.

Well, dad, I have been in the trenches from last Friday until Tuesday and would have enjoyed it very much only for the Rain which made us look like Mudlarks. We had a few narrow escapes—last Sunday the Germans sent us a few presents from the Kaiser, they were Shrapnel Shells or as we call them Jack Johnsons,* they came very near our trenches but never hurt anybody, and the boys were laughing every time one Bursted, there seems to be no Fear in the old Lincolns. No one seems to Realize it is Active Service.

P.S. We get a nice Drop of Rum every day.

'The trenches'—there can be little doubt that that phrase was the most emotive to emerge from the vocabulary of the Great War. For the generation of 1914–18—as indeed for every generation since—the words had and have a unique ring. To have been 'in the trenches' put a permanent mark on a man: he had been admitted to a special, private world, the reality of which, as many were aware at the time, could only be fully understood by those who had been part of it. Men outside that fellowship longed and feared to join it; those inside it tended to 'buck' to their less favoured

---

* A Jack Johnson was a heavy shell that gave off a considerable amount of black smoke—named after a famous Negro pugilist.

comrades about their experiences within it. Private W. T. Colyer expressed the typical reaction of the newly arrived soldier awaiting his blooding: 'Since being here have listened to at least 158 ghastly stories of the firing line from chaps who have just come from it. Want to go home!'

But there was no mistaking the fascination of that now-so-near Western Front: of his billet near St Omer into which he and his fellow Artists' Rifles were moved on their way 'up the line', the same man wrote: 'It had been occupied by French *poilus* [French infantrymen] who had left two days before for the trenches; and such was the magic glory of that word "trenches" that we were proud to occupy their beds.'

The phrase 'the trenches', in fact, covered a unique reality. The war of brisk and spectacular movement, as envisaged at the outset in August 1914, lasted only a matter of weeks. As early as mid September the order to 'entrench' was given by the French Commander-in-Chief, Joffre, and by the winter of 1914–15 a continuous line of trenches ran some 450 miles across Europe from the Belgian coast to the frontier

'Funk-holes' in the line (above) and (opposite) billets behind the line. The men in the funk-holes are soldiers of the Border Regiment in Thiepval Wood, on the Somme, in 1916. The soldiers in the ruined barn are Canadians at Villers au Bois in 1917.

'We were accommodated in farmhouse buildings and I was appalled to find that the French farmer took the handle off the pump, so that we could not obtain water. Consequently sixteen of us had to wash out of one bucket.'

Private Thomas Bickerton, 3rd Bn Royal Sussex Regt

of Switzerland. There had been trench fighting in other wars, notably the American Civil War, but nothing on this scale. As Churchill wrote: 'All the wars of the world could show nothing to compare with the continuous front which had now been established. ... It was certain that frontal attacks unaccompanied by turning movements on the flank would be extremely costly and would probably fail. But now, in France and Flanders for the first time in recorded experience there were no flanks to turn. ... Neutral territory or salt water barred all further extension of the Front, and the great armies lay glaring at each other at close quarters without any true idea of what to do next.'*

For four years the trenches were to remain more or less along the line established in those first traumatic months. Salients would be pinched out here and there; the 'Big Pushes' of 1916 and 1917 would throw the Germans back over a few miles of snarled up countryside; the Germans would retaliate in kind in March 1918; occasionally the German commanders would alter the geography of the front by retiring to better positions (notably on the Somme in early 1917)—but for the most part the line drawn with astonishing swiftness in the autumn of 1914 held until the final breakthrough in the summer of 1918. When Sergeant F. W. Billman, 9th Bn East Surrey Regt, noted in his diary in the Loos salient on 25 October 1916 'Here exactly thirteen months after, we are holding trenches on the same ground that we fought on, on the memorable 25th and 26th September 1915' he was chronicling a by no means extraordinary experience. The front had its perpetual shifts and spasms, but the same names—the same towns, villages, hills, woods, rivers, streams—occurred again and again in the story. The war in the west in fact resolved itself into a static, apparently interminable slogging-match, the essential element of which was (to quote Churchill once again) 'ramparts [hundreds of] miles long, ceaselessly guarded by millions of men, sustained by thousands of cannon'.

'The trenches', therefore, became the classic experience of this war and the classic location. Many of the most famous paintings, poems, novels and plays which it produced were set, inevitably, in or around the trenches. Whenever people in Britain—or people of the other major western combatants for that matter: France, Germany, the United States—think of the world conflict of 1914–18, they think first and foremost of the trenches of the Western Front.

The system favoured by the British consisted of three lines of trenches: front line, support and reserve. Barbed wire entanglements lay between the front-line trenches and No Man's Land; on the other side of No Man's Land, which might be anything from twenty-five yards to half a mile (the average was 250 yards), was the enemy, behind his own wire and bedded down in his own particular trench system. Communication trenches, roughly at right angles to the three basic lines, linked them together and led back to the safer areas behind. Trenches were built in zig-zags to reduce the

* Winston S. Churchill, *The World Crisis 1911–18*, Chapter XVIII, 'The Deadlock in the West'.

effect of shell-fire. Here and there little trench extensions ran out, for snipers, for example, or more humbly, for latrines. Dug-outs were normally (though by no means exclusively) for officers or senior NCOs: ordinary soldiers often had to make do as best they could—in funk-holes (holes carved out of the side of the trench) or under waterproof sheets. The Germans built splendid dug-outs for their soldiers, but then they intended to stay where they were, whereas the British intention was to shift them out and send them packing. Comfortable quarters, which might encourage the Tommy to settle down and 'live and let live', were therefore not encouraged.

An infantry battalion permutated through three basic locations: in the line, that is, in the front and support trenches; in billets (usually some ruined village or farm just behind the line) where they would act as local reserves; or in a rest camp clear of the fighting zone. A typical pattern would be a fortnight spent commuting between the line and the billets, followed by six days out at rest. Relief of battalions in the line was always carried out at night; in fact, most activities at the front were, for obvious reasons, nocturnal.

The artillery was ranged behind the trenches: their task, very broadly, was to pound the enemy lines with shrapnel and high explosive and, ultimately, to prepare the way for the advance of the infantry. They worked in close collaboration with the infantry: their Forward Observation Officers and signallers (the latter endlessly paying out their bales of telephone wire) were always to be seen in the front line trenches.

Life in the line was not one of constant furious activity: far more often than not it consisted of the dreary round of trench routine. There were 'cushy' trenches and quiet times as well as appalling conditions and moments of 'hell let loose'. Even so on average a British battalion (roughly a thousand strong) lost about thirty men a month through death, wounds and sickness. In big set-piece battles, of course, battalions could and frequently did, suffer virtual annihilation.

The Grimsby Chums, the 10th Bn Lincolnshire Regt, had their first taste of trench life near Armentières in February 1916. Major Walter Vignoles wrote a full account of it in a letter home. Like Second Lieutenant Lillywhite and Private Sweeney, he found his first spell of real warfare more agreeable than it might have been.

> It has been quite an interesting experience and our men were very bucked and quite enjoyed it, and I must say I did too. The trenches were on the whole in very good condition and there are wooden footboards practically everywhere, and with the dry weather too, it was really quite comfortable. One could not QUITE get a bath! as of course everything has to be carried up to the trenches by hand, but apart from that one could carry on, at least the officers could, very nearly as well as in camp, with the one exception that one has to sleep in one's clothes. We had a very quiet time, and I will say that the Boche behaved in a very gentlemanly-like manner while we were in, and did not give any shells nor any of his fancy contrivances, only rifle and machine gun fire. One has to look after the top of one's head, as they

Aspects of Trench Warfare

A scene in the trenches opposite Messines near Ploegsteert ('Plugstreet') Wood, January 1917. The soldiers are Lancashire Fusiliers; the sentry is looking through a box periscope.

Latrines

The sanitary arrangements usually consisted of a pit, or series of pits, perhaps approached by a short trench and equipped with buckets or large biscuit tins which were emptied at night by the company 'pioneer'. The whole place was liberally treated with chloride of lime which provided a never-to-be-forgotten smell associated with trench life.

Private Harold Horne, 6th Bn Northumberland Fusiliers

Latrines were always dangerous places because of the regularity with which they had to be used. Jerry soon came to spot such places, and, believe me, they were not places in which to linger.

Private Archie Surfleet, 13th Bn East Yorkshire Regt

A First Visit to the Firing Line

Yesterday afternoon I went right up into the front line fire trenches and walked along for nearly a mile. They are most beautifully made in this part of the line and are fortunately quite dry just now. I looked through the periscope at the Boche front line trenches, which in places were quite close, and saw our shells bursting above them. I hadn't been right up into the fire trenches before and it was all most interesting to me. I was very careful darling, and went up with an officer who knew the ropes and at the time of day when there is not usually much 'strafing' going on ...

From a letter of April 1916 written by Captain Rice-Oxley,
2/1 Field Ambulance, 56th London Division

The trenches from the air. In this photograph, taken on 15 July 1915 west of Auchy-lez-la-Bassee, the British trenches are bottom left, the German trenches top right and No Man's Land is the white zone in the centre. The strange pustules in the ground in the bottom right of the picture are mine craters. The zig-zag patterning of the trenches can be clearly seen. The German trench system appears to be more elaborately and systematically constructed than the British—as was usually the case.

'Only God and the Royal Flying Corps saw the trenches properly in daylight. As for the infantry, in the daytime one was *in* them, and one went up to them, as a relieving unit taking over, or as working party, by night.'
Lieutenant H. E. L. Mellersh, 2nd Bn East Lancashire Regt

These photographs—never previously published—show with remarkable clarity and precision of detail what trenches were like in the early days of the 'Western Front'. They were taken (contrary to regulations, though these were regulations that, to the great benefit of posterity, were occasionally ignored) on the camera of a young Lieutenant of the Royal Field Artillery, Cyril Drummond. Now Brigadier Drummond, Retd, he has kindly allowed some of his photographs to be used in this book and has supplied the accompanying information.

▲ November 1914. Royal Dublin Fusiliers' trench at St Yvon (Ypres Salient). 'It must be realized' writes Brigadier Drummond, 'that they had only been dug a few weeks before and there had been little opportunity to make them better. The soldier in the trench is looking through a periscope. Rum jars are prominent ornaments.'

◀ January 1915. Making the tea in the front line at St Yvon. Brigadier Drummond adds: 'It will be seen that by now the trench has been made much more presentable with the aid of sandbags. I think much of it was done during the Christmas Truce, during which both sides worked upon their trenches undisturbed.'

Good Trenches . . .

At Ypres the trenches we were in from time to time were very poor; in some cases they had only been in existence a day or two and only resembled scratches in the ground. At Neuve Eglise and Armentières the trenches were splendid: they had been in existence for nearly a year, were very thick and deep, had lateral trenches running the full length in the rear, plenty of dugouts, and good communication trenches which made it possible to leave during the day and return to billets in the town. These trenches had trench boards to walk on, fire platforms to stand on, drains and sumps with pumps, shelters for lookouts with rifle racks, rubbish shoots, gas alarms, rifle batteries, loop-holes, periscopes, etc., and war could be carried on in a comparatively safe manner. Dug-outs, like trenches, varied considerably. At Ypres they were mainly holes in the ground and no cover. At Armentières they were all shell splinterproof and, in some cases the officers' dug-outs were like little dwelling houses, fitted with beds, tables, chairs, pictures and stove.

From the 1915 Notebook of Sgt E. W. Cotton

and Bad Trenches . . .

We moved forward to the site which had once been the village of Rochincourt, a most hopelessly forsaken hole without a single house standing. Real devastation! Billeted in trenches, and such trenches! Many French and Germans (and a few British) buried around here and the whole area is a veritable rabbit warren of trenches and old dug-outs in which we lived when not on working parties up the line. The top step of our particular stink-hole consisted of a kind of soft bagging which, when wet with rain, exuded a red fluid which trickled down the steps. We found it better to ignore it, for conjectures are not pleasant when you come across more than one poor soul buried in sand-bagging and forming part of the trench side, as we did in that area. To dig around about was most unpleasant. Poor devils: used even after death.

From the diary of Private Archie Surfleet

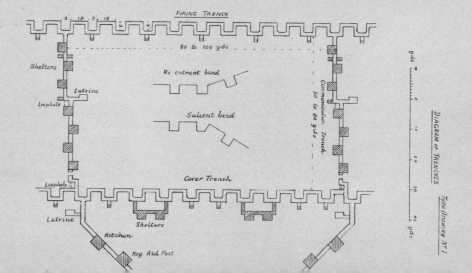

Trench warfare soon became a systematized science, as this diagram shows. Even dug-outs and latrines had to be built according to textbook patterns.

are very expert at making the bullets skim the top of the parapet, but THEY DID NOT HIT ANYONE IN MY COMPANY.

The snipers are always busy, but they do not hit what they aim at by a long way. It is queer to hear the bullets snapping overhead, but usually there is no danger, as one is behind thick parapets or in dug-outs. They say 'every bullet has its billet'—that is true, but it is nearly always in Mother Earth.

In the daytime there is not much firing, but as it begins to get dusk, the men start to fire over the parapet, a few shots at a time; this is usually kept up during the night, sometimes it dies away, and then we suspect the Boche is working in front of his parapets, or up to some mischief!

While the rifle fire keeps spluttering away quietly, a machine gun suddenly opens—'rat-tat-tat' and the bullets come snapping overhead or 'tap-tap-tap' against the parapet, and we try hard to see from whence the gun is firing. We see the flashes and take a compass bearing so as to be able to look at the place next day, and if it is located ask the guns to knock it out.

In a letter written after a further spell in the line, Major Vignoles describes the basic pattern of trench routine.

At dawn we 'stand to arms', every one turning out. When it is light, all rifles are cleaned and inspected, and the men have a tot of rum. Then breakfast, after which I let them turn in to sleep till dinner, with the exception of the day sentries, just a few men watching the enemy's line through periscopes. After dinner the men turn out for work in repairing periscopes, etc., and put in about three hours at that.

We 'stand to' again at dusk. After dark, we have to get over the parapet to do any repairs that may be required to the wire entanglements, or repairs to the front of the parapet. In the salient here there is a good deal of work to be done, and there are several places where the trenches are old and broken, from whence one can peep at the enemy; we filled and put in position nearly 4000 sandbags while we were in the trenches.

Conditions were not quite so 'cushy' as on their previous spell in the line, because of some very bad weather, with snow falling on the first of their four nights in the line and lying about afterwards. Major Vignoles felt particularly sorry for the 'poor fellows on sentry go'.

We have a certain number of sentry groups on duty in the front line trench; each group consists of six men, two keeping watch while the others sit on the firestep, trying to sleep or walking about trying to keep warm.

The two on the look-out change every hour so that each man has one hour on and two off. It is not so bad in warm weather, but rotten in winter or in snowy weather, as they are not allowed to go into their dug-outs during their time off, the reason being that they are so tired that once asleep in a dug-out it would probably be impossible for the other men to wake them in case of an attack. The Boche might get into the trench in a surprise rush

and they would very likely be killed in their sleep in their dug-outs. That is what has happened to the Boche in some of OUR raids.

For some men trench life soon became a routine like any other. Sergeant F. W. Billman, 9th Bn East Surrey Regt, wrote in his diary in June 1916 after almost ten months in France: 'After six days out at rest we came back into Brigade reserve for six more and then up into the line again. It gets just like going to an ordinary day's work.' But the Western Front was in fact a very extraordinary place with the perpetual hazard even in the quiet times of death or maiming from a sniper's bullet or a sudden stray shell. Billman himself was very much aware of such dangers, because of an incident of which he had been an exceptionally fortunate witness on Good Friday 1916:

> I had a very narrow escape from death, by a shrapnel shell bursting over me, while talking to three other chaps in the trench. One of these was killed outright, and the other two were very badly wounded, and I was left standing there, untouched. It was the only shell that came over that part of the line that day and as long as I live to see 'Good Fridays' I shall remember that. Such a thing as that is not reported in the papers each day, while the official news says, 'All quiet on the Western Front'.

Lance Sergeant Elmer Cotton, 5th Bn Northumberland Fusiliers, recorded a similar event at Zillebeke behind Hill 60 in May 1915.

> Imagine a bright May morning and a platoon (about 55 men) busily engaged in washing, cleaning up, cooking and some sleeping. Suddenly a tremendous explosion, a deathly stillness as if all were paralysed, then fearful screams and groans and death gasps. What had happened? A high explosive German shell had fallen right into a wide part of the trench where many men had been. The sight of the wounded shedding their blood from gaping wounds and their agonized cries—one asking to be shot—would have convinced any humane man that war is an impossible way of settling national questions— or *it will be* in the near future. It was on May 2nd that this incident took place and this single high explosive shell *killed 7* and *wounded 18*—yet the day before 400 shells came over and dropped immediately behind this trench within 10 yards and no one was hurt—but this one shell bursting right in the trench accounted for a *total of 25 men*. The trench after the dead and wounded were removed presented a ghastly sight—it was red with blood like a room papered in crimson while equipment lay everywhere.

6

'Rats as Big as Rabbits'

What soldiers in the trenches were always subject to: the sudden arrival of an enemy shell.

Private Kenneth Garry, of the Honourable Artillery Company, wrote a jaunty account of his first experience of the trenches to his 'Dearest Mother' in January 1916. Like all infantrymen* he went into the line fully loaded.

> We had two days' rations to take, and the 150 rounds of ammunition we always carry. I only took an extra pair of socks, but I wished before I got back that I had taken three extra pairs. We wore our great coats, with full equipment on top of this. Our mack we put on top of the pack. Our water bottle was full and of course we carried our mess tin, also mug and cutlery. The one blanket we were allowed to take was rolled in the ground sheet, and slung like a horse collar round our necks. I carried in addition my pocket primus, and a tin of paraffin, two small tins of Heinz baked beans, vaseline (three tubes, one each of pure white, capsicum and carbolated), a Tommy's cooker and a tin of re-fill; a pair of gloves, mittens and a muffler (in my great-coat pocket). Beside this, we carried our rifle. I wish you could have seen us. We looked like animated old clothes shops.

As behind the line, so in the line the inevitable basic means of transportation was Tommy's feet. Mule-drawn limbers or pack-mules would bring the necessities of trench life to a dump some distance behind the front, but from that point forward everything—equipment, guns, ammunition, sandbags, screw-pickets, barbed wire, duck-boards, food, water—had to be carried by manpower and invariably in the dark.

Major Vignoles of the Grimsby Chums expressed in a letter home his sympathy for the hard lot of the ordinary soldier:

> The men are very fit on the whole but they have a rough time going in and leaving the trenches, carrying heavy loads, slipping and scrambling about, and, I am sorry to say, cursing as a rule in a language that would make a bargee turn pale with envy, but it doesn't mean anything! No 'arm!

Feeding the troops in the trenches was never an easy problem, though like all other aspects of service life it had its regular routines, as Private Harold Horne, 6th Bn Northumberland Fusiliers, recalls:

* The Honourable Artillery Company was a Territorial Regiment which consisted of two artillery batteries and one infantry battalion. Garry was a member of the infantry battalion. He was later commissioned in the 13th Bn Northumberland Fusiliers. He died of wounds in June 1917.

Infantry marching order. Going into battle infantrymen normally carried over 60 pounds of equipment, including such items as picks, shovels, wire cutters and, of course, bombs.

Extract from the 1915 Notebook of Elmer Wilfred Cotton, Private, Lance Sergeant and Sergeant of the 5th Battalion Northumberland Fusiliers:

WHAT AN INFANTRY SOLDIER CARRIES:

On his body:

1 pair of boots
1 pair of braces
1 service cap
1 pair drawers
1 pair service trousers
1 pair puttees
1 service jacket
1 field dressing
1 service pay book
1 identity disc
1 clasp knife
1 shirt
1 vest (in winter only)
1 pair socks
pouches, basic equipment and belt
2 smoke helmets
1 iodine in bottle
1 waterproof sheet
1 cardigan jacket or waistcoat (in winter)
1 mess tin and cover
1 rifle and sling
1 oil bottle
1 pull through
1 bayonet and scabbard
1 entrenching tool head
1 entrenching tool helme
1 entrenching tool carrier
1 water bottle filled with water
1 haversack
1 valise & supporting straps
150 rounds ·303 cartridges

Infantryman in marching order (his ammunition is not in webbing pouches as in the display opposite but in leather ones).

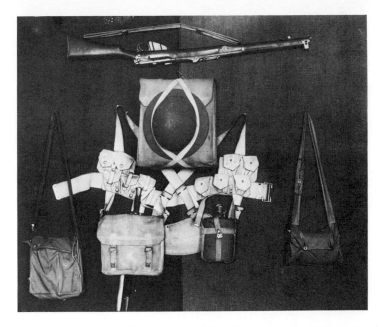

In Valise:

1 cap comforter
1 *holdall* containing
   1 hussif
   1 tooth brush
   1 razor
   1 comb
   1 shaving soap
   1 pair spare braces
   1 piece soap
2 pairs socks
1 shirt
1 towel
1 pair drawers
1 vest (in winter only)
1 greatcoat
1 blanket (in winter)

In Haversack:

1 table knife
1 table fork
1 dessert spoon
1 tin bully beef   ⎫ Emergency
1 tin tea and sugar ⎬ Rations known
1 lot of biscuits   ⎭ as Iron
                   Rations

'The amount of kit & equipment carried by an infantryman makes up an almost impossible weight. It proves a terrible burden on the march, the shoulders and back ache severely; a route march being thus made into a most torturous operation ...'

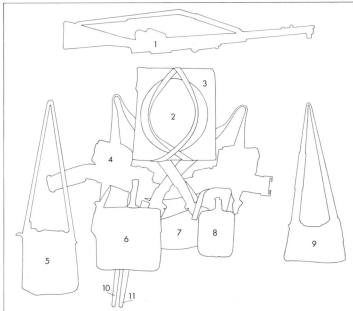

1 Short Muzzled Lee-Enfield Rifle	7 Entrenching Tool, Head Container
2 Tin Hat	8 Water Bottle
3 Large Pack	9 Gas Helmet
4 Webbing with Ammunition Pouches	10 Entrenching Tool Handle
5 Small Box Respirator	11 Bayonet
6 Haversack (or Small Pack)	

Ration parties from each company in the line went to carry back the rations which were tied in sandbags and consisted, usually, of bread, hard biscuits, tinned meat ('bully') in 12 oz. tins, tinned jam (Tommy Ticklers plum and apple), tinned butter, sugar and tea, pork and beans (baked beans with a piece of pork fat on top), cigarettes and tobacco.

Sometimes we got 'Maconochie Rations'. This was a sort of Irish stew in tins which could be quickly heated over a charcoal brazier. This was quite good at first but one got satiated before long.

When it was possible to have a cookhouse within easy reach of trenches fresh meat, bacon, vegetables, flour, etc. would be sent up and the cooks could produce reasonably good meals and food and tea was sent along the trenches in 'dixies' (large iron containers the lid of which could be used as a frying pan). In 1916 large containers on the thermos principle, which could be carried on the back, appeared in which the hot tea or stew could be carried up to the trenches from Battalion rear HQ where the cooks could work under better conditions.

In winter there was a ration of rum, one or two tablespoons per man; this was a strong, black spirit which was usually issued during the morning 'stand-to'; it was very welcome on a cold winter's morning. It was supplied in a 'grey hen', a heavy earthenware jar marked SRD (translated as Service Rum Department).

In summer there was a ration of neat lime juice supplied in the same kind of jar. There were reports that some unfortunate unit had received this in winter in mistake for rum, nearly causing a mutiny.

Water was sent up the line in petrol cans. We were not supposed to use untreated water so each battalion had water carts and the medical officer was responsible for ensuring that it was chlorinated before use.

Food in the trenches had an eternal sameness about it. And with the limited means of cooking that were available, the taste of one meal became an immediately identifiable ingredient in the next. As Private W. Carson Catron, of the Hull Commercials, put it, his principal memory of trench food was of 'the monotony of bully beef and biscuits, and plum and apple jam and biscuits, washed down with tea flavoured from the previous meal, cooked in the same container as the water was boiled, onion being predominant'.

The soldier was not likely to starve, for if the worst came to the worst he could always fall back on his iron rations. These, however, were only to be eaten *in extremis:* when Tom Macdonald, 9th Bn Royal Sussex Regt, asked his officer 'when do we eat our iron rations?' he received the following memorable reply: 'You don't eat your Iron Rations until your belly button hits your back bone and your hip bones show out of your trousers!'

In the circumstances, there was inevitably much reliance on parcels sent from home. One of the supreme privileges of service on the Western Front, as opposed to such other foreign fields as Salonika, Italy or the Middle East, was that mail, post and   78

LIST OF ARMY RATIONS
1 Man Per Diem

Meat (bully beef)	1 lb
Bread (or Biscuits)	1¼ lb
Bacon	¼ lb
Tea	½ oz
Sugar	2 ozs
Jam	2 ozs
Cheese	1 oz
Butter	¾ oz
Potatoes (+Vegetables=1 lb)	¾ lb
Salt	1 oz
Pepper	1/36 oz
Mustard	1/20 oz

From Elmer Cotton's 1915 Notebook

Serving out stew to men of the Lancashire Fusiliers in a front-line trench opposite Messines, in the Ypres Salient, in March 1917. Front-line fare was, inevitably, the butt of much humour and criticism, but there were times—after an action or the failure of a ration party to get through or in foul weather—when it could seem the food of the gods. Perhaps the classic statement is Sydney Rogerson's in *Twelve Days*: 'Did not a mess-tin of stew or a tot of rum, or whisky and water in a tin mug taste more like divine nectar than the best champagne drunk out of the finest cut glass?'

parcels came very quickly to the soldier in the trenches. It was possible to ask and receive within days.

> If you can manage it occasionally cakes and sweets (cheap ones of the hard nature) would be quite welcome for the little dug-out mess. They would have to be packed securely though because they come by a rough road.
> *Second Lieutenant Geoffrey Lillywhite, 9th Bn East Surrey Regt*

> I have got a cardboard box with extra food, which I am husbanding very carefully. I have got some Bivouac cocoa and beef-tea squares, which are excellent and really invaluable. Will you send out a lot more of both as soon as possible? Even if I don't want them, the men would be delighted to have them, as they haven't got any extra delicacies.
> *Second Lieutenant Arthur Gibbs, 1st Bn Welsh Guards*

Lieutenant Gibb's last statement was perhaps a shade sweeping: parcels were by no means exclusive to officers.

> On June 20th we were working all night taking ammunition to the guns and the next day, being my 21st birthday, I slept all day, as we were to go

One of the highlights of Western Front life: the arrivals of parcels and post from home.

> ... I have been very lucky in the way of letters and parcels—folks seem to be taking a new interest in me since I left for the front.
> *Private Peter McGregor, 14th Bn Argyle & Sutherland Highlanders*

out again the following night. Somebody woke me up about midday and handed me a parcel from home; I opened it and found it contained cakes, which I shared out amongst the others, who wished me many happy returns of the day, then I went to sleep again.

Driver R. L. Venables, Royal Field Artillery

This is a red letter day. My parcel came this morning with a tin of peaches, loaf and butter, fish paste, tobacco, sleeping helmet, chocolate, a pair of socks and a towel. Had peaches for sweet at dinner and fish paste for tea. *Grand.*
Private Frank Bass, 9th Bn Norfolk Regt

If you are sending any eatables amongst yourselves, you might put in some tooth powder as I have not cleaned my teeth for 3 weeks, also should like some of your jam if you have any as it makes the hard biscuits eat better, especially on Sundays.

Private A. H. Hubbard, London Scottish

It is, of course, undeniable that officers fared better, particularly those with the right social connections. Second Lieutenant Cyril Rawlins, 1st Bn Welsh Regt, listed in a letter home some of the delicacies which had enriched his life at the front: 'Fortnum & Mason's Fresh Cod Roes and Preserved Ham, Chicken in Jelly, Whole Roast Pheasant, various soups: very rich Turtle Soup last night when I returned with the convoy at midnight.' And any officer, supplied with loving and generous relations or not, was likely to fare particularly well at the high seasons of the years. On Monday 25 December 1916, Captain Harry Yoxall, 18th Bn King's Royal Rifle Corps, noted in his diary:

At seven-thirty we had our Christmas dinner. The Menu was as follows:

Tomato Soup

Curried Prawns

Roast Turkey & Sausages
Roast & Mashed Potatoes

Christmas Pudding   Minced Pies
Devonshire Cream   Rum Butter

Scotch Woodcock on Toast

Cheese   Caviare

Apples   Oranges   Tangerines   Almonds & Raisins   Nuts
Candied Fruit   Chocolate

Coffee
Veuve Cliquot 1906
Whiskey   Rum
Port
Liqueur Brandy 1891
Rum Punch

Christmas dinner—presumably with a somewhat less extensive menu than that described—being served in a shell hole at Beaumont Hamel, 25 December 1916.

> With crackers and everything. Oh! to be in service now the food controller's here. Three courses only for soldiers in Blighty. But I'd give a good deal to be in Blighty all the same. Lord, how I'm getting weary of this war.

By contrast, an ordinary soldier might be lucky to receive a very modest reminder of the arrival of the Christmas season, Corporal James Brown Gingell, Royal Engineers, for example:

> Xmas Day, day off. Not much to do, we only had our ordinary rations with the exception of a bit of Xmas pudding.

At a previous Christmas, however, he had been able to put a happier note in his diary:

> 25/12. Day off we had a good feed and a decent concert at night.

Such gargantuan meals as those referred to by Captain Yoxall were not easy to prepare in the conditions of the trenches. Private Jack Sweeney, 1st Bn Lincolnshire Regt, was for much of his time on the Western Front an officers' cook: the picture he paints shows the other side of this glittering coin.

My luck is in—I have the employment of officers cook again but it is not such a nice time as I had before as I have to go into the trenches and cook for them there, but it is better than doing sentry duty. It is very hard cooking on an old pail with coke, and the officers expect five course dinners just the same—well I do my best for them and I have suited them very well up to now.

His officers, however, made no allowance for conditions, which, particularly in winter, were often atrocious.

Last time we were going into the trenches I had a terrible lot of goods to carry—all the tinned food the officers buy and I could hardly manage the lot but I had to get there somehow. There was myself and four other officers servants, and it was so dark we could not see our hands before us. We were going along a communication trench known as 'Lovers Walk'—I can hardly tell you for laughing but I did not laugh when I went into the water—it covered me and I lost the bag of food, but my mates managed to get me out. I did swear, my Word, I called Fritz everything. Afterwards we went on and then two of my mates fell in. It was a game and also a very cold bath. I arrived in the firing trench at last, then the officers wanted their dinner cooked. They saw the state I was in and only laughed—my face was all mud and I had lost my cap. I was in a state: it is a good job I am used to it.

Private Sweeney's expertise as a cook was also appreciated by his comrades. His letter continues:

I have a nice dug-out where I cook and after the officers have had their dinner I let as many of the boys who are not on duty come in and have a warm and I make them a drop of hot tea, the officers get plenty of food, they waste a lot but the boys are glad to eat all they leave. The boys are so happy when they can have a warm and makes me feel happy to be able to give them a little comfort—you should see the steam rising off their clothing it is the only way they can get their clothes dry.

Every army, as Napoleon said, marches on its stomach. When an army is not marching, but standing still in holes in the ground, it is likely to have obsessions about other things than the source of its next meal: for example about the weather. In fine, dry conditions life could be tolerable, but the Western Front was particularly vulnerable to the depradations of the rain. Rain damped spirits as well as uniforms. It soaked men to the skin in circumstances in which it was virtually impossible to dry out. It helped to induce that painful condition from which so many men suffered known as 'trench feet'. It was so disagreeable a component of trench life that it seemed to be always there.

A flooded dug-out in a front-line trench occupied by Lancashire Fusiliers opposite Messines, near Ploegsteert Wood, March 1917. It was conditions such as these that gave rise to 'trench feet'. Sergeant Harry Roberts, RAMC, spent six days and nights holding a flooded 'strategic' front-line trench before the opening of the Somme offensive and came out with 'trench feet'. This is his description of that painful condition:

> If you have never had trench feet described to you, I will tell you. Your feet swell to two or three times their normal size and go completely dead. You could stick a bayonet into them and not feel a thing. If you are fortunate enough not to lose your feet and the swelling begins to go down, it is then that the intolerable, indescribable agony begins. I have heard men cry and even scream with the pain and many had to have their feet and legs amputated. I was one of the lucky ones but one more day in that trench and it may have been too late.

An Australian officer wading through the mud at Gueudecourt, on the Somme front, December 1916. Winter conditions could be not only dispiriting but exhausting as well. In December 1916, in the same sector of the front, Lieutenant Arthur Gibbs, 1st Bn Welsh Guards, wrote in a letter home: 'It would make you cry to see the state the men are in when we come home out of the line. There are men from many regiments sitting or lying in the mud and crying like babies because they can't move any further. They are absolutely beat to the world. They must have 20 or 30 lbs of mud on them.'

Private Kenneth Garry wrote to his mother in January 1916, in the account quoted at the beginning of this chapter: 'It need not be said that it was raining; in fact it will save a lot of time in this chronicle if you assume that it is always raining except when otherwise stated.'

Captain Harry Yoxall, writing home in January 1917, put the same point with the aid of Shakespeare:

Dearest Mater,
    With a hey-ho, the wind and the rain,
      The rain it raineth every day
Except when it's snowing!

But it was what rain did to the surface of the land and to the trench system that made it such a key participant in this stalemate war. It turned battlefields into quagmires and even firmly constructed trenches into alleyways of slippery, treacherous mud. In some places on the front men compared the mud it produced to caramel; in others it laced the terrain of the battle zones with muddy lakes and pools into which it was all too easy for men and horses to slide and fall. Once in, it was almost impossible to get out unaided; and many men lost their lives in the mud of the Western Front. It was a pathetic way to fall for one's country.

Private Tom Macdonald was in the Ypres Salient in early 1916.

The Salient in winter was like Dante's Inferno. Shell holes full of slime, mud everywhere. Many men were wounded and trying to get back to Dressing Stations slipped in holes and were drowned. The Menin Road up to the Salient from Ypres they reckon claimed 900 a month.

The trenches in the chalk uplands of the Somme survived better than those in low-lying Belgium, but even here conditions could be all but impossible after rain.

We left those Mericourt trenches yesterday. It was a pretty wood but the trenches were very wet in the rain and crumbled in a good deal—in fact in the relief two men had to be dragged out of the slush by force from above, so hopelessly did they get stuck up to their thighs in sucking sloppy mud.
Second Lieutenant Kenneth Macardle, 17th Bn Manchester Regt

There was something about the rain of this part of north-west Europe that seemed to give it a special malignance. Lance Corporal Roland Mountfort, 10th Bn Royal Fusiliers, described in a letter home a spell in new trenches in February 1916.

The weather kept fine for a day and then broke. It rained for two nights and on the third, between 3 and 6 a.m. it surpassed itself. It blew great guns, it snowed till the wet ground was covered 3 ins deep; it rained again and washed it away; sleet fell and froze as it fell; it rained again and washed *that* away. In the morning the trenches fell about our ears.

At the end of four days they relieved us and we waded out knee deep

Christmas Day on the Somme, 1916.

It was of the mud of the Somme that Sydney Rogerson wrote, in his classic war-book *Twelve Days*, that it became 'the arbiter of destiny, the supreme enemy, paralysing and mocking English and German alike. Distances were measured not in yards but in mud.'

The picture is also a reminder that more transport in the Great War was drawn by horses than by vehicles, and that horses and pack-mules were as vulnerable as men. Official figures state that 484,143 animals were killed or died serving the British forces in the war. Many men found the sacrifice of animals unbearable. In October 1916 Captain Harry Yoxall wrote in a letter home about 'a heart-breaking horse I saw lying wounded near High Wood. It seems such a shame to drag animals into the mess we've made of things.'

as of old. We struggled out somehow and crawled to a village about three miles back, the rain still coming down in BUCKETSFULL.

Perhaps not surprisingly Roland Mountfort's letter began with the statement: 'I don't like writing other than cheerful letters, but If I could compose one now I should be one of the most deserving VC heroes of the war.'

> It has been raining here every day this week which makes things very uncomfortable, heaps of mud and lice including rats of course, but getting quite used to same now, my skin is quite raw owing to keeping on rubbing myself, haven't had a chance of getting water to wash a shirt out but hope to do something towards comfort tomorrow.

So wrote Private A. H. Hubbard, London Scottish, from the Somme front in May 1916, putting into one sentence all the major natural scourges of trench life. Lice and rats became an inevitable, unforgettable component of service in the line. Almost everyone was lousy. As one subaltern, Second Lieutenant James Dale, 2nd Bn Liverpool Scottish Regt, put it: 'I have become a base depot for sundry lesser fauna who crawl and bite.'

Lice—or 'chats', as they were often called— got into clothes and once there were virtually immovable. Men ran lighted matches up the seams of shirts and enjoyed the crackle of incinerated livestock, but this, though it afforded sweet revenge, was only a temporary sweeping back of the tide.

> If you're nearly frozen, they keep quiet; as soon as you warm up those blasted lice start to bite like the devil. It's horrible. I often think it is one of the worst things we have to endure out here.   *Private Archie Surfleet*

> I had a lice hunt this forenoon and oh my I caught thousands—quite big fat ones—and wee fellows—they get into the folds of your kilt, down the seams of your shirt—the devils, how they get there I don't know—nothing kills them—powders etc. have no effect—the only way is to heave a few Rum Jars at them.*
> *Private Peter McGregor, 14th Bn Argyle and Sutherland Highlanders*

And then there were the rats.

> There are millions!! Some are huge fellows, nearly as big as cats. Several of our men were awakened to find a rat snuggling down under the blanket alongside them!   *Major Walter Vignoles*

> There are the greatest old rats in the trenches that you ever saw. They are so tame they won't run away but just toddle along in front of you just out of reach. One of our men went up to one the other day and kicked it like a football.   *Second Lieutenant Geoffrey Lillywhite*

---

* Not literally. Rum-jars in soldiers' slang were German trench mortar bombs.

Where the rats came from was a mystery. Good regiments like ours kept their trenches clean and tidy, so far as they could, and the only unwelcome smell was the salutary if unpleasant one of chloride of lime in all the appropriate places. But they were everywhere. There was one old fellow who was quite well known in our sector. I met him one day in a communication trench. He could walk on top of the mud into which I sunk at every step. He was enormous, with ferocious and venomous eyes, and I freely admit I flattened myself against the trench wall and let him go past, which he did without turning his head.

Lieutenant Cyril Drummond, 135 Battery Royal Field Artillery

Whilst asleep during the night we were frequently awakened by rats running over us. When this happened too often for my liking I would lie on my back and wait for a rat to linger on my legs, then violently heave my legs upwards, throwing the rat into the air; occasionally I would hear a grunt when the rat landed on a fellow victim.   *Driver R. L. Venables*

In one of the dug-outs the other night, two men were smoking by the light of the candle, very quiet. All at once candle moved and flickered. Looking up they saw a rat was dragging it away—fact. Another: very quiet and saw rat washing itself like a cat just behind the candle. Some as big as rabbits. I was in the trench the other night and one jumped over the parapet. Made sure it was a German's head looking over, so kept still and watched, and found it was a rat.   *Private Frank Bass*

An Artilleryman's Viewpoint

'The trenches here are quite impossible—about four feet of mud and water in most of them & they have nearly all been abandoned . . .' This is not a letter from an infantryman but from a young officer, Lieutenant Colin Faviell, of the 51st Battery, Royal Field Artillery. It is only fair to make clear that it was not only the Poor Bloody Infantry who were bogged down in the mud of France and Flanders. Faviell's letter—written incidentally to an infantry officer friend—continues: 'Of course, the infantry never stay for more than six days & then they only have two companies as firing line and supports, the other two being back in reserve. The poor old gunners don't matter, they stay for six weeks or six years if necessary.'

Extract from the diary of Corporal Albert George, 120th Battery, Royal Field Artillery, 11 December 1915:

Raining nearly all night—terrible storm, rain coming in dug-out—blankets wet through, heartily fed up—Reveille 6–0 a.m. SATURDAY DEC. 11th. Glad to get up as it isn't very pleasant lying in a wet *bed*—still raining—mud about 6 inches deep—horse lines in terrible state—exercising horses 8–45 still raining slightly—water and feed horses 12–0 noon. Dinner 1–0 p.m. (Stew). Time 3–30 p.m. in my dug-out, just remembered—last Saturday this time, was in GLOBE Theatre and enjoying myself with MABEL—what a difference this Saturday—up to my knees in mud and very downhearted—never mind must CHEER UP and think of the future. MAIL up 4–0 p.m., expecting a letter from someone—but no luck—left off raining at last but very windy outside. 6–0 p.m. feed and hay up horses. 6–0 p.m. last Saturday M & I were on our way from VICTORIA TO OXFORD—makes me grieve to think about it—have a talk among ourselves about our adventures on the retreat and advance until 9–0 p.m. BED 9–30—Still raining hard. 2 a.m. Sunday a big rat runs over my face and wakes me up—Still Raining.

Extract from the diary of Second Lieutenant E. J. Ruffell, 342 Siege Battery, Royal Garrison Artillery; during attachment to Belgian Army, Oostkerke, Belgium, November 1917:

> I have never seen a more depressing, desolate country than the part we were in—the mud was black and of the clinging variety, its usual depth being about 9 inches. When the guns fired, the whole earth—or rather mud—shook like a Blanc mange . . .

> Walking around the guns was about as much exercise as we could get—apart from the long tramp to the OP—it was not much pleasure to pull each foot in turn with both hands out of the mud, especially when being shelled and 50 yards from cover and progressing at the rate of 1 yd per minute.

Mud created prodigious problems when guns required to be moved. The photograph shows a 6-inch howitzer, weighing 26 cwt, being manhandled through the mud of the Somme battlefield near Pozières in September 1916.

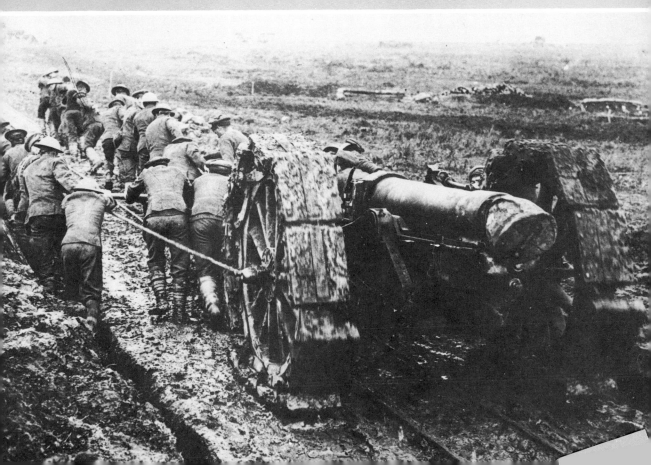

Field Postcards and Green Envelopes

Letter of Major Walter Vignoles, 16 February 1916:

It is splendid getting letters from home. . . . It makes one feel nearer home when they arrive and for a few minutes one forgets that there is a war, until reminded by the boom of a 'Heavy' firing at the Germans from just behind one.

Letter of Second Lieutenant Cyril Rawlins, 15 June 1915:

Those soiled envelopes with their sprawling smudgy addresses from sequestered country villages, from smoky clanging factory towns, each with a message of hope and comfort, from wife, sweetheart or parents, how eagerly they are searched for, and how crestfallen the man who draws a blank! Do people at home realize how much a line from them is worth? The men rip open the envelopes and gloat over the contents, puzzling out the words, then you hear them telling their mates—'Little Joe's started school', 'Our Jinny got married last week to that chap wot etc., etc., etc.'; laughing amongst themselves they fade away into the labyrinth . . .

The fact that a soldier's letters were censored by his officer could lead to potentially embarrassing consequences, as this story—from the memoirs of Private Tom Macdonald—indicates. 'Down in the dumps' because his girl friend had gone off with a wounded soldier, he tried to think of a girl in his home town with whom to exchange letters:

Well Leana Dean was her name, so I wrote to her and she replied and our letters gradually got from the Dear to Darling stage and I wrote one and put a lot of Bull in it about how much I loved her etc. Could not get a green envelope because you were only allotted one now and then. Now as a rule my officer would let mine through, but I guess he saw it was to a girl, he censored it and had a bit of fun doing it I guess.

Well Leana sent a part of it back to me and on it was written in his handwriting 'Don't you believe him'. First I was furious and I accosted him and asked him if it was his handwriting. He said it was, then we both burst out laughing.

The field postcard (below) could be sent at any time; they were an effective, though very limited, means of communication. Letters in ordinary envelopes could also be sent as often as a soldier cared to write, but they had to be censored by the officers of his battalion. If the soldier wished to write confidentially he had to wait until he was assigned a green envelope; this would not be censored by the man's officers but might be subject to a spot-check examination at the Base. Green envelopes were precious as they were only available at irregular intervals—in some cases as rarely as once a month. They were normally issued on application to a man's Company Headquarters, but only when out on rest.

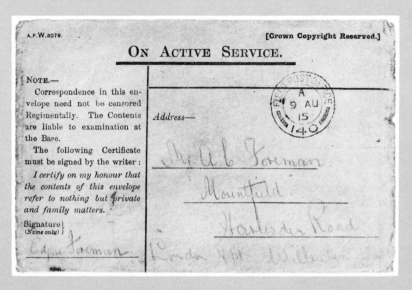

'Dear Dad and Mother,
'I'm afraid you must be getting a bit worried because I haven't written you for some time, but really I find it very difficult to get a letter off while in the trenches and it's so easy to send a field p.c.'

This envelope and card were sent by the soldier who wrote the letter quoted above, Private Edgar Foreman, Civil Service Rifles. The letter was in fact to be his last: he was killed by a stray shell the next day. The main substance of his last letter—a jaunty account of a visit to a bath house—is given in Chapter 8.

'... Edgar when writing to us gave us very little information concerning himself but devoted himself to cheering us up with bright breezy epistles ...' *From a letter by his father after his death*

7

'Keep the Hun on his Toes!'

A sentry of the East Lancashire Regiment sap-head at Givench January 1918.

Mud and vermin were the lesser enemies in this war; the real enemy was the human one, a matter of yards away, in his own muddy, rat-infested trenches.

> At night we would be on sentry, head and shoulders above the trench gazing into No Man's Land, which was lines of tangled barbed wire in front of ours and also in front of the Germans. Only yards at times separated us. In fact so close you could hear a chap coughing.
> *Private Tom Macdonald, 9th Bn Royal Sussex Regt*

Variously known as Jerry, Fritz, the Boche,* or the Hun, it was the German whom Tommy had come to fight, outwit and kill. Launched by 'Kaiser Bill' into unprovoked attack in 1914, he had arrogantly seized territories that were not his own. The purpose of trench warfare as far as the British were concerned was, initially, to prevent him from seizing any more; ultimately, to send him packing to Berlin; and, in the meantime, to harass and discomfort him with every conceivable ruse or device.

There were times and places where the French were content to 'live and let live'. Even the Germans were happy at times to follow this philosophy. But for the British this was merely playing at war. They favoured the doctrine of the offensive: there must be continual raids on the enemy lines to seize prisoners and cause casualties; there must be regular 'strafes' by the artillery; it must be the aim of the British battalions to dominate No Man's Land, to justify the claim that 'the German wire is our front line'. In official parlance, time in the trenches was to be 'utilized not for passive defence but for exhausting the enemy's troops'. The Hun must be kept on his toes.

In 1915, Private Harold Horne and his comrades of the 6th Battalion of the Northumberland Fusiliers moved south from the Ypres Salient, 'where the trenches were fifteen yards apart and we and "Jerry" could call to each other', to Messines:

> Things had been quiet there for some time and the trenches were clean and tidy and dry with fields of poppies behind us and in front of us in No Man's Land which was three or four hundred yards across. When we took over this sector our Brigadier told us that the trenches were like a garden but, as we were soldiers and not 'bloody gardeners' we had to liven things up.

95   * Boche (also spelt Bosche or Bosch) was French slang for 'German'.

The night hours, inevitably, were the time chosen for putting into practice the philosophy of the High Command. The 'free firework displays' often referred to by the Tommy were an essential component of this nocturnal activity, as in each front line sentries peered through the unnatural glow of flares and Very lights to see if they could make out what the enemy was doing. For men out in No Man's Land, whether carrying out a reconnaissance or a raid or, more humbly, engaged in such routines as the repairing of the barbed wire defences, the sudden illumination of this dangerous zone could be extremely unnerving.

> Very lights were trying, it is so natural to want to duck as these terrors of the working party streak upwards, but our platoon sergeant told us to remain motionless. And what a sight it was over the top in the sickly glare of those lights. Everything seemed to stand out: the barbed wire, the posts, the shell-holes—all bare and desolate, a spectacle of utter devastation.
> *Private Archie Surfleet, 13 Bn East Yorkshire Regt*

Perhaps those most able to take in the unique atmosphere of No Man's Land were men pushed out into listening posts between the lines. Rifleman A. H. Young, 1/18th London Regt, London Irish Rifles, went out to one at Givenchy in May 1915.

> We could hear the Germans talking quite plainly. It was a curious experience listening to our own and German bullets whistling overhead and to be right in the centre of things, as it were. The only company I had besides my companion, was the dead piled all around, Germans, British and Indians, and the odour was indescribable, especially as a lot of the 23rd were lying there who had only recently been killed.

The philosophy of the offensive has been much argued about. There are those who claim that its losses outweighed its gains, that, because of its inevitable casualties, it drained good and energetic battalions of their most enterprising officers and men, that it inspired COs to launch acts of bravado to provide worthwhile entries for the battalion diary and evidence of keenness for their superiors. The defenders of the philosophy assert that it kept the British as well as the Germans on their toes, that as well as wearing down the enemy it trained and honed Britain's largely amateur army for the set-piece battles, the big pushes, that were bound to come in the fullness of time. As for those who had to carry out the doctrine in practice, many loathed and feared the whole business, but others found in it a remarkable personal fulfilment. For Lieutenant W. T. Colyer (formerly a Private of the Artists' Rifles and now a junior officer in the 2nd Battalion Royal Dublin Fusiliers) this was what trench war was about. In April 1915 he found himself covering for a working party in No Man's Land.

> How different it feels to be doing something! Back there in the trenches I feel like a rat in a trap, because I can't move out of it, however many shells they send over, and can do nothing in my own defence. Here, though a hundred yards nearer the Boche and quite exposed, I feel pretty much

96

as if I were walking down the back garden at home. I don't feel any more frightened of Fritz than if I were playing hide-and-seek in the dark with him. Kingsley is severely critical of what he evidently regards as my foolhardiness in wandering about in such a brazen way while so close to the enemy lines. For something to do I visit each one of my men and ask him if he has observed or heard anything of interest. I know jolly well he hasn't, beforehand; for if he had I should have noticed it myself. Still, an occasional question helps to keep them on the alert.

Second Lieutenant Kenneth Macardle, 17th Bn Manchester Regt, was another young subaltern who found exultation and satisfaction in these nocturnal war games. He confided to his diary in May 1916:

I love being out of trenches and searching for adventure in No Man's Land at night. . . . Now that Carter has gone home on special leave I have to go out every night myself. They try to pamper me—expect me to suffer from nervous strain but I don't. I have breakfast in bed and sleep again; I live in HQ in great luxury and sometimes when I am out on a fighting patrol, the Colonel sits up for me!!

Patrolling at night was an acquired craft: taking greenhorns out 'in search of adventure' could produce strange results. Macardle took twenty-five men out one night on the Somme front in May 1916 when unexpectedly a white mist came down. Some of the men began 'to see things'.

A message was sent up to me from one that we had a Hun cornered and would I surround him. We converged with lowered bayonets upon the prostrate form lying in the grass—a fallen log. But it had raised a fatal ripple of excitement—too much for the untrained men from the company—two of them suddenly shot away, ran fiercely into the mist and plunged their bayonets into a very obvious hummock of grass. Then a message reached me that a patrol was approaching through the fog. My own Corporal came up and said the Company was all windy and overstrained—one can't patrol dangerous land with men like that—they are apt to loose off at the man in front; so I took them home.

But even after this curious outing there was a moment of warm satisfaction when they returned to their trenches, with the sense of a dangerous exploit boldly undertaken and a companionship shared. 'We sat in the light of two candles and smoked—everybody smoked; the great calm and good humour of these occasions settled down on me.' It is sad to have to add that this brilliant young officer was killed in No Man's Land some weeks later shortly after the beginning of the Battle of the Somme in 1916. Indeed, tragically but not unexpectedly, some of the best accounts of daring raids into No Man's Land are to be found in the accounts of young men who did not survive. The following is taken from a letter to his mother by Second Lieutenant Ian Melhuish, 7th Bn Somerset Light Infantry, written on 21 October 1915, just six days before he was killed when on a later patrol.

Raids were occasionally carried out in daylight. The photograph shows the 9th Cameronians going over the top during a daylight raid near Arras on 24 March 1917. Such a raid, unlike the slow secretive night raids, would be carried out in a carefully planned dash across No Man's Land after a short artillery and mortar barrage. Once in the enemy trenches bombardiers would bomb from traverse to traverse and the infantry would follow up to kill Germans or take them prisoner. Apart from the taking of prisoners to gain intelligence (from pay-books, uniforms, identity discs and personal letters) attempts would be made to destroy machine-gun posts or trench-mortar positions. Obviously all means of identification were left behind by the attacking troops.

Whilst in the trenches I had to take out 2 Patrols: my object both times was to capture a Boche alive.

The first time I took 3 men with me, but one only cared about coming all the way with me. We went right up to their barbed wire and located a working party. We could also hear the Huns talking. There was no one however to capture. We crawled about in the grass from 6 p.m. to 2 a.m. and then made our way home.

The second night I took out 2 men whom I could trust and this time located a listening post from which they were sending up flares. Unfortunately the sentries caught sight of us and turned some machine guns on to us. We lay v. still in the grass and after some time they thought we had either gone away or been killed, for they only fired now and then.

Then a thick fog began to develop and we were able to creep quite close to the wire of the post and throw in 3 bombs, all of which failed to explode. (These bombs are v. terrible if they do explode and they blow everything near them to pieces.) Well, after the bombs had been thrown we bolted for a ditch and remained there till after they had finished searching for us with rapid fire, when we returned home.

The worst part was that the Boche had succeeded in killing and wounding two of our men in the trenches with bullets aimed at us.

If raids which succeeded produced their own satisfaction, raids which failed did not. In May 1916 Private Jack Sweeney wrote in a letter to his fiancée:

It is simply murder at this part of the line. There is one of our officers hanging on the German barbed wire and a lot of attempts have been made to get him and a lot of brave men have lost their lives in the attempt. The Germans know that we are sure to try and get him in so all they have to do is to put two or three fixed rifles on to him and fire every few seconds—he must be riddled with bullets by now: he was leading a bombing party one night and got fixed in the wire—the raid was a failure.

Lance Sergeant Elmer Cotton, 5th Bn Northumberland Fusiliers, described the tragic loss of another young officer in his notebook in August 1915.

We were in no. 78 trench—the Germans had built a dummy hedge and it was necessary to find the reason why. Accordingly on the night of the 23rd Lt Winkworth, Sgt Coppick and Pte Longworth left our trench, word was passed down the line and all firing ceased, no flare lights were put up from our trenches. They would normally be out about $\frac{1}{2}$ an hour but an hour passed and they had not returned. I was Sgt of the line from 9 to 12 midnight and at 11.0 p.m. I became anxious and was about to send out a search party when a sentry in a bay challenged a figure in front of his trench. It was Pte Longworth and he came in minus his hat or rifle and with a revolver in his hand. He reported the Lt shot and lying between the lines in 'no man's land'. The Captain, myself and 5 bearers then went out to his aid. We stumbled through our own barbed wire and then along a hedge, fell down

The Enemy

Postcards such as these were designed to show the Tommy what his enemy was like and inspire him with a suitable hatred. It was in fact very rare for the Tommy actually to *see* the enemy. Being unseen, it was possible to imagine the worst. Hence, in the words of Sydney Rogerson, in his powerful book *Twelve Days*, the Germans became a legend—'savages, Huns, blond beasts who gave no quarter, who crucified Canadians and bayoneted babies, raped Belgian women, and had built Kadaver wards where they rendered down the bodies of their dead into fats'.

Of course many did accept wholeheartedly the standard view. A young Guards officer wrote in a letter home in 1915:

> Perhaps you have noticed that I have never used the word 'German' when referring to the enemy. The word 'German' seems to be absolutely taboo out here, as being too good a term to apply to the people that we are fighting. We always call them Huns or Boche and the men usually call them Fritz or Allimans, the last obviously being from the French.

However, the received propagandist view of the inhuman enemy often gave way to a more realistic attitude. The Tommy had no wish to be in trenches killing Germans and he realized that the German almost certainly had no wish to be in trenches killing Tommies. A camaraderie of the victim grew spontaneously between: they were both there because they were there! Particularly when British soldiers captured German trenches and found in dug-outs or the pockets of dead soldiers just the kind of photographs that they might have owned themselves, they saw the enemy as—after all—a human being. The top pictures opposite were picked up in captured German trenches.

The enemy cartooned. Such cards could be bought by the Tommy in France.

'The Day'—'Der Tag'—was, by repute, the most common and most meaningful of German military toasts: it was held to be convincing evidence of a long-held intention to go to war.

"PUTS THE GERMANS TO FLIGHT."

THE BRITISH BULL DOG.

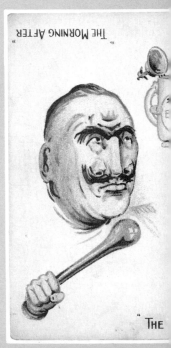

"THE MORNING AFTER"

"THE

Young German soldiers in cheerful mood wearing their 'pickelhaube' helmets.

The soldier who found this picture captioned it: ▶ 'German machine gun mounted for Anti-Aircraft. The man on the right is an NCO.' The NCO looks fairly formidable—but then no Tommy would have found anything strange in that.

Peace on Earth...
The Tommy knew that there had been a time when British and German soldiers saw each other face to face and did *not* fire: the legendary Christmas truce of 1914. This photograph of German soldiers in No Man's Land was taken by Second Lieutenant Cyril Drummond, Royal Field Artillery.

The following is from Second Lieutenant (now Brigadier) Drummond's account of the occasion:

... that day I discovered that places where we were usually shot at were quite safe and looking down towards the trenches it was just like an Earls Court Exhibition. There were the two sets of front trenches only a few yards apart and yet there were soldiers, both British and German, standing top of them, digging or repairing their trenches, without ever shooting at each other. It was an extraordinary situation.

In the sunken road I met an officer I knew and we walked along to a point where we were only about 70 yards from the German front line. One of the Germans waved to us and said, 'Come over here'. We said, 'You come over here if you want to talk.' So he climbed out of his trench and came over towards us. My friend and I walked out towards him. We met, and very gravely saluted each other. He was joined by more Germans, and some of the Dublin Fusiliers from our own trenches came out to join us. No German officer came out, it was only the ordinary soldiers. We talked, mainly in French, because my German was not very good, and none of the Germans could speak English well, but we managed to get together all right. They were very nice fellows to look at, they looked more like university students than soldiers, and one of them said, 'We don't want to kill you, and you don't want to kill us. So why shoot?' They gave me some German tobaccos and German cigars and they asked us whether we had any jam; and one of the Dublin Fusiliers got a tin of jam which had been opened but had had very little taken out and he gave it to a German who gave him two cigars for it ...

The Christmas truce was unique. Apart from those involved in trench-raids and set-piece battles, British soldiers were only likely to set eyes on Fritz when he was captured. Gunner Hiram Sturdy watched a group of prisoners being brought in in the first stages of the Battle of the Somme:

Our prisoners were not big savage hulks of men with bristling whiskers or criminal foreheads. They were young men, bandaged and battered, who when the wee Seaforth guard gave them a shout 'Right Turn' fustled and jumped, a solid bunch of nerves after having I expect been through this hellish bombardment. The most savage comment I heard while watching the prisoners came from an infantryman. That was 'Poor buggers!' It makes one feel glad to belong to a fighting force where 'poor buggers' is said about enemy prisoners. Fancy seeing it in print in the morning newspapers: 'Our infantrymen are sorry for the enemy prisoners and wonder why he has to kill them.' Those who printed it would be on parade next day.

German prisoners being brought in, 1 July 1916

an old trench and finally found the brave officer with the Sgt who had already carried him about 50 yards from the dummy hedge towards our line. He said they had crawled up to the hedge and the Lt had raised himself up to see better but they had been seen and a machine gun sprayed them with bullets, one hitting Lt Winkworth in the elbow and passing into his stomach. We got him onto a stretcher, gave him 2 grains of morphine and carried him safely back to our own trenches. One or two bullets were fired at us but we got back safely. The brave Lieutenant, who though a newcomer promised to become a very good officer, died the next day.

Deaths at the hands of the enemy were expected; deaths of comrades by bullets from one's own side made men angry and bitter. Yet in the darkness of the trenches, with all the possibilities of confusion, misunderstanding and panic that inevitably existed in this dangerous twilight world, such deaths were far from uncommon. Private Archie Surfleet's battalion, the 13th East Yorks, were about to pull out of the line for the last time when

on that last night, that tragedy happened. One of our Sergeants went out on patrol just in front of our line. They had done the job and were coming in when, owing to a misunderstanding over the pass-word, our company Lewis gunners opened fire, killing the sergeant and two men. They had got no reply to their challenge; raids by the enemy were very frequent then so, fearing an attack, they thought to do their duty by opening fire on the supposed raiders. The dreadful pity of it is that today I have been told that this damned good soldier, the sergeant in charge (who had been out here since 1914) was somewhat hard of hearing and it seems almost certain that he failed to hear the challenge. This most regrettable incident has cast a gloom over the whole Battalion; it has taken what little wind was left clean out of our sails.

Captain R. S. Cockburn took part in a raid which ended in a somewhat similar disaster, though here the cause was the failure of the appropriate officer in Cockburn's battalion, the 10th King's Royal Rifles, to inform the battalion next in line that the raid was to happen. The next battalion's listening post opened up and Cockburn's Corporal Hadley fell at his feet. Cockburn stood up and shouted in the darkness:

'Stop that firing! We're the 10th KRR.'
When I turned to look at the still figure on the ground, I knew that Corporal Hadley had been shot. I caught hold of him under the arms, and the other man with me, Smith, took his legs; we carried him with some difficulty back to our own sap, and sent for a stretcher bearer. But it was too late, as Corporal Hadley was already dead. He had been shot through the head and must have been killed instantly—a very brave and upright man who was never replaced.

103 The unhappy footnote to this story is that this particular escapade—the idea of which

was to attack an enemy listening post—had been devised at the last moment by the Colonel because a previous scheme had been found to be impracticable. The Colonel had decided that he would 'think of something else to do that night'. Cockburn added the comment: 'In those days it was the commonest thing to carry out little operations like that for the sake of doing something, although their value might be questionable, and their risks not at all questionable.'

'Our fellows hate the Boche like anything.' So wrote a young officer at the height of the Battle of the Somme. But many men had an enormous respect for the German as a fighting soldier, and it is on the whole remarkable how little animosity was felt for the men in field grey on the other side of the wire.

> The Hun is a strange fellow. We are constantly gingering him up with raids and artillery shots. On the whole he fights very well against odds and I can't help admiring him.
>
> You can't think how deep an interest you feel in those people across there, separated from us only by that narrow strip of bog and those two entanglements of rusty wire. And somehow one doesn't—or at any rate I do not—feel much rancour. 'With malice towards none' . . . 'Forgive them, for they know not what they do'—and they do it jolly well. That is as far as the actual combatants are concerned; but we shall not forget the people who made the war.   *Captain Harry Yoxall, 18th Bn King's Royal Rifle Corps*

> I was shocked to hear that Tom had been wounded. One thinks that I would feel anger, burning anger, against the Germans. Not so! The whole damned show is so impersonal that one cannot (at least I cannot) feel any personal emotion (except, perhaps, fear) when in the thick of things. Hope, revenge, anger, contempt—any of these would be a sustaining emotion in action, but very few experience them, I believe.
>
> *Sapper Garfield Powell, Royal Engineers*

The enemy was, however, indisputably there to be wounded and killed. The whole purpose of all those months of cheerful manly training in rifle and bayonet drill was that eventually a German would be in the sight of one's rifle or vulnerable to the exultation of a bayonet charge. In practice it was not always so simple. Sapper Garfield Powell (quoted above) was trained to disable and kill by gas. He wrote in his diary in June 1916: 'What a difference there is between the war of visions and the actual thing. In a few days we go up to let off the gas. More dirty work or rather more help towards the triumph of Right over Might.' Gas, however, was impersonal. Killing with bullet or bayonet made one acutely aware of the human being whose life one was taking.

104

Private Jack Sweeney killed two Germans during a trench raid on the British lines in the small hours of 21 November 1916. He was in a dug-out with two other officers' servants when the raid began after a flurry of shells and shouting.

> They began to throw bombs down into the dug-out but we were safe as long as we kept clear of the stairs. Presently I heard someone coming down the stairs—I shouted 'Who are you?'—he said something but I pulled my trigger and he said no more, he rolled down to me with two men very much alive following him up. I let go at them, one I killed, the other died later, the other two servants shot five, and one was wounded.
>
> The German that I shot who died afterwards was a fine looking man, I was there when he died, poor chap—I did feel sorry but it was my life or his, he was speaking but none of us could understand a word he said, to tell you the truth I had a tear myself—I thought to myself perhaps he has a Mother or Dad also a sweetheart and a lot of things like that, I was really sorry I did it but God knows I could not help myself.

Lieutenant R. A. Chell, 10th Bn Essex Regt, killed his first enemy in September 1915 at Mametz on the Somme. He spotted a bullet-proof sniper's plate on the other side of a newly created crater some seventy yards away.

> After about fifteen minutes quiet watching—with my rifle in a ready position—I saw a capless bald head come up behind the plate. The day was bright and clear and I hadn't the slightest difficulty in taking a most deliberate aim at the very centre of that bright and shiny pate—but somehow I couldn't press the trigger: to shoot such a 'sitter' so deliberately in cold blood required more moral courage than I possessed. After a good look round he went down and I argued with myself about my duty. My bald-headed opponent had been given a very sporting chance and if he were fool enough to come up again I must shoot him unflinchingly. I considered it my duty to be absolutely ready for that contingency. After about two minutes he came up again with added boldness and I just did my duty. I had been a marksman before the war and so had no doubt about the instantaneousness of that man's death: aim and trigger pressure were as deliberate as when I'd been grouping at 100 yards at test ranges in 1913 and 1914 and that bald head was a perfect target. Still, I felt funny for days and the shooting of another German at 'stand-to' the next morning did nothing to remove those horrid feelings I had.

Gas

There were many types of gas—chlorine, phosgene, chloropicrin, mustard (which caused the most casualties), prussic acid (used occasionally by the French), tear gas. The men in this photograph, taken on 10 April 1918 at an Advanced Dressing Station at Bethune, are suffering from tear g this caused temporary blinding or

'A strange green vapour, a surging mass of agonized fugitives, a four-mile gap without a living defender.' So wrote Liddell Hart of 22 April 1915, the date of the first significant use of poison gas in war. The location was the Ypres Salient. The gas, launched by the Germans on a favourable wind at dusk, was chlorine. The bulk of it fell on an Algerian division, which panicked and took a French territorial division with it. Only darkness, the curious unreadiness of the Germans to exploit their advantage and the prompt action of the Canadians in attempting to seal the gap, prevented a worse disaster.

Lance Sergeant Elmer Cotton described the effects of chlorine gas in his 1915 notebook:

> It produces a flooding of the lungs—it is an equivalent death to drowning only on dry land. The effects are these—a splitting headache and terrific thirst (to drink water is instant death), a knife edge pain in the lungs & the coughing up of a greenish froth off the stomach and the lungs, ending finally in insensibility and death. The colour of the skin from white turns a greenish black and yellow, the tongue protrudes & the eyes assume a glassy stare. It is a fiendish death to die.

Cotton was not talking from theory; he himself experienced a gas attack on Whit Monday 1915. His company of Northumberland Fusiliers was attached to a South Lancs battalion for trench training, when they received orders to reinforce the front line. On their way up they passed an advanced dressing station:

> Propped up against a wall was a dozen men—all gassed—their colours were black, green & blue, tongues hanging out & eyes staring—one or two were dead and others beyond human aid, some were coughing up green froth from their lungs—as we advanced we passed many more gassed men lying in the ditches & gutterways—shells were bursting all around.

Then Cotton and his comrades came under a gas attack themselves. He had already been affected by a whiff of gas caught earlier in the day; this forced him to spit and he had to take off his respirator to clear his throat.

> My respirator fell to pieces with the continual removal and readjustment—the gas closed my eyes and filled them with matter & I could not see. I was left lying in the trench with one other gassed man & various wounded beings & corpses and forced to lie & spit, cough & gasp the whole of the day in that trench.

Eventually he was evacuated by motor field ambulance to hospital: 'That was a fearful day for the British—they sustained 3000 "gas" cases alone not to mention the wounded & dead due to shellfire & rifle & machine gun bullets.'

Once gas had been used—and odium for using it had fallen on the Germans—the British used it themselves.

Captain Reginald Leetham, 2nd Battalion the Rifle Brigade, witnessed the launch of a gas attack on the Somme front shortly before 1 July 1916:

> At 9 the Engineers got the message to liberate gas at 9.15. I was in our Company dug-out at the time, so I hurried down to my platoon and had just the time to get every man to put his helmet on.
>
> I was caught bending myself as I saw an Engineer turning the tap on before I had put my helmet on. I asked him to wait a second but he refused. The gas belched forth and I got a nasty whiff in my lungs which left me gasping and choking for the next minutes.
>
> For the next hour and a quarter we had to remain with our helmets on. In my platoon frontage, fifty cylinders were let off, some of which leaked and filled the trench with gas. It was like moving about in a fog.
>
> My men behaved splendidly and kept quite cool. The Engineer officer congratulated me on their behaviour. One sapper lost his head and took his helmet off for half a minute.
>
> He got awful pains in his stomach when he got to the hospital and has since died.

British troops in anti-phosgene masks manning a Vickers machine gun on the Somme front in July 1916. Deservedly one of the best-known photographs of the war.

8 'Out on Rest

British soldiers purchasing geese for their Christmas dinner in the market place at Bailleul, December 1916.

After its allotted period in the front line, a battalion would move back to reserve trenches. The normal pattern was four days in followed by four days out, but, as one soldier put it, 'you must not think those four days were spent lounging about'.* At the very least there were fatigues, which often included exhausting trips up to the front with supplies. At the most there were operations of very considerable danger. Private Edgar Foreman, 1/15th Bn London Regt (generally known as the Civil Service Rifles), described a particularly hazardous assignment in a letter home written in September 1915.

> When we were in reserve our whole Company had to form a covering party to another Battalion, who came up to dig a new fire-trench at night-time. As soon as it was dark we went out in front until we were midway between the German and English trenches, where we lay down at about 20 paces interval between each pair of us: the first night we were by ourselves at 10 paces. Our job was to form a screen so that the working party could not be surprised. We were there from 8 until 2 a.m. The first night was the most exciting, the Germans shelling our trenches and our artillery replying; we could hear the pieces from the shrapnel dropping all round us and a large number of stray shots whizzing through the long grass, it was the longest six hours I have ever spent, but the only casualties in our party were an officer and a private who were shot by our own men mistaking them for Germans; they were both killed.

By the time this task was completed, there had been more deaths, including several fatalities caused by that formidable German weapon, the 'Minenwerfer',

> a contrivance the Germans have which can throw a bomb 200 lbs in weight and 5ft long a distance of 1000 yards, it explodes like a mine and kills by concussion.† They sent several over every day and killed a good many. One of the four men of our Battalion who were killed that way I knew quite well, he was the last of five brothers all of whom have been killed in the war.

*Private Henry Bolton. His diary entry continues: 'You could often hear the remark "I would rather be in the firing line" and more than once have I passed that remark myself.'
† The Germans were well ahead of the Allies in the use of trench mortars. They had 150 'Minenwerfer' available when the war began and they were precision pieces very effective in trench fighting. Their reputation was well deserved.

Normally, however, reserve trenches meant hard rather than risky work, to be borne with weary resignation, or, as in the case of this sixteen-year-old, Private Frank Birkinshaw, Royal Warwickshire Regiment, writing home in May 1915, with breezy if cynical good humour.

> We are relieved tonight and go back for four days rest. I think it must be a little joke to call it rest, for we do twice as much work as in the trenches. Every night we 'man' the reserve trenches until two o'clock in the morning. After that we lie in the woods until six o'clock: then we march back, sleep, eat, have rifle inspection and wonder why we ever joined the army: until six o'clock at night when the same thing happens again.
>
> In our spare time we go and mend roads or pick up jam tins which other regiments have left behind.

But sooner or later the moment would arrive when the battalion would withdraw to rest billets well clear of the battle zone.

> There was no more delightful sensation in those days, than marching on a good hard road under a bright moon to rest billets far behind the line. You were so glad to be away from the shells; you could look forward to sleeping in a bed, perhaps between sheets; you knew that you might, if it was summer time, procure fresh eggs and milk and vegetables; you might wear your soft cap again, instead of the steel helmet which was such a fearful weight. Your peace of mind was only interrupted by thoughts of what the Battalion was, when it last came out for a rest.
>
> *Captain R. S. Cockburn, 10th King's Royal Rifle Corps*

Perhaps most important of all at such times was the reassurance both to the eye and the ear that there was another world still continuing only a matter of miles from the zone of barbed wire and devastation from which they had just emerged.

> After living in holes in the earth, sometimes waterlogged, wet through to the skin, it was delightful to arrive in a town without war scars, even though the women moved about like sacks of potatoes tied around the middle. Nevertheless their feminine voices were pleasant to the ear, after those of strident sergeant-majors and their kin, linked as they were to the discordance of bursting shells. *Private W. Carson Catron, Hull Commercials*

For men being relieved after a hard spell in the trenches a slog of several miles with heavy kit was a tough beginning to their time of rest, but, as Private Henry Bolton, 1st Bn East Surrey Regt, wrote after such a march,

> We were well repaid for our walk, for Locre was a beautiful place with a grand old church and it had not been shelled. The first morning I was there was Sunday and the bells of the fine old church rang out their welcome and the Belgian people (of course mostly ladies or very aged men) flocked to their call dressed in their best and it made one think of Dear old Home and the Loved ones we had left behind.

Bath-house routine. Men of the 2nd Australian Battalion waiting outside a bath house at Ypres, 1 November 1917.

This was a time when trench-hardened soldiers found supreme satisfaction in simple, ordinary things.

> Imagine my feelings when I got onto a straw mattress that night! To be able to sit at a table and have a plate to eat your food from, well—it reminds you of once upon a time.
>
> *Private Albert Johnson, 11th Bn Royal West Kents*

> We don't need much, now, to make us happy: a pile of clean straw, a clean shirt, ten francs, an estaminet out of Jerry's range and we are as happy as sandboys. *Private Archie Surfleet, 13th Bn East Yorkshire Regt*

To be clean again, not to be lousy, to feel for a while like a decent human being— these were among the best pleasures of being away from the trenches. The Army recognized this need and had its own special rituals to provide for it. Private Edgar Foreman described the experience of getting cleaned up, army style, in a letter of November 1915.

> We got a hot bath in on the Sunday morning, it was one of the best organized things I have yet seen in the army. They *do* you in batches of 12 (I had the

luck to be in the first 12). You first of all throw all your clothing into a trough under your own number (1 to 12), it is taken in charge by an RAMC man, who only deals with your special number, the underclothing is changed and the khaki brushed and the seams ironed. While this is being done you are allowed five minutes in a tub of hot water. (The twelve men soaking in twelve steaming tubs would be a good photo for the *Daily Mirror*.) When you are turned out for the next lot to get, you go to another trough to find clean underclothing and your brushed khaki all ready for you.*

Others, however, found the Army's bath-house routine much less organized and a good deal less satisfactory. Private Archie Surfleet and his comrades of the 13th Battalion of the East Yorkshire Regt, for example, in February 1917:

We marched to the bath-house (the usual converted brewery) and stripped in an outhouse. The bathroom was a large, bare place, floored with duck-boards, the sort used in the trenches, and we trooped in, standing in lines like so many shivering jellies, for the boards were covered in *ice*. Then after the usual wait, with much spluttering of air in the pipes, a thin stream of scalding hot water shot down on us. Note that: stood on ice—scalding hot water on your head! It struck me as a likely idea for the next Spanish Inquisition, I wonder we did not drop dead from shock, but after the scramble for your togs, out we went into the snow!

Gone too along with the individual bath-tubs was the scrupulous laundering of individual uniforms of the kind that had delighted Private Foreman in 1915. As the Army grew in size and complexity, there was less time for such civilized niceties. Now when dirty, lice-infested shirts were discarded at the bath-house, it was anybody's guess whose allegedly clean shirt you were issued with as you left. Private Archie Surfleet voiced a common reaction when he wrote in his diary in July 1916:

Speaking of 'chats', lots of the lads say they prefer to 'keep their own'— which sounds a pretty damnable comment to be forced to make, though I tend to agree with the sentiment! How the hell they expect anyone to put on fresh shirts when they are already at least as lousy as those discarded beats me!

Despite such drawbacks, time out from the trenches had its very special quality. The same man, Archie Surfleet, summing up his whole experience as a soldier, wrote: 'I think the happiest times I had during the 1914 war were with the PBI when we were at rest in those pleasant villages like Saint-Venant, Robecq, Camblain-Chatelain and a few more.'

* Unhappily this was Private Foreman's last letter home. He was killed by a shell together with two others of his battalion on 10 November 1915, the day after this letter was written. [See pages 92–3, also Ch. 13: 'The Terrible Price'.]

A village behind the lines on the Somme front: it was to places like this that the infantry battalions returned after their visits to the trenches. Unsophisticated, austere, they provided havens of rest for men whose most normal landscape consisted of shell holes and barbed wire.

Captain Wilfred Nevill, 8th Bn East Surreys, describes the pleasures of being out on rest in a letter of November 1915:

> Cheer ho,
>
> All correct. I'm just going to have a hot bath; in fact, $\frac{1}{2}$ a beer cask has just come in and now Markey, my altogether excellent new servant, has gone to the cooker where Cpl Parr, the cook corporal, a goodly soul, has boiled me a 'dichie' (pronounced 'dixy') of water. Wow.
>
> I found I had not forgotten how to undress, it all came quite naturally. . . . Also I've just had a haircut & shampoo.
>
> I've not been out the whole day because, for once, I've had nothing to do all day; I've not even put my boots on. . . . I had breakfast in my pyjamas about 8.30 and have simply lazed in front of a fire with books & mags the whole blooming day. By Jove, it is good.

Among the 'few more' Private Surfleet did not name was the village of Longuevil-lette, where he spent a particularly happy time in January 1917 in spite of 'quite the coldest weather I have experienced'.

It is daylight now and a wonderful winter's day. When we are off duty, which is frequent, both officers and men spend most of the time sliding on the frozen pond; great fun on a really first-class slide. The old folks come out of their cottages and stand around while we dash about; they seem a bit

Dear Rose

88 ROUEN. — La Seine et la Rue Ste Catherine. — LL.

'10 January 15

'Dear Rose, this is where we are at present where the cross is, don't forget to answer and send me something nice with love from Sid × × ×'

Sid Lewis began sending postcards to his fiancée Rose from the moment that he landed in France.

His messages were always simple and cheerful. He was invariably in the best of health and concerned about the well-being of his family and friends back in Shepherd's Bush, London.

'11 April 15

'Dearest Rose, I am in the pink of condition regarding health, hoping you and all at home are the same. Yours ever, Sid × × ×'

AMIENS - 1915 - Place René Goblet

Now Sid and Rose are married.

'2 October 15

'Dearest I am in the pink & I hope you are alright safe & sound. Dearest I had no letter last night what have you forgot me. Cheer up my dear and be happy, I will be with you soon if all keeps as well as it is now. ... Lots of love & kisses from your loving husband for ever × × ×'

As in the case of most of Sid's postcards the censor has attempted to remove the name of the town; but not, in the card shown left, the address of the printer.

Love from Sid

'6 August 16

'Dearest, have not received any letters today Monday. Still in the pink hoping you are feeling better. Don't forget to write freely and Rose I am broke. Darling one, this time two years ago we were happy, never mind roll on the finish. Cheery Oh lots of Love & Heaps of Kisses, yours for ever Sid × × × Cheery Oh.'

RENINGHELST-DORPPLAATS

'2 February 17

'Dearest, I am still A1 don't send any letters to me yet, but I will let you know when. Cheer Oh, Keep smiling, I will send you a letter tomorrow, yours for ever Sid × × × Lots of Love & Heaps of Kisses × ×'

Undated

'Darling Rose, where you see the × is the place where we used to stand our cars and wait for orders. Really I wish I was with you, I am still yours for ever. Love & Kisses Sid × × × Save all these cards.'

was Sid Lewis's last card to his wife. [ot]her hand has added the end of the [story:] 'Killed by gas. Age 23.'

surprised to see our officers mixing so readily with the men. (I must say our officers are very good sports.) I hope this life will continue.

A few days later he wrote again in the same vein:

I have been waiting, half afraid, for something to put an end to this wonderful time and I suppose this has made me delay writing up my diary. It has been almost too good to be true and we are becoming so 'civilianized' the keeping of a diary seems absurd.

Almost the supreme pleasure of being out on rest was simply 'taking it easy'. Sapper Garfield Powell, Royal Engineers, wrote in his diary on a May day in 1916:

Am writing these notes in a field at the back of the billet. Nearly all the section are here— sprawled out in the sun. One Elphick (called Sopey owing to a fancied resemblance to a Spaniard)—is trying to play a piccolo. Another—Jenkins G. E. (called Eddie, George, Ted, Ned and many other things, mostly bad)—is stripped to the waist and washing in a tin—evidently enjoying it. A few seconds ago he was looking carefully at his shirt—for diamonds? Davies D. J. is listening to Elphick talking (he has given up the piccolo to indulge in his usual pastime). The others are watching the sky— except myself, of course, who is writing (should it be 'who am' or 'who is'?).

Being British soldiers, it was inevitable that they should resort to traditional British sports; if the necessary equipment was not available, it could be invented. Lance Corporal Roland Mountfort, 10th Bn Royal Fusiliers, wrote in a letter of June 1916:

Some enterprising person being possessed of a red tennis ball our latest recreations are tennis with entrenching tools on a hard court about as level as a rockery and cricket with the aid of a biscuit tin and a piece of packing case. After all I don't see why a monotonous dead level and faultlessly turned implements are necessary to sport. You get so many more variations from our method.

In fact the British affection for ball games was irrepressible. There is at least one authentic case of football being played on the Arras road between 4 a.m. and 5.30 a.m. on a September morning (Rifleman A. H. Young, 1/18th Bn London Regt, London Irish Rifles, in his account 'My Experiences on the Western Front', written in 1915).

Inevitably, the tiny country villages of France and Belgium became well known to the Tommy and he to them and in particular it was to that peculiarly French—or Belgian—institution known as the *estaminet* to which many of them were drawn. The *estaminet* was not at all like a British public house, but it provided the same service: it offered company, a chance to let the hair down, and, for the persevering, a brief oblivion. Lance Corporal Roland Mountfort described the three which he and his fellow 10th Royal Fusiliers were allowed to visit as:

much of a muchness, both as to appearance or stock in trade. The latter consists almost entirely of a fearful thin beer sour as vinegar, vin rouge, vin blanc and cognac. The bar is in the front room and is merely a small dock, like a county court witness box, in one corner with a few shelves behind. I have not encountered an inhabitant who speaks English yet, but almost all of us know enough French to carry on an entente cordiale. English money is taken at the rate of 10d a franc; beer is two sous a glass and red wine 1 franc 75 a bottle. The latter is a sort of claret and not bad stuff.

But for those who regularly found their satisfactions in these sparsely furnished, unsophisticated village drinking-houses, they could hold, at least in retrospect, a not unromantic glow. Writing many years afterwards, W. Carson Catron, former Private in the Hull Commercials, put into his affectionate description of one representative *estaminet* the essence of many convivial evenings with his battalion comrades.

Within the estaminet oil lamps shone dimly on a dozen or so beer drinkers seated around a large table. Smaller tables occupied the corners.

Madame struggled to the large table with an outsize jug on the side of which were painted two flying angels. She poured the frothless, spineless fluid the jug contained into the empty glasses to the accompaniment of a bedlam of voices. She laughed as she poured, each time lightening the weight of her jug, meanwhile jerking out 'Oui Monsieur' to all enquiries, regardless.

The last glass filled, she rested the jug at her feet as dirty pieces of paper, like overworked blotting paper, were pushed around the table to her. She took them up, examined them, then placed them in her pocket, before collecting the metal coins some of the men were offering her. Finally, with a 'Merci beaucoup', she turned and hurried off to recharge the jug as quickly as her legs and her ample proportions would allow.

Back in the room she watched those around the table hold up their charged glasses high. A voice called out, 'All set? Go!'

Heads were thrown back, mouths opened wide and down it went, followed almost immediately by pandemonium. The last man to bang on the table had to pay for the next round. Madame stood by, hugging her replenished jug to her bosom, awaiting instructions.

This kind of performance could have only one result where weaker heads were concerned. Tommies lurching back to their billets the worse for liquor were not uncommon sights on French roads.

It was one day towards the end of March 1918; several of us were walking along the road towards St Omer. Perhaps two hundred yards away was a Tommy whose unsteady gait was unmistakable. As he drew slowly but surely nearer a young French peasant girl came abreast of us. She saw the Tommy even as we did and as she spotted that unmistakable gait she said, partly to herself, partly to our little group and partly to the universe at large 'ANGLAIS SOLDATS BEAUCOUP ZIGZAG TOUS LES JOURS!' 'Ziz-zag' himself drew

near, then passed beyond us, talking to himself. . . . That was all of sixty years ago but I can still see Tommy, and still hear the almost sad note in Ma'amselle's voice.

Private W. G. Brown, 2/3rd Field Ambulance, 59th (North Midland)
Division

It was, of course, while out on rest that the British Tommy and the French or Belgian civilian came into contact. The obvious question that must be asked is: how well did they get on together, thrust as they were into close proximity by the fortunes of war? In fact, this is an area where generalizations are difficult. Experiences varied widely. Some soldiers report favourably on their relations with the local people, others much less so. The evidence is, perhaps inevitably, somewhat contradictory. Sometimes, indeed, a soldier will write in one vein in one letter and in a totally opposite vein in another. Second Lieutenant Ian Melhuish, 7th Bn Somerset Light Infantry, for example:

It is v. nice here. The French people we come across are v. pleasant.
Letter of 26 July 1915

I am afraid the much vaunted generosity of the French people is on the wane. They are not anxious to give much away, in fact their chief object seems to be to make as much as possible out of the British.
Letter of 11 August 1915

Melhuish's second, sourer note is, it must be admitted, frequently struck by soldiers who felt that they had been less than justly treated by the local shopkeepers, aware that they had what would in modern terms be called a captive market. Second Lieutenant Arthur Gibbs, 1st Bn Welsh Guards, for example, writing in August 1916:

There is quite a big town near here where we dined last night. We did a little shopping and got some very nice fresh fruit, for which we were charged much too much. Some idiots at the beginning of the war spoilt all the shop-keepers, the result is that we are all robbed.

Or there is Private Jack Sweeney, 1st Bn Lincolnshire Regt, writing home less legibly than usual in November 1915:

I have just paid a Franck [*sic*] for this Rotten pencil, it is not worth a penny. The French people here do put the pence on to us, they rob us every way they can, there are not many English soldiers that will give them a good Name. I cannot say much for them myself.

There is then an abrupt change in Sweeney's handwriting from pale, barely distinguishable maroon to ordinary, legible graphite. The letter continues: 'I cannot write with that thing. This bit I have is not as big as my little finger but it is English.'

On the other hand, Private Archie Surfleet, 13th Bn East Yorkshire Regt, could   118

A typical *estaminet* of northern France. They were quite unlike the public houses of Britain, but they had their own special and—for many soldiers—highly memorable atmosphere. It should be remembered, however, that this was a time when Temperance was a very powerful cause in Britain: many soldiers would never dream of darkening an *estaminet's* door. By the same token, there were many officers who could not conscientiously collaborate in the distribution of rum to the troops in the trenches.

nterior of an *estaminet*—a photograph taken by a young British officer. It had been diverted from its original purpose to serve as an officers' mess, but its furniture, stove and general appearance were unchanged.

In spite of the difference of language, relations between the Tommy and the *estaminet's* Madame could be close and sympathetic. Private Archie Surfleet recorded in his diary in November 1917:

'Charlie Gold and I have just witnessed a very distressing scene. We went over to Maroenil this evening after tea and called at Madame's little estaminet. We had just been paid a mingy ten francs and, splitting a bottle of Vin Blanc between us, had just settled down to a quiet drink when the poor old soul appeared with tears streaming down her wrinkled face. 'They'—the French Army—had fetched her youngest son. Poor old lady: husband at Verdun, another son in some other blood-soaked bit of France and now the youngster off. God! it seemed rotten: luckily we miss *that* part of the war. . . .'

not praise too highly the generosity of certain French villagers whom he met when out on rest during the Battle of the Somme in 1916.

> We called at a house in a little place called Neuf Berquin and asked the people if they would do us a meal, for which, of course, we intended to pay. We were welcomed with open arms and ushered into the best room whilst a beautiful little dinner was got ready for us. When it came to parting, these kindly folks absolutely refused to accept anything at all for it; one does not meet many like that in any country.

Of course, these were ordinary civilians with no commercial interest. Perhaps it was more tempting for those who had the commercial power, however limited, to try in their own way to do well out of the war.

But unfair dealing was not necessarily a monopoly of perfidious Frenchmen: the Tommy could have his perfidious moments too.

> Billeted at Bus-les-Artois, a most respectable village. Some of the inhabitants made a small fortune by providing 'café au lait' for the troops, but at the same time they probably lost a good many spoons and cups! Unfortunately some of the men looked upon this as desirable plunder, for future use in their billets. This was undoubtedly one of the reasons for the attitude of suspicion shown by the country folk in many places—an attitude which was most strongly condemned by the very men who caused it.
>
> *Private Clifford Carter, Hull Commercials*

The relationship between soldier and civilian was inevitably complicated by the problem of communication. Lance Corporal Mountfort and his comrades of the 10th Royal Fusiliers—mostly city men from London—might find it relatively easy to maintain an *entente cordiale* with the local people, but for most men the French language presented a major problem, if a problem with rich possibilities for comic misunderstanding.

> I expect this is supposed to be a very nice place in peace time but I think myself it is not half so good as good old England. If you ask the people any question here all they say is 'NO COMPREE', if you want to buy an Egg you have to think of a horse and say 'HOOF'. Bread is *Du Pain*, butter is *De Burr*, from morning to night it is 'No Compree'.
>
> *Private Jack Sweeney*

> The men's 'French' is most amusing: the usual remark in passing through a town or village is 'Bong joor, madam, how's your father?' or 'Commont ally voo? Bocoo prommynade!' *Second Lieutenant Arthur Gibbs*

Some men, in fact, resorted to sign language. Second Lieutenant Cyril Rawlins, 1st Bn Welch Regt, described the resourcefulness of his batman in a letter of June 1915:

My man Bobett nearly makes me die with laughing sometimes as he gesticulates to the peasants for eggs: squatting down, flapping his arms and squawking. He then grunts and makes as if he were slicing bacon. For milk he says 'moo, moo', but you should see him trying to get boot polish.

One thing that always won the admiration of the British troops was the extraordinary resilience of so many French and Belgian civilians and in particular their determination to carry on their normal lives even within range of the guns. Major Walter Vignoles, Grimsby Chums, wrote in a letter of February 1916:

> There is a house close by where a mother and a daughter are still living. The mother refuses to budge although two shells have burst in the farm, one in the yard outside their living room and one actually in their bedroom. They keep chickens and sell coffee to the soldiers, but appear to have no other means of livelihood.

But the people who won Major Vignoles' supreme accolade were two French ladies who ran a tea-shop in Armentières, even though the town was 'all but deserted, with street after street shut up', and 'notwithstanding that a few shells are sent into the town almost every day'.

> On each side of it the shops are closed, but in the window of this one was an oil lamp lighting up boxes of chocolate, and a card marked 'Tea Room'. Inside there was a room that would not disgrace London and two charming Mesdemoiselles to serve us.
>
> We were late so there was no crowd. We had a chat with the pretty Mlle, who must be known and admired by several thousands of British officers! The house has already been hit by five shells and the upstairs rooms have been wrecked, but there is no sign of this in the tea room. Parker and Anderson of course made eyes at her, and told her we had come quite especially to see her, which she seemed to think quite natural, and one of the two said: 'That is the sort of girl I could easily fall in love with.'
>
> Parker played the piano and it was surprising to see how the men who were there turned round at the tables, to listen more easily. I had noticed before how men appreciate any music, however simple, when they have been in the trenches.

OLD HUN LINE.

9

'It's Unlucky to be Killed on a Friday'

'Smile boys that's the style ...'
British troops in buoyant moo
a captured German trench at
Serre, on the Somme, in Marc
1917.

As the soldier approached the front for the first time he was inevitably curious as to how he would stand up to the presence of danger. This is how Private W. T. Colyer of the Artists' Rifles recorded his reaction to his first shell, which exploded at a distance of thirty yards.

> And was I panic-stricken? No. Not in the least. It would be hard to analyse my feelings as I gazed at the ugly brown hole in the green field. Astonishment, excitement, realization, relief, foreboding, curiosity and even a morbid kind of satisfaction—these emotions possessed me almost simultaneously and left no room for the sensation of fear.... Nothing to be frightened of in fact—provided it did not burst any closer, that is to say. Ah, that was the question: where was the next one coming?

The real test came when a bombardment was not sporadic but sustained, and when it was virtually impossible to dismiss the thought that the next shell might be considerably nearer than the last. On a September night in 1915 Second Lieutenant Cyril Rawlins led a ration party with six pack-mules up the line through steady shell-fire. He described his own and his men's reactions in a letter to his mother.

> The men laugh and joke with each other and speculate on the possibilities of getting a 'blighty' wound. Some of them sing little songs under their breath and try not to think about the bullets: I think we all envy the mules who don't know what it all means. I suppose I must be a bit of a coward myself after all, because I would give anything to be able to run and hurry along, anything but that slow crawling walk: or I would like to get down in a ditch whenever the glaring star shell rises: I want to stoop and hang my head and get down as low as possible. But one must stride along as nonchalantly as if out for a moonlight stroll at home!! I wonder, do other men have these weird feelings?—things one does not talk about except to one's intimates.

The problem with a man of Rawlins' sensitivity was that he could not avoid the mental speculation as to what might happen when exposed to shot or shell. 'I have too vivid an imagination for a soldier; it's so hard to keep one's mind off the "feel" of bullets entering various parts of one's anatomy.' But his own highly charged and sophisticated reactions led him to comment, perhaps too facilely, on the difference

123

of response, as he saw it, between officers and men—though it is perhaps fair to add that he wrote this in a letter written two months before the journey up the line described in the extract above. 'Our soldiers have no nerves, no imagination, and only one fear, being without a "fag".'

There is no evidence that fear and imagination were only confined to the well brought up and the highly educated. Indeed a vivid awareness of the possibilities of pain and death could strike any thoughtful soldier whatever his rank. Private Archie Surfleet, 13th Bn East Yorkshire Regt, analysed his feelings in his diary when out on rest after a number of particularly hazardous visits to the line.

> It is easy to sit here in the sunshine all nice and quiet, and write it up now, but there is something akin to great nervous strain to trek there and back, shelled at intervals, losing men killed and wounded on each journey. I don't suppose I shall ever lose my nervousness of shelling and though I may not panic I always have a secret fear at the back of my mind; not maybe, unnatural in a chap raised in peace and security.

There was another element in his anxiety which many others would have understood:

> I keep thinking of the old folks at home. They really are a worry to me and, windy as I am, I think I am more distressed at the thoughts of their feelings *if* the worst comes to the worst, than I am afraid for myself.

Equally comprehensible, and no doubt equally widely shared, was the attitude expressed by Private George Morgan, 1st Bradford Pals:

> I was afraid—everyone must have been afraid, but I was more afraid of showing it. I didn't want to let the side down. I hoped I would be able to do what I was expected to do.

Yet there were undoubtedly men who claimed never to be afraid; men who never experienced 'the wind vertical'; men who were able to adopt a totally fatalistic attitude to danger. If a shell or a bullet had your number on it, you would get it; if it didn't you would survive. It was as simple as that.

> I was never frightened. If you were scared you were done for. Thank God I wasn't. I don't know why—I've no idea. As a signaller in the Artillery I often had to go forward with the infantry, paying out my signal wire, but I can't remember ever worrying whether I would be able to do my job or whether I would get to wherever I had to go. And often I had to be on my own, in places where if you had somebody with you it wasn't so bad, but if you had to go forward on your own under heavy shelling you would be bound to think that if you got knocked out there would be no one to help you. But I was never nervous.
>
> How you didn't get blown to atoms you never knew. Your life wasn't yours, it wasn't even yours to think about; it was in the hands of Fate. You were to go or you were not to go; you either got wounded or you didn't.

124

And under no circumstances could you jib or run back: you couldn't. And you couldn't take cover if you were told to go forward. You had to go forward even if you were blown to pieces.

Gunner J. J. Daniells, Royal Field Artillery

Perhaps most remarkable of all was the attitude of such a young officer as Lieutenant Alex Wilkinson, 2nd Bn Coldstream Guards, when he went into battle on the first day of the Third Battle of Ypres, 31 July 1917:

I felt wonderfully confident about the show. Never for one moment did I have the least anxiety. I knew from the start that I was going through without a touch and in spite of the appalling discomfort I enjoyed it enormously. I would not have missed it for anything. I am only looking forward to the time when we have to do another show.*

It might be thought that, among those who took a less fatalistic view, time would make it easier to live with the pressures and dangers around them, that they might even become blasé. Such may have been the case with some men, but with others precisely the opposite was true. When Private Jack Sweeney had his first experience of the front line in November 1914, his reactions were decidedly jaunty—'there seems to be no Fear in the old Lincolns', he had commented in a letter home—but by October of the next year he was writing in a very different vein: 'I find now that my nerves are all gone and I tremble every time I hear a shell. It is not because I am frightened but I cannot help it at all.' Six months later his mood was equally sombre: his battalion had just gone through a bombardment by trench mortars, a gas attack and a German trench raid: 'I had one of the closest shaves I have ever had but I am safe though badly shaken. I am sure this war will send us all mad, people at home cannot realize what the lads out here have to go through.'

In January 1917 he wrote home reporting

a very bad time in the trenches at Xmas, but the lads that relieved us had it worse, old Fritz took 51 prisoners. I am pleased to tell you that we are resting for a long time, yet I have often wondered how I stick it but I really feel done now and my nerves seem to have all gone but after resting I expect I shall be fit again.

He still had many months of hard fighting ahead, including what he dreaded most of all—a return to 'Hell', as he always called Ypres, during the long-drawn-out battle of 1917 usually known as Passchendaele. On 3rd November, just three days before Passchendaele was captured in almost impossible conditions by the Canadians, he wrote from the Ypres Salient to his fiancée:

I laughed at you, dear, getting the wind up when I was home but you should see me shaking like a jelly. Yes this is quite true dear I am not joking. 'Struth

---

* For further references to the question of fear in battle see the remarkable account by Private Henry Russell in Ch. 11.

125

The Cartoons of Bruce Bairnsfather

" —— these —— rations."

Bruce Bairnsfather was the 'artist-laureate' of the Western Front. He went to France in 1914 as a subaltern in the Warwickshire Regiment, but his cartoons caught the earthy, half-bored, half-frightened cynicism of the ordinary Tommy with remarkable accuracy. His pungent and uncompromising wit was too much for the authorities at first and he was subject to official censure. Later they gave in and from 1916 he was attached to the War Office as an officer catoonist.

SITUATION SHORTLY VACANT
In an old-fashioned house in France an opening will shortly occur for a young man, with good prospects of getting a rise.

A.D. NINETEEN FIFTY
"I see the War Babies' Battalion is a coming out."

There could be no better or moving evidence of the popularity—and relevance—of Bruce Bairnsfather's cartoons than the following story, told in his *Personal Record of the War 1915–1916–1917* by Brigadier-General H. C. Rees, DSO. The story concerns the first day of the Battle of the Somme, 1 July 1916, and in particular the Commanding Officer of the 1st Battalion the Hampshire Regiment, Lieutenant Colonel the Hon. L. C. W. Palk, who was to become one of the many senior officers killed on that heroic and tragic day. His battalion suffered very badly in the attack, all 26 officers and 559 men becoming casualties.

Col. Palk said that this was the greatest day the British army had ever had and that therefore every Hampshire man should take part in it. He, on the day of the attack, dressed himself in his best clothes, put on white gloves and led the whole of his battn Hqtrs across No Man's Land, when he himself and most of those with him became casualties. While lying mortally wounded in a shell hole, he turned to another man lying near him and said, 'If you know of a better 'ole, go to it'. That kind of spirit does great things and it is lucky for the Germans that they were able to prevent us getting on even terms with them.

uce Bairnsfather's most famous
toon—it appeared in the first edition
The Bystander, and was often
eated in subsequent issues. It
oduced one of the most frequently
d quotations of the war.

"Well, if you knows of a better 'ole, go to it."

it is a rotten war. Fancy lying down under a sheet and the sheet is the only cover to stop the bits of bombs, not very comforting is it dear. Well we all get the wind up and no mistake.

Sweeney was fortunate: a month later a not-too-serious wound but one bad enough to get him back to 'Blighty' put him out of action for the rest of the war; but for men with badly frayed nerves who found no such relief there were worse torments waiting. 'Shell-shock' was a condition to which many men succumbed which produced, and sometimes not only temporarily, a complete disintegration of personality. Curiously enough, it took two years for the military authorities to recognize that 'shell-shock' existed as a definable medical state: the term only became official in 1916. In late 1917 Bombardier Harry Fayerbrother, Royal Field Artillery, found himself with a gun-crew in the Ypres Salient with a seriously shell-shocked comrade.

He upset all of us. There were just five or six of us in our dug-out and every time a shell came over he went haywire, shouting and screaming as if he wanted to tear the place to pieces, and tear us to pieces too. We just couldn't put up with it, so I grabbed him by the scruff of the neck and took him down the duckboard track to the dressing station. He was quite a mild little fellow, in fact quite a sweet-natured sort of chap.

It must be readily admitted that this is a very difficult area in which to draw conclusions or attempt generalizations. Men reacted in a wide variety of ways to the extraordinary circumstances in which they found themselves: some could take them in their stride, some could adjust to them with the help of discipline and comradeship, some simply could not cope. Perhaps the best way to conclude this selection of disparate and indeed contradictory experience is to quote from two soldiers—one an NCO and one an officer—who wrote, at the time, thoughtfully and with insight about their part in the war.

Lance Sergeant Elmer Cotton, 5th Bn Northumberland Fusiliers, made this statement in his notebook of 1915:

The British soldier is a man who knows fear but overcomes it—when in the fight he can be relied upon to see it through but before it begins he is anxious.

Captain Harry Yoxall, 18th Bn King's Royal Rifles Corps, wrote this in September 1916 during the Battle of the Somme:

Don't believe stories which you see in the papers about troops asking as a special privilege not to be relieved. We stick it, at all costs if necessary, as long as ordered, but everyone's glad to hand over to someone else. And anyone who says he enjoys this kind of thing is either a liar or a madman.

To a later generation, perhaps over-conditioned by the disenchanted war poetry of writers like Siegfried Sassoon and Wilfred Owen and by the explosion of anti-war 128

literature of the late twenties and thirties, it is a revelation to realize that the Tommy found much to tease his humour in the life of the Western Front. Sassoon might write of the 'hell where youth and laughter go'; but in that hell laughter, if somewhat grimly, managed to survive.

> Even in the most dire circumstances, shell-fire, machine-gun fire, knee-deep in mud and water, with short rations and pay-day just a distant memory (4/8d a week in my case), most of us still found time for a laugh and a joke.
> *Private A. L. Atkins, 7th Bn Middlesex Regt*

Second Lieutenant Cyril Rawlins spent some time as battalion censor; he found the reading of his soldiers' letters to be more than merely a tedious chore.

> One gets a good insight into the inner working of the Tommy's mind in this way: there never was a more cheerful, philosophical, kindly creature than the British soldier; his humour is inimitable and equal to any emergency.

Postcards like this one, though obviously produced with the propagandist purpose of showing that nobody was downhearted at the front, nevertheless catch something of the genuine spirit of the Tommy's humour. The caption on the reverse reads: 'Our grand artillerymen like to address a shell before they fire it. This shell, being of the biggest size, is addressed to the biggest Hun.' Shells as 'presents' to or from the enemy was a standard concept (see, for example, Private Jack Sweeney's first letter from the front line in Ch. 5). Cards of this kind could be bought by the soldiers in the villages and towns behind the line.

122. A PRESENT FOR THE KAISER.

"Daily Mail"
Official Photograph
Crown Copyright reserved

British Tommies in cheerful mood at the end of the Battle of the Somme, sporting that most prized of souvenirs, the German 'pickelhaube'. These picturesque items of headgear were soon to be superseded by the 'coal scuttle' steel helmet.

The humour is not music-hall; it provokes the resigned smile rather than the belly-laugh; it comes right out of the situations in which the men found themselves. Major Vignoles, Grimsby Chums, collected one or two of the spontaneous witticisms of his men and recorded them in his letters home.

> Our ration party was paddling along in the water one day, carrying their bags on their shoulders, all very quiet being very tired, when some wag at the front says: 'Pass it on, KEEP A SHARP LOOK OUT FOR SUBMARINES', and so the message was passed on by every man, perfectly solemnly without laughing at all! The Tommies are very quaint sometimes.

Sloshing through mud and water seems to have produced a rich vein of comment at all times. Sergeant R. MacKay, 109th Field Ambulance, 36th (Ulster) Division, was on his way to the front just before the opening of the Battle of the Somme when he and his comrades came to

> a very deep shell-hole. I waded in until the water was up to my arm-pits

130

and was just getting out on the other side when I heard a loud laugh and splashing behind me. I looked back and could just see a tin hat moving across the surface of the water. One of the others called out, 'This is our first casualty, not shot but drowned!' Gradually, however, a head, and then the remainder of the body emerged from the muddy water, and I realized it was Joe Allen. Joe was only about 5 feet 2 inches in height and he had sunk into the deepest part of the shell-hole.

At times, however, the context could be positively macabre. The following are memories of autumn 1916, during the Somme battle.

Along the road was an unburied hand of a soldier, some of our 'wags' would pretend to shake hands with it—a bit of humour along the way.
Lieutenant Fred R. Wells, 47th Bn Canadian Expeditionary Force

On the day we took Thiepval—it was one of the greatest days in our Battalion's history—our movement to the forming up line was by a communication trench called Pip Street. At one point a dead soldier's lower leg was protruding from the side of the trench. It was covered, to some extent, by what had obviously been a green silk sock; the good quality of the article was still obvious. With a loud 'Lor' Bill! What a toff!' one of our men, a worthy from Stratford E., passed on to his battle position.
Captain R. A. Chell, 10th Bn Essex Regt

By contrast the Tommy was not above a bit of innocent fun to amuse the local people.

We marched back to Bethune and some of our men afforded amusement to the inhabitants by wearing German helmets with sausages stuck on the spikes, which they found in the captured German dug-outs.
Rifleman A. H. Young, 1/15th Bn London Regt, London Irish Rifles

But humorous reaction to the life of the trenches was not confined to the spontaneous asides of wits and wags or the occasional outburst of boisterousness while away from the firing line. It had its more formal aspects. Every connoisseur of First World War literature is familiar with that remarkable production *The Wipers Times*, sustained over two-and-three-quarter years with various changes of title (for example, *The Somme Times*, *The BEF Times* and finally, and perhaps most brilliantly, *The Better Times*—for its edition of December 1918). But the paper was founded by officers and the humour was largely officerial in character. It had all the hallmarks of the public school end-of-term magazine. The following items, whose origins are almost certainly lost in the folk-memory of the front, have an earthier ring. Here surely is the droll, tongue-in-cheek attitude of the Poor Bloody Infantryman, authentically preserved.

STANDING ORDERS FOR BRITISH INFANTRY IN FRANCE

131   1. The Colonel is thine only Boss; thou shalt have no other Boss but him.

Concerts

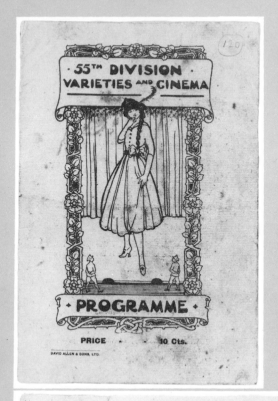

55TH DIVISION VARIETIES AND CINEMA

PROGRAMME

PRICE — 30 Cts.

DAVID ALLEN & SONS, LTD.

Concerts

A typical concert programme of the Western Front—and one particularly well supplied with still available jokes.

It is perhaps noteworthy that the programme 'announcements' give due prominence to two subjects of very special interest to the soldier—leave, and the green envelope. It requires little imagination to deduce why the Leading Lady was 'out of bounds' to all ranks.

In spite of—indeed, perhaps *because* of—the imminence of danger, concerts and film shows (which were equally popular) were often hilarious affairs. 'The audience is always out to enjoy itself, no matter what the programme is; & the talent of the entertainers who provide the "varieties" & the merits of the various films have really nothing to do with the success of the evening. Everybody is ready to laugh at everything & mirth is the predominant feature of the whole performance.'

2nd Lieutenant E. W. Jacot,
14th Bn Royal Warwicks

¶ Discussions on LEAVE are prohibited, as the Artistes are "Full of Hope."

★ ★

¶ The Shell-hole adjoining the Theatre is the property of the Company and must not be taken away.

★ ★

¶ Any member of the audience showing one or more green envelopes does so at his own risk.

★ ★

¶ ALL Ranks are notified that our Leading Lady is "Out of Bounds."

★ ★

¶ Patrons are requested to note that they can pay without coming in, but cannot come in without paying.

★ ★

¶ During the remainder of the War no person will be admitted to this theatre in Evening Dress.

★ ★

¶ Patrons are requested to refrain from falling off the balconies.

★ ★

¶ Our Shrapnel is the best, refuse all imitations.

★ ★

¶ Working parties supplied with (very) light

The 55th Divisional Theatre Coy.

PRESENT

Their Third Revue

ENTITLED

"THUMBS"

IN THREE SCENES

WRITTEN AND PRODUCED BY THE COMPANY

Wigs by W. CLARKSON
Costumes by W. CLARKSON and MORRIS ANGEL.

FOR THE DIVISIONAL THEATRE:

Stage Manager and Carpenter	Sapper A. HORRIDGE
Electricians	J. HURLEY & Pte. ROBOTHAM
Engineer	Pte. C. HALL
Cinema Operators	Trooper REYNOLDS, Ptes. BUDD & RAMSDEN
Scenic Artist	Lce.-Cpl. G. PAGE

Orchestra under the Direction of Pte. COUPE, consisting of
A. HONDERWOOD, R. ROBINSON & J. FULLERTON

Prices of Admission:

Officers—Box Seats		2 Frs.
Balcony		1 "
Sergeants		50 Cts.
Other Ranks		30 "

'Our wonderful show of the 1st Army'—
Les Rouges et les Noirs—also known,
English style, as *The Reds and the
Blacks*. The 'ladies', of course, are
soldiers in drag.

'... Another day I walked to Arras and
I spent the evening at the Theatre
where the First Army Concert Party
was performing. This was a real treat,
by far the finest show I had seen in
France & compared with some I had
seen in Blighty.'

Gunner J. H. Bird

'Gwen'—a leading 'lady' of *Les Rouges
et Les Noirs*. In a world without women
such concert-party heroines were often a
great success. Major R. S. Cockburn
describes in his memoirs one 'Kitty
O'Hara—a young girl of infinite charm
and beauty, prettier than most girls
whom you see on the London stage. It
was impossible to think of her as
anything else but a delightful flapper.
She was really an ordinary, simple
Canadian lad of some twenty years who
had been "over the top" nine times.'

2. But thou shalt make unto thyself many graven images of officers who fly in the heavens above, Staff Officers who own the Earth beneath, and of Submarine Officers who are in the waters under the earth. Thou shalt stand up and salute them for the Colonel thy boss will visit with Field Punishment unto the 1st & 2nd degree on those that salute not, and shower stripes on them that salute and obey his commandments.

3. Thou shalt not take the name of the Adjutant in vain for the Colonel will not hold him guiltless who taketh the Adjutant's name in vain.

4. Remember thou shalt not rest on the Sabbath day. Six days shalt thou labour and not do all thy work but the 7th day is the day of the CRE;* on it thou shalt do all manner of work & thy officers & thy NCO's & thy sanitary men & the Kitchener's Army who are within thy trench for instruction.

5. Honour the Army Staff that thy days may be long in the Corps Reserve where one day they may send thee.

6. Thou shalt kill only Huns, slugs, lice, rats & other vermin which frequent dug-outs.

7. Thou shalt not adulterate thy Section's rum ration.

8. Thou shalt not steal or at any rate not be found out.

9. Thou shalt not bear false witness in the orderly room.

10. Thou shalt not covet the ASC's job, nor his pay, nor his motors, nor his wagons, nor his tents, nor his billets, nor his horses, nor his asses, nor any cushy thing that is his.†

Also in the same cynically humorous vein are these 'Soldiers Superstitions'.

It is unlucky for 13 to sit down to a meal when rations have been issued for only 7.

If the sun rises in the East, it is a sure sign that there will be stew for dinner.

To drop your rifle on foot of a second lieutenant is bad luck—for him. To drop ditto on foot of sergeant major is bad luck—for you.

To hear lecture on glorious history of your Regiment indicates that you will shortly be going 'over the top'.

If a new officer, on taking over trench, announces that he has learned all about it at Cadet School, sign that he is about to get a surprise.

Perhaps a special place of honour should be reserved for the superstition which normally appears at the head of the list quoted above:

It is considered very unlucky to be killed on a Friday.

---

* The Senior Engineer Officer in each division was known as Commander Royal Engineers—CRE for short. Each division also had a CRA, i.e. Commander Royal Artillery.

† The Army Service Corps was the object of much envy on the part of the men nearer the firing line. Their pay could be as much as six times as high as that of an ordinary infantryman and they were usually well clear of shells and bullets. It seems curious to a later generation whose sympathies go first and foremost to the men in the trenches that the pay of the PBI—the Poor Bloody Infantry—was lowest of all.

10

'Just a Line to say I go "Over the Top" Tomorrow'

Fixing scaling ladders in trenches on the day before the Battle of Arras, 8 April 1917.

However much he might become accustomed to the routines of trench warfare, the Tommy knew that in time he would almost certainly have to face a still greater ordeal. Sooner or later the moment would arrive when he would have to leave the relative security of his trenches and advance towards the enemy in open battle.

The intention behind the British doctrine of maintaining the offensive spirit even in the quieter times and the cushier trenches—and behind the acceptance of trenches recognizably inferior in quality to those on the other side of the wire—was to instil in the soldiers the firm understanding that he was only there for the time being—until his leaders could mount the massive assault which would put the enemy to flight and drive him back towards Berlin. Trench routine, in fact, was merely a holding operation; the essential act of war was the set-piece battle—in the parlance of the time, 'the Big Push'.

Major Walter Vignoles of the Grimsby Chums put the point in young officers' language before the 'Push' of 1916—the event that was to become known to history as the Battle of the Somme. As the great preliminary bombardment continued day after day, he wrote: 'When one thinks about it all, or stops to analyse it, it seems an extraordinary "game"—the awful waste—but the only thing to do is to go on and try to "biff the Boche".' It was, indeed, the only thing to do, so long as the Western Front remained, as it did remain, the principal theatre of the war. It was here that, to borrow Churchill's phrase, the 'World Crisis' was to be resolved. And it was to be resolved by the energy, the fighting capacity, and, as everyone knew, the sacrifice of thousands and thousands of men.

For the infantryman this was the ultimate experience: it was for this he had joined the Army. He had not volunteered to hold alien ground indefinitely in a muddy warren of rat-infested trenches, but to right the wrongs of France, avenge little Belgium, and, in C. E. Montague's phrase, 'reclaim the world for straightness and decency'. To achieve these ends he had to attack the enemy and beat him; and to do that he would have to go 'over the top'.

'Over the top', 'over the lid', 'over the bags' (i.e. the sandbags that formed the trench wall)—there were a number of versions of this 'fateful phrase', as one infantry- 136

man called it, but whatever expression he used it expressed a daunting concept for the soldier. The prospects of being killed or mutilated were high. If a man was wounded in a trench stretcher-bearers were usually on hand to take him quickly down to the dressing station. If he were wounded among the shell-holes and barbed wire entanglements of No Man's Land, he might bleed slowly and painfully to death with no one to help him or relieve his sufferings. But these possibilities had to be faced if the goal for which everyone had trained and striven over the weeks and months of preparation were to be achieved.

The letters and diaries of the time show no unanimity of reaction among the soldiers about to go into battle. Predictably men faced the prospect of action in a wide variety of ways: some with jaunty heroism, many more with a thoughtful and reconciled awareness, others with unashamed loathing and apprehension.

The extracts that follow all date from the last days before the opening of the Battle of the Somme on 1 July 1916. This was a particularly significant and emotional time for the volunteer soldiers of Britain. It was to be the first blooding of the men of Kitchener's Army. The Pals Battalions were there in strength. Confidence was, on the whole, remarkably high. The preparations, it seemed, had been as thorough as they could be. Throughout the last weeks of June—during which period most of the letters that follow were written—a bombardment of colossal intensity, reputedly the greatest the world had ever seen, pulverized the enemy trenches. The optimistic forecasts of the commanders predicted a virtual walk-over. (Indeed, the tactics chosen by the General in charge of the opening phase of the battle, Sir Henry Rawlinson, dictated that the attacking troops were *literally* to walk across No Man's Land, heavily laden with equipment, at 7.30 on a summer's morning.) Everyone knew, however, that the German was a formidable opponent. Even if the first wave were to stroll to its objectives—which in the event it did not—there would be bound to be fierce resistance sooner or later and, inevitably, many casualties.

This letter was written by Lieutenant Robert Sutcliffe, West Yorkshire Regiment. At thirty-eight Sutcliffe was older than most: a successful Bradford solicitor, a well-known amateur golfer and a distinguished old boy of Bradford Grammar School. He had joined up as a member of the Public Schools' Battalion and later been commissioned in the 1st Bradford Pals.

> Just a line to say I go 'over the lid' tomorrow. My company are in the first line of attack and hope to do great things. We all naturally hope to come through all right, but, of course, one never knows, someone's bound to go under and it's the only way to end the war. It's a great thing to be in, and I'm glad our division is one of the first chosen to go over.

Sutcliffe was badly wounded on 1st July and died at sea while being evacuated by hospital ship to England. He is buried not with his 'Pals' of the 16th Battalion of the West Yorkshire Regiment in the cemeteries on the Serre road in Picardy, but in a quiet graveyard in the Pennine Hills a dozen miles from Bradford.

Bombardment

Scenes from the great bombardment which preceded the opening of the Battle of the Somme. The bombardment lasted a whole week and was audible in England.

Major Walter Vignoles, Grimsby Chums, attempted to describe this great artillery cadenza in his letters:

'The noise is terrific, as we are just in front of some of the guns, the shells passing right over us. I cannot describe the noise accurately; it is a series or succession of huge bangs, developing at times into a continuous roar. This ceaseless bombardment of the enemy lines has been going on now for some days, and as our fellows say, we have given him SOME stick. ... The whole air throbs with the sound ... it seems to come in huge sudden stabs. ... It is impressive to watch the vicious puffs of smoke as the shells explode on the enemy's lines, smoke of all colours from white to green and black and yellow; at night times it is even more impressive as the lines are outlined in the darkness with the bursting shells'.

A 9.2-inch gun firing.

Before Battle

'A most magnificent entertainment' was how Lieutenant Kenneth Macardle described the great bombardment in his diary, writing on 26th June:

> The abused, overworked, underpaid infantry has come into its own at last; now that the push is in sight and dirty work to do we have the front row of the stalls in the theatre of war, and the gunners, working hard behind the scenes, can't even see the show they are putting on. But they do it uncommonly well. All along the Bosch front line black & yellow, white & grey puffs of smoke dance in mighty cruel glee; fountains of brown sand or black clay shoot up high carrying with them a bunch of stakes all tangled up with wire. . . . The heavy shells throw black volumes of smoke some 300 feet into the air.

German front line under artillery barrage at La Boiselle prior to the attack of 1 July 1916.

What no postcard could convey was the shattering experience of firing guns of this weight and power through a long bombardment such as that which preceded the Battle of the Somme. The continuous appalling noise concussed the mind and made men bleed from the ears. In the words of one artilleryman, Gunner H. Sturdy, Royal Field Artillery: 'Firing the guns themselves was enough to turn strong men into deaf nervous wrecks.'

For the infantryman the colossal pre-Somme bombardment was often something of a revelation. Captain Reginald Leetham, 2nd Bn the Rifle Brigade, came out from the trenches shortly before the battle and saw the artillery at full stretch: 'All the way home to our billets we saw another side of the war and passed battery after battery loosing off shell after shell. As we passed in front of one, only forty yards from us, it fired a 12 inch shell over our heads; the explosion and vibration was terrific.'

Second Lieutenant O'Sullivan, 6th Bn Connaught Rangers, witnessed a later Somme bombardment: 'We worked our way through in front of the British field artillery where every gun was barking away in a perfect frenzy. Their hellish noise directly behind us was so stupefying that to talk with one's neighbour meant shouting in his very ear . . .'

A BRITISH HEAVY GUN IN ACTION.

Cards on sale at the time of the Battle of the Somme. The caption on the reverse side reads: 'This heavy gun on the British Western Front, seen in action, is a unit in the tremendous siege which we are making, "not on a place, but on the German Army".'

FIRING A HEAVY HOWITZER IN FRANCE.

This card is captioned: 'One of the earth-shaking howitzers on the British Western Front.'

This letter was written by a Kitchener volunteer of forty-nine to his fourteen-year-old son.

> To my Own Dear Boy Jimmy,
> . . . I am well contented knowing my loved ones at Home are thinking of their Dad & doing the best they can to brighten one another's lives. Your Sweet Mother tells me that you do try & be a Comfort to her & it takes the weariness off my shoulders over this War and I can fight with a better heart when everything is going on all right at Home. So now my Dearest Boy Look Upward & Go Forward in the Right is the Earnest Wish of
> Your Affectionate
> Father.

The writer was reported missing in the battle and later presumed dead: he became one of the 73,000 dead of the Somme whose bodies were never found.*

This letter was written by Lieutenant William Clarke, Sheffield City Battalion, to his fiancée, on 29th June.

> My Own Sweetheart,
> I have just been busy sending off letters to various people & before lying down must send my wee girl a few lines.
> I got your letter today & you seem quite cheery so as long as Dora's all right 'All's well with the world'.
> Now my sweetheart I am going off to get some sleep. All my love darling girl and keep a brave heart for my sake & just pray that this war will soon be over & I can come back to take care of you & never leave you any more. All all my love & lots of sweet kisses.
> Willie

* This simply expressed but profoundly moving letter, faithfully preserved for sixty years, was lent to me by the writer's son, Mr James Hargreaves. Mr Hargreaves wrote: 'I am proud to show you the calibre of these men who gave their lives for their country on that fateful day in 1916.'

Lieutenant Clarke quoted above with members of his platoon in the early days of the Sheffield City Battalion. His fiancée later married a soldier of the Battalion—who lost the sight of his eyes in the attack which killed Lieutenant Clarke.

'I went to Communion this morning and knelt in the long grass beneath the blue sky ...' (Lance Corporal Roland Mountfort, 10th Bn Royal Fusiliers, shortly before going into battle in July 1916).

The photograph shows a church parade of the 17th Battalion the Liverpool Regiment at Carnoy Valley just behind the Somme front on 29 June 1916. For many men Communion before battle was more than merely a ritualistic formality:

> We had a service in the orchard with H. C. [Holy Communion] after in the barn, most impressive it was, equipment & rifles lying around and pigeons flying above in the rafters. Padre referred to our work to come reminding us it might be our last chance of Communion; it was quite sad and many men had wet eyes. It however gave me courage for the days to come.
> *Lieutenant Lionel Ferguson, Cheshire Regt, Sunday 25 June 1916*

Lieutenant Clarke was killed in action on 1st July. His battalion attacked almost eight hundred strong and suffered over five hundred casualties.

The following extracts are from a letter written by Private A. H. Hubbard, London Scottish, to his two sisters. The letter was begun on 29th June.

> Hope we shall be successful on Saturday morning July 1st at dawn when you are all fast asleep in driving the Huns out of their present position, and without any bad luck to myself. I have got to go over with the first batch, and assist in cutting the barb wire [sic] which hasn't been destroyed by our artillery during the past few days heavy bombardment. . . . I should be in my glory if the news came through to cease firing and pack up. . . . I can imagine how everything looks at home, and the garden as you say must be almost at its best, you will soon be having beans I presume. I shall imagine I am in heaven when I get home, what a treat it will be to feel nice and clean, at present it is up to your neck in mud, which all helps to make you feel miserable. I am sorry to have to state all this, but I don't feel inclined to tell you a pack of lies, if the truth were told a bit more often, I don't suppose the war would be on now, when you land over here, they have got you tight and treat you as they think.*
>
> *Friday June 30th.* We are just going to have an open air Church service, and are going to the trenches this evening, ready for the attack in the morning, so I think this is all I have to say until this affair is over, hoping to write a longer letter to Heather & you all on Sunday if I get through alright, which I very much hope I shall successfully, so must close with my best love to you all at home.
> > I Remain,
> > > Your Affec Brother
> > > Arthur.

Private, later Corporal, Hubbard survived the battle and the war but never recovered from his experiences at the front. He committed suicide some years later. His family is convinced that this was a direct consequence of the psychological dislocation induced by his war service.

Private Jack Sweeney, 1st Bn Lincolnshire Regt, wrote this in a letter to his fiancée also written on 29th June.

> I am trusting in God to let me come out of this big attack safely. I do not mind getting wounded as long as I get one so that I can help myself. I do not want to lie on the field for hours wounded and then a shell to come and finish the job. Keep a good heart as the boys out here are all sure that there is going to be a great victory.

* Private Hubbard's unhappy letter also includes an account of an episode by no means unique before a great battle: 'I was 20 yds from one of the Kensington's 13th Lon. Regt. last week, when he shot himself through the foot just to get back to England out of it, of course he will get about 84 days field punishment for it, after the wound has healed up. I went over and fetched assistance to him and extracted the empty case out of his rifle, what a feeling he will have later on if it takes a long time to heal up and to know he (has) done it himself, but still he is not the only one that has done likewise.'

Private Sweeney survived, but was one of those soldiers whose nerves slowly deteriorated with the passage of time. A 'Blighty' wound, received in December 1917, was his salvation.

Second Lieutenant Kenneth Macardle, 17th Bn Manchester Regt, wrote the following in his diary shortly before the battle opened. He was the archetypal young officer who found great exhilaration in war (Chapter 7); he was already famous in his battalion for his expertise and coolness in No Man's Land. His diary reflects the high optimism that was the prevalent doctrine of the time; there is no hint of personal doubts or uncertainty.

> Rumour says we are to smash the Hun line altogether, shove in our army de chasse and finish the war. . . . Rumour also says that we have given Germany four days to declare peace or take the consequences. I am not addicted to boasting but I think if he could see all the guns behind, all the grenades, trench mortars and other stores in front, if he knew how thoroughly ready we are . . . and if he could conceive how we are longing for 'the day'—I think if he knew, the Kaiser would cut his losses and—take poison.

Second Lieutenant Macardle was to be killed just a few days later in the opening stages of the great battle.

There could be few more moving accounts of the thoughts and experiences of a young and highly sensitive man about to face the ordeal of battle than that left by Second Lieutenant Roland Ingle of the 9th Lincolns. His all-too-brief diary begins at 5.30 p.m. on Saturday 24 June 1916 and ends at 7 p.m. on Friday 30th June, just twelve-and-a-half hours before the first-wave attack.

Saturday June 24th
The bombardment for the 'great push' has just begun: I am sitting out here on an old plough in a half-tilled field watching the smoke of the shells rising over the German lines. In the hollow straight in front lies the town with its broken church,* with the long straight road leading to the rear: there is the village that I was in last Saturday in a hollow to the right, with its small church spire intact showing among the trees. It is a pleasant rather cloudy day, after a night of heavy rain: and the light breeze blowing from the west lessens for us the sound of the guns, besides being a protection, as far as we know, against gas. . . . On the whole the evening is 'a pleasant one for a stroll'—with the larks singing.

Sunday June 25th
I went up the hill again last night after mess—about 10 o'clock. . . . It was of course a wonderful sight: flashes right and left caught your eye in quick succession, and all the time beyond was the red burst of the shells falling

---

* The town was Albert; the broken church was the basilica of Notre Dame de Brebières, with its famous 'Leaning Virgin'.

Second Lieutenant P. S. Worner, 9th Devonshire Regiment, killed 4 September 1916 on the Somme. Buried at Bernafay Wood.

It became common practice to print the last letters of fallen soldiers in local newspapers, particularly when they showed the kind of courage and high patriotic spirit displayed in the example below.

LIEUT. PERCY WORNER

Prominent Exeter Athlete Killed in France

News was received from the War Office this morning by his parents, residing at 9, Edgerton Park-road, Exeter, that Second-Lieut. Percy Worner was killed in action in France on Tuesday. He was an only son, and the report of his death will be received with deep regret by a wide circle of his friends in Exeter.

When war broke out he was an assistant teacher at St. Sidwell's School, where he had previously been a pupil and then a pupil teacher. He underwent a course of training at St. Luke's College, and there became a very clever Association footballer. His college chum and inseparable companion was the International footballer, Lieut. Evelyn Lintott, who was killed in France in July. Worner first of all joined the Public Schools' Corps, and was at the Front over six months while a member of it, taking part in several big actions. Then he was sent home to train for a commission, and recently was given a second-lieutenancy. He was in Exeter on leave before going to France last month, and was then quite enthusiastic about his new duties. He took up military life, in fact, very seriously, just as he did anything to which he put his hand. It was his quiet earnestness on the sports' field which made him such a warm favourite with everyone, while it is safe to say that at St. Sidwell's School he was held in quite affectionate esteem by all his pupils.

Only this week a football was sent out to him from the Mayoress of Exeter's Depot. He had written there asking if he could have one for his Company, amongst whom he was hopeful of forming a Soccer team. His letter was full of cheery optimism.

This is the second member of the St. Sidwell's School teaching staff who has laid down his life for his country, the other being Sergt. Emrys Jones, the well-known Rugby County player.

SPLENDIDLY ENGLISH

The Last Letter of Lieut. Worner of Exeter

The last letter sent home by 2nd-Lieut. Percy Worner, the Exeter schoolmaster and athlete, who was killed in France a week ago, was addressed to his parents, and now makes the more impressive and stirring reading. It is splendidly English. "I have been appointed to a Company," he wrote, "whose officers are practically all Exonians. . . . They gave me a great welcome, and have done everything they can to make me at home and comfortable. . . The men out here are so grand that, whatever my fate may be, I shall be ready for it. The only thing one fears when one finds he has to lead such fine men is that one may funk at the last moment. What is most striking of all out here is the utter cheerfulness and confidence of the men, many of whom have been in France since the beginning. To be among them is the finest thing imaginable. Their cheerfulness and confidence are most infectious. They have been out for a short rest since their last strafe, and yet they are keenly looking forward to another 'go.' If only the Kaiser could see and understand the spirit of these men he would realise that the game was up so far as he was concerned. Nothing on this earth can defeat their spirit, and I feel it an honour to be privileged to serve with them. . . . Probably before I hear from you I shall have been in action—leading men this time. Please give me all your thoughts and all your prayers that I may not lead these fine fellows amiss. . ."

No letter could more strikingly reveal the spirit of the former St. Luke's College student than this. News of exactly how he was killed has not reached his parents yet, but that he died a gallant death none who knew him can doubt.

146

on their target. I stood some time looking and two sergeants came up—we talked the usual gossip that we had all heard: any story passes these days and the funny thing is that no one seems to mind if it is something in our favour or decidedly against us. I have heard two distinct rumours that the anxious would find unpalatable—one, that a doctor went over to the Germans from the division on our right, of course, with plenty of valuable information: another that our latest and most wonderful aeroplane settled peacefully behind the Huns' lines. Nobody worries if they are true or not. As the time for us to move approaches I suppose we shall be excited and nervous, but now for most people, and I should think for the most thoughtless and unimpressionable, it is just a contemplative pause and a rest. Excitement braces the muscles in healthy people, and that is the feeling you have at the thought of the 'great push' beginning. As an alternative to trench warfare it is welcome—to me especially, with my doubtful powers of endurance.

Someone made the inevitable remark in the mess the other night that we are taking part in what may be a historic event—for us, personally, of course, historic but also possibly in years to come a historic event of the Great War. One man's part in any move nowadays is so small that he is not likely to be nervous about the effect of his work on the final result: and fortunately the habit of 'carrying on' (that immortal phrase) is by this time so ingrained in him that in spite of great shattering of everything else [sic] he has a hope that he will be able to do it. And no one should forget that a free throwing of yourself into a forward move gives the thing a momentum that nothing else can—beyond any mechanical discipline. If the least thoughtful could analyse his feelings, he would say, I suppose, that provided he was hitting hard he didn't care what happened to him. And the men who are going to be knocked out in the push—there must be many—should not certainly be looked on with pity: because going forward with resolution and braced muscles puts a man in a mood to despise consequences: he is out to give more than he gets: he really dies fighting, and a man who is used to sport, takes things—even in the great chance of life and death—as part of the game.

This is a remarkable statement and is perhaps worthy of comment. To a later generation—groomed to a diametrically opposite view of war by precisely the kind of event in which Ingle was about to be engaged—to write of a major battle as though it were a somewhat more than usually vigorous soccer or rugby match might seem quaint and naive. It would, I believe, be uncharitable to think it so. Roland Ingle was a product of the British public school system and of Oxbridge: an old boy of King's School, Ely; a former open scholar at Cambridge; and in the last years before the war a Worcestershire schoolmaster. Like so many of his kind he was a keen sportsman, a cricketer ('a splendid field, especially at point', according to his family) and a good soccer player (he missed his Cambridge Blue through injury). But at twenty-eight, and known as a highly intelligent and sensitive young man, he was no doughty jingo eager to kill Germans and have a crack at the Hun. He had joined up because

it had seemed his patriotic duty to do so. To go into battle was a necessary corollary of that decision. And for a man brought up in this particular tradition, with no thought of becoming a soldier until the sudden crisis of 1914, what other comparisons were there than the field of sport, with its tensions, its pre-match nerves, its requirement to perform stylishly and to effect and its obligation to attempt to achieve victory? It was, indeed, almost automatic at the time to compare war to a game. 'It seems an extraordinary game,' Major Vignoles wrote, less than half a mile away from Ingle, in the same week. Several miles to the south-east Captain Wilfred Nevill, at about the same time, presented two footballs to the leading companies of the 8th East Surreys, so that they might kick them 'over the top' at zero hour (Ch. 11). Elsewhere a battalion was to advance to the attack on 1st July to the sound of a hunting horn. The long months of attrition ahead would put paid to such sporting gestures, but it is entirely comprehensible that they should have been made at this time—before the new, highly dangerous game established its own brutal rules of play.

Having resolved his philosophical attitude, Second Lieutenant Ingle then proceeds, reasonably calmly, with the preparations for the battle. There is only one further reference to the prospect of action. 'Everyone is pleased with the idea of going forward: it should relieve the pressure on Verdun, which has been applied purely with the object of delaying and embarrassing our offensive.' For the most part he is content to chronicle the pattern of the days' events—bouts of last-minute training, company 'pow-wows', superintending the moving of ammunition up to the forward emplacements (he was an officer in a Trench Mortar Battery). There are moments of half-amused irony:

> I went up the hill again last night, with three or four others and a gramophone; we took up a position and watched the bombardment, which was still lively and had increased to a continuous roar by the time we came down at 11.0; the gramophone discoursing 'Comfort ye, comfort ye, my people'! was a curious accompaniment to the guns.

He describes a nearby military cemetery:

> The cemetery lies on the right of the road going up to the château; whenever you go by, there is some mound of new earth thrown up. The graves are beautifully kept, and the crosses made in various patterns—all carefully done by the pioneer battalion who are responsible for these things. Often you see figures or inscriptions carved in chalk placed on the graves, or, on the cross itself the dead man's cap. Often there are flowers, and men—pals from the dead man's company—tending the graves. The cemetery is in a quiet open space in the middle of the wood, just by the road: on one side were the cookers'—the field kitchens—on the other concealed guns, firing their perpetual salute over the graves.

He visits the battalion 'canteen village', as he calls it:

> I got to the village in time to draw 125 francs from the field cashier and

This picture was taken on 28 June 1916, and shows men of the 10th East Yorkshire Regiment (the Hull Commercials) on the march near Doullens on their way to the line.

13

WILL.

In the event of my death, I give the whole of my property, effects & credit to my mother & Father,

Mrs & Mr. W. Atkins,
75 Summerhill Rd
West Green
Tottenham
London. N.15.

Signature _A. Atkins_

Rank and Regiment _L/Cpl. 198 M.G.C._

Date _October 25th 1917._

Regimental No. 106613.

A soldier's will, written on a page of his pay-book. Another form of pre-battle preparation encouraged, not without reason, by the Army. This soldier survived and has in fact been one of the major suppliers of material for this book.

149

The picture shows the 1st Lancashire Fusiliers being addressed by their Divisional Commander, General de Lisle, before the Battle of the Somme, on 29 June 1916.

Pep-talks by senior officers before a battle were standard. One veteran claims to have heard a Colonel address his battalion in the following terms: 'Up to now this Battalion has not made a name for itself; now, tonight, you will have this opportunity. Should you be slightly wounded, make your way on your own to Base, don't take up valuable Ambulance Service space, and if too badly injured, crawl away to a shell hole and die.' It is perhaps fair to add that this story almost certainly emanates from a later and more cynical period of the war and that pre-battle addresses were normally couched in somewhat more encouraging terms.

then I went to tea at the officers' tea-shop where was a great squash: I read a paper, *The Daily Chronicle* of Wednesday, while waiting for tea and after tea bought milk and fruit and bread, butter and coffee for our mess. Madame stowed the tins in my haversack on my back and I carried some in a side-haversack and I came away.

Later the same day he records

'a fat meal' as the result of my shopping—tinned chicken, very little and very expensive at 3 francs: tinned apricots and condensed milk.

He also notes, in the same entry, the death of a friend:

Today one of C Company officers of the Lincolns (the Company I was in) was killed: Rowe his name was. He acted as second in command of the company during the move from Gandspette. I liked him, he was good-natured and straightforward.

His last entry, which he signed at the end so that it could be sent home as a letter,

An advanced field ambulance—symbol of another necessary form of preparation for a great battle. Second Lieutenant Ingle, in the diary quoted in this chapter, wrote on Wednes-day 28 June: '... the road from our canteen village was fairly busy with transport, and there were many ambulance cars "packed" by the side of the road, with various inscrip-tions—"A gift from the County of Meath"—"The Derbyshire Miners Association"—"The gift of the Hellenic Community in London" ...' These ambulances were to be in very great demand on the first day on the Somme.

131. AN ADVANCED FIELD AMBULANCE.

Second Lieutenant Roland Ingle, 1886–1916.

Ingle's Commanding Officer wrote in his letter of consolation:

'At the time when Roland was killed he was attached to a Trench Mortar Battery. All the TMB's were unable to get much beyond the front line, so intense was the German machine-gun fire. ... The fire that officers and men had to face in this battle was terrible, and your son led his men through it till he fell.'

A Corporal wrote to Ingle's father:

'Only one in the battery escaped injury. It was so awful to see them cut down as they were. ... Sir, I trust to God I shall soon be at home and share with others a peaceful life.'

is written quite coolly and without any demonstration of emotion. The tone, if it can be interpreted at all, is one of quiet acceptance.

We are moving up to the château to-night and having breakfast there at 3.30. We moved 200 rounds from dugouts to our gun emplacements this afternoon, which took from 3.0–5.30. Our guns were firing all the time and the Huns making some return.

It was a lovely afternoon with a fresh wind blowing: some of the trenches were badly knocked about. I looked over into Hunsland as I came out—the wood in front looking like currant bushes with the blight.

Some trees were down in our wood. I passed the cemetery as I came back and looked at Rowe's grave. I am moving up by myself at 8.30, having a little time here to wash and have a meal. I had three letters to-night and the *Observer*, rather delayed, all posted on Sunday.

This ends the diary before the push as I must pack up.

Ever yours,
Ro

Second Lieutenant Ingle was killed on the morning of 1st July. He is buried in the cemetery which he had described with such careful detail just a few days previously.

11

Into Battle 'A Great Thing to be In'

Ready to go over—th[is]
famous photograph s[hows]
Canadian infantry wa[iting]
for 'zero' on the Som[me in]
the later stages of th[e]
battle, in October 191[6]

'How the time dragge[d]
on. Would it never c[ome?]
At last, "One minute [to]
get ready." Now for [it,]
either death or glory, [or]
perhaps a nice woun[d]
good enough to get [me]
across the water.'

Corporal F. W. Billm[an]
9th Bn East Surrey

Just before dusk on 30 June 1916, a young Lieutenant of the Royal Field Artillery, Cyril Drummond, rode towards the British trenches opposite Thiepval to reconnoitre the route by which his battery was due to advance if the attack went well the following morning. His purpose was to see where and for how long the battery would present a target to the enemy's artillery. It was a relatively quiet and peaceful evening; the British guns were firing but there was no response from the Germans and everything seemed relaxed and outwardly calm. Somewhere in the dead ground behind the trench lines he received a harsh reminder of the reality of war.

> Lying beside a pile of boxes was the body of a soldier who had been killed earlier in the day. He was covered by a blanket, but one corner was awry, exposing an arm, torn, shattered, and dusty. Suddenly, for the first time, the thought crossed my mind, 'Shall I be looking like that this time tomorrow?'

Everywhere about him along the eighteen-mile front—to the north as far as Gommecourt, to the south-east as far as Montauban—thousands and thousands of men were preparing themselves for battle, some in the trenches, some on the march, some waiting in their billet villages for the order to move forward. Apprehensions of the kind experienced by Lieutenant Drummond must have afflicted many at this time.

At Bus-les-Artois, the 93rd Infantry Brigade, which consisted of four Pals Battalions from the north of England, gathered on the village green and listened to a concert by the Band of the Leeds Pals. Sixty years later a Bradford Pal recalled the mood of the occasion.

> Although I cannot remember the programme played on that lovely summer evening so long ago, I certainly have an abiding memory of one piece—Schubert's *Unfinished Symphony*. Because of this, every performance that I have heard of it since takes me back to that evening in Bus, still quite clear in my mind's eye, with all those Leeds and Bradford Pals sitting around on the grass, quietly listening, and with all of them no doubt wondering, as I certainly did, what awaited us at daybreak the following morning.

Private W. Slater, 2nd Bradford Pals

Elsewhere men were marching. A stretcher-bearer in the 19th Division, watching the divisional infantry march off from Laviéville towards the trenches near Albert, was much taken by the fact that

> men of the Welsh Regiments sang most of the time; sang quite softly and—strangely enough—hymns. Accompanied by the muffled shuffling of many feet, this singing in the darkness intensified the eerie unreality of it all.
> *Private A. L. Linfoot, 5th Field Ambulance, 57th Brigade*

But a battalion of Northumberland Fusiliers heard a very different sound that evening: a raucous anonymous voice which hailed them as they marched towards the front line:

> You came of your own accord,
> You didn't have to be fetched;
> You *bloody* fools!*

Generally, however, this was a time when, whatever private apprehensions men might feel, the mood of the majority of soldiers was one of optimism, and morale and hope were high. The previous night, 29th June, Major Vignoles, Grimsby Chums, had parted from the officers of his company who were not to go over in the attack.

> They shook hands with us all when they left, and went off not at all pleased at being out of the show. We, on the other hand, were in very good spirits: I don't know why, for we all knew that there was a good chance of many being killed or wounded, but we WERE in good spirits and they were not assumed either—even those who grouse as a rule were cheerful. I think the fact that at last we hoped to get to close quarters with the Boche and defeat him accounted for it.

Private Linfoot, watching his comrades of 19th Division assemble on the last night before the battle, sensed a similar buoyant mood.

> They were massing to go 'over the top'—fateful words for all infantrymen. They were intensely excited yet quietly confident. This was to be the big breakthrough to end the stalemate; to end the war. The timid were less fearful, the bold more exultant, and were thrilled and intensely alive as they 'fell in' on the evening of 30 June. In Laviéville a troop of cavalry trotted past them two by two. Sombre enough in their drab khaki, but in the eyes of their trench-dwelling comrades romantic and splendid. A good omen, surely!

The cavalry, in fact, were to play virtually no part in the ensuing battle; the infantry were to be cut down in their thousands. On the following day, 1 July 1916, there would be almost 60,000 British casualties, of whom a third, about 21,000, would lose their lives. It was to be a day like no other in British military history.

---

* I am indebted to former Private John Anderson, 18th Bn Northumberland Fusiliers, for this story: he heard the original shout.

When attempting to describe the mood of the men of 1914–18 when going into battle, there is some case for differentiating between the Somme—in particular its catastrophic first phase—and the other major battles of the war. The effect of the Somme on the morale and attitudes of the British Army is a subject of continuing and often rancorous controversy. There are those who see the Somme as the tragic massacre of a generation, as an event so cataclysmic that it killed the breezy, crusading spirit of 1914–15 at a stroke and destroyed once and for all the grand, heroic view of war. This was when Siegfried Sassoon's 'happy legion' was happy no longer, when in the telling words of C. E. Montague—in a book whose title, *Disenchantment*, carries its own highly charged message—a web was woven across the sky and a goblin made of the sun. There are others, however, who dismiss this interpretation as naive, if romantic nonsense, exaggerated out of all proportion by the international acclaim that has surrounded for several decades the clique of young poets who most ardently expressed it. They claim that the British Army, despite the shattering defeat on the first day, came out of the Somme battle blooded, honed and confident, and that, by contrast, it was the German Army which had lost its cutting edge and its zest for battle. This is not the place to explore these arguments, each of which has its compelling pieces of evidence and its passionate expounders. It is sufficient for the purposes of this book that for many 1 July 1916 *was* a major watershed, and that there was among many battalions—particularly the amateur ones of Kitchener's Citizen's Army*—an incontrovertible feeling that nothing would ever be the same again. Lieutenant Robert Sutcliffe of the Bradford Pals could write of the forthcoming battle that it was 'a great thing to be in'. But many of the New Army battalions were to be virtually annihilated on that dreadful first day, and the mood of the survivors was to be distinctly elegiac rather than heroic in retrospect. 'So ends a Golden Age' was the comment on that day by the official history of the 9th York and Lancasters, a Kitchener battalion which lost 423 men in its first battle.†

Before 1 July 1916, it was possible, if misguided, to believe that the Big Push would be the first step on the road to Berlin, that, in spite of the sinister warnings of Loos and Verdun, the Boche could be 'biffed' and beaten in one great show. After 1 July 1916 it became increasingly clear that the way would be long and hard and that the war would only be won at the cost of continuous and staggering losses. Before 1 July 1916 the new soldiers had only touched the fringes of war; they were now to experience it at its most savage.

All the accounts which follow in this chapter relate to that horrific first day. Ironically it was one of the most beautiful days of the war. Second Lieutenant Siegfried Sassoon wrote in his notebook that the weather 'was of the kind commonly called heavenly'.

* Ironically Kitchener had just died—drowned in HMS *Hampshire* off Orkney while on a mission to Russia.
† Quoted in Martin Middlebrook, *The First Day on the Somme*. This book is the essential work on the opening phase of the Somme battle. For a brief but impressive analysis of its importance see John Keegan, *The Face of Battle*, also hailed as a major work on the subject of war.

157

The Face of Battle —
The Somme 1916

'Over the Top'

'There was no lingering about when zero hour came. Our platoon officer blew his whistle and he was the first up the scaling ladder, with his revolver in one hand and a cigarette in the other. "Come on, boys," he said, and up he went. We went up after him one at a time. I never saw the officer again—his name is on the memorial to the missing which they built after the war at Thiepval. He was only young but he was a very brave man.'

Private George Morgan, 1st Bradford Pals

These two photographs are unquestionably among the great classic images of the
First World War: the ritual of going into battle superbly caught by the camera. The
picture on the left was actually taken by a movie camera; it is a still frame from the
British official film *The Battle of the Somme* which was being shown in the picture
palaces of Britain as early as August 1916—only a matter of weeks after the great
attack of 1st July. There has been much discussion as to whether the event it
purports to record was 'zero hour' on 1st July or a staged assault laid on for the
cinematographer—certainly the men are not carrying the heavy equipment carried by
most of the attacking infantry on that day. But it conveyed the experience of going
over the top to the cinema audiences of 1916 and will unquestionably continue to do
so for future generations.

The picture above is less controversial. It seems to catch with documentary reality
the dash of a confident and well-trained battalion (these are Canadians, who gained
a high reputation for their courage and tenacity on the Western Front) at the moment
of going into action.

Two scenes taken by the same photographer at almost the same spot, near Beaumont Hamel on the morning of 1 July 1916.

In the top picture he is looking towards the German lines at precisely 7.20 a.m., as a huge mine explodes underneath the German-held Hawthorn Redoubt. The explosion killed or entombed many Germans but it alerted the other German regiments in the area to the imminence of the British attack. At zero hour they were ready and waiting for the infantry of the 29th Division who went 'over the top' into withering machine-gun fire.

Zero hour was 7.30—just ten minutes after the top photograph was taken. Between the taking of these two photographs, some 66,000 British soldiers of the first wave had advanced into No Man's Land towards the enemy lines.

The bottom picture is a record of the consequences of the fatal error described above. What it shows is not men advancing but the remnants of the 16th Middlesex falling back. The time is 7.45. These scattered figures hurrying and stumbling back towards their own lines are all that are left of the once-proud Public Schools' Battalion, as the 16th Middlesex was usually known. Twenty-two officers and 500 men became casualties on that day out of an attacking force of 700–800.

The photographer is looking slightly to the right of the view in the picture above. At this point the British front line dog-legged, giving the photographer a grandstand view of the ridge.

When war broke out in 1914 the general expectation was of a brisk, brief and picturesque campaign—almost certainly over by Christmas—in which there would be much dash and bravery and the cavalry would sweep into action in a manner worthy of the great traditions under which it had been trained. (Almost all the generals in high command were cavalrymen, including Sir Douglas Haig, Commander-in-Chief for most of the war.) In the event the warfare of the Western Front became the reverse of picturesque. 'For the onlooker,' wrote Charles Carrington, in *Soldier from the Wars Returning*, 'battles of the First War were rarely spectacular. A great noise and a smoke cloud filled the valley, in which now and then one saw distant figures moving, like ants in a disturbed anthill.' There could be no better illustration of Carrington's observation than the photograph below, which shows the British attack on the German front line near Mametz on the early morning of 1 July 1916.

The tiny specks against the white chalk are infantrymen—probably the Gordon Highlanders—crossing No Man's Land shortly after zero hour.

```
S P E C I A L   O R D E R   O F   T H E   D A Y
                        By
BRIGADIER-GENERAL H. C. REES, D.S.O.,
        Commanding 94th Infantry Brigade.
        ----------------------
                                            \

                                Bde. H.Q., 28-6-16.


    You are about to attack the enemy with far greater numbers

than he can oppose to you,  supported by a **huge** number of guns.

    Englishmen have always proved better **than** the Germans were

when the odds were heavily against them.   It is now

cur opportunity.

    You are about to fight in one of the greatest battles

in the world, and in the most just cause.

    Remember that the British Empire will **anxiously watch**

your every move, and that the honour of the North Country

rests in your hands.

    Keep your heads, do your duty, and you will

utterly defeat the enemy.

                                        Captain,
                                Brigade Major,
                                94th Infantry Bde.
```

These two documents—special orders of the day issued just four days apart—tell in brief the tragic story of the opening phase of the Battle of the Somme. The one left indicates the high pride and confidence with which the British Army went into battle on 1 July 1916. In the one right the pride is still there, but it is pride not in victory but in heroism in defeat.

162

What lay between the issuing of these two orders was vividly described in the journals of the man who wrote them, Brigadier H. C. Rees. He saw his brigade—which consisted of four 'Pals' battalions from the north of England—virtually annihilated before his eyes. Their point of attack was the heavily defended village of Serre, just to the north of Beaumont Hamel, where the Hawthorn Redoubt mine was prematurely exploded. He was, it is worth adding, handing over command of his brigade (see the order below) not because of its defeat but because its permanent commander had just returned from sick leave.

Our opening bombardment was magnificent. The trenches in front of Serre changed shape and dissolved minute by minute under the terrific hail of steel. Watching I began to believe in the possibility of a great success, but I reckoned without the Hun artillery. This ten minute intense bombardment combined with the explosion of twenty tons of dynamite under the Hawthorn Redoubt must have convinced any enemy observer that the attack was in progress, and, as our infantry advanced, down came a perfect wall of explosive along the front benches of my Brigade and the 93rd. It was the most frightful artillery display that I had seen. ... At the time the barrage became intense the last waves of the attack were crossing the trench that I was in. I have never seen a finer display of individual and collective bravery than the advance of that brigade. I never saw a man waver from the exact line prescribed for him. Each line disappeared in the thick cloud of dust and smoke which rapidly blotted out the whole area. ... I saw a few groups of men through gaps in the smoke cloud, but I knew that no troops could hope to get through such a fire. ... The whole brigade had been destroyed as a fighting unit. ...

SPECIAL ORDER OF THE DAY

By

Brigadier-General H.C. REES, D.S.O.
Commanding 94 Inf. Bde

On giving up command of the 94th Brigade to Brig General Carter-Campbell, whose place I have temporarily taken during this great battle I wish to express to all ranks my admiration of their behaviour.

I have been through many battles in this war, and nothing more magnificent has come under my notice. The Waves went forward as if on a drill parade, and I saw no man turn back or falter.

I bid good-bye to the remnant of as fine a Brigade as has ever gone into action.

B.H.Q.
2-7-16

Brig-General, Comdg 94 Inf. Brigade.

Bombardier R. H. Locke, Royal Horse Artillery, writing about it before the sixtieth anniversary of the battle, remembered it as a day without equal.

> It was really a pity to have a war on July 1st, for in all my time it was the most beautiful day we had. Sky was cloudless and the sun shone. The sky-larks were singing as they flew heavenwards and unknown to them thousands of our soldiers were on their way there too.

Zero hour was 7.30. At 6.25, wrote Major Vignoles, Grimsby Chums, 'the artillery, which had been firing in a desultory manner, began to speed up, and within fifteen seconds there was a perfect hurricane of sound'. His account continues:

> We had an hour to wait, so lighted pipes and cigarettes while the men chatted and laughed, and wondered whether the Boche would wait for us. I had a look round but could not see much; the morning was fine and the sun shining, but the enemy trenches were veiled in light mist made worse no doubt by the smoke from the thousands of shells we were pumping into his lines. Nearby I could see our machine gunners, out in the open already, trying to get the best position from which to enfilade certain parts of the Boche line.
>
> There was a kind of suppressed excitement running through all the men as the time for the advance came nearer.

Vignoles himself did not go over with the first wave—and when he did attack he was almost immediately wounded—but in that short time he was able to see an infantry attack of the Great War in its most classic form:

> The mist had lifted slightly, and the picture before me, combined with the uproar, gave me an impression which I am not likely to forget.
>
> Looked at broadly, there was nothing horrible about it; the ground fell from where I was into Sausage Valley,* rising again beyond covered with enemy trenches. No shells were falling on these, as our barrage had lifted, but dark green figures could be seen moving forward on the right, while No Man's Land was littered with men apparently lying down. At first it was difficult to realize that these were all casualties, and that what was left of the Battalions had pushed on.

Dark figures moving forward, other figures lying down—all seen from such a distance that the horror of what was actually taking place was quite disguised. But what was it like to be one of those far-off figures?

Second Lieutenant Kenneth Macardle was in the attack on Montauban, several miles to the south-east, at precisely the same time that Major Vignoles was watching the attack on La Boiselle. His account forms one of the striking entries that fill the last pages of this remarkable young officer's diary.

* Sausage Valley was a name given by the troops to a depression just to the right (looking eastwards towards the enemy lines) of La Boiselle; predictably there was a Mash Valley on the left.

All around us and in front men dropped or staggered about; a yellow mass of lyddite shrapnel would burst and a section of men in two-deep formation would crumple up and be gone. We advanced in artillery formation at a slow walk. We led our sections in and out of the stricken men who were beyond help or whom we could not stop to help; it seemed callous but it was splendid war. Men crawling back smiled ruefully or tried to keep back blood with leaky fingers. We would call a cheery word or fix our eyes on Montauban—some men were not good to see.

In spite of the high casualties, this attack on Montauban was going well—too well, for Macardle's 17th Manchesters had to wait for forty minutes under heavy shell-fire before they rushed the village at the assigned time of 9.56. By the time they moved forward 'A' Company was all but wiped out; their Sergeant-Major was killed, and only one officer was on his feet and he had been wounded. Macardle's 'B' Company came up with him as he ordered the survivors of his stricken company forward.

I caught a glimpse of young Wain, his face haggard with pain, one leg soaked with blood, smoking a cigarette and pushing himself forward with a stick. His voice was full of sobs and tears of pain and rage. 'Get up you ——s! Blast your souls—get up!' I waved to him and he smiled and dropped— he knew it was not absolutely up to him any longer. We of 'B' Company took over. We were enfiladed from our left (where another Battn had failed to advance) by machine guns and rifle fire, but we took the village from a fleeing and terror-struck enemy. The village was by then a monstrous garbage heap of stinking dead men and high explosives.

Private Lawrence Crossland, 2nd Bn Seaforth Highlanders, went over at Beaumont Hamel, advancing from slit trenches just behind the British front line which his battalion had previously dug on night working parties. He was in the second wave, carrying materials for consolidating the new positions that were supposed to be taken in the first-wave attack. In addition to his usual kit and loaded rifle he carried on his shoulder 'two corkscrew-ended iron stakes piercing a roll of barbed wire plus a Mills Bomb in each of my tunic pockets in case of need'.

On the given signal we left the trench by means of roughly-made ladders and advanced under a hail of fire from rifle, machine gun, high explosives and shell—just Hell let loose.

My companions fell left and right but we had been told in no circumstances were we to stop and help a comrade. The fire came from the right so I well remember tilting my steel helmet sideways to protect my face. I got as far as our front line which I endeavoured to jump when I was hit in the shoulder with a bullet which penetrated my lower spine causing temporary paralysis. I fell face downward in the trench amongst wounded and dead, helpless and unable to move, saturated with blood which I was also vomiting. Afraid of losing consciousness I dug my nails in the earth and fought the nausea with every ounce of my strength as I realized that in my

'I Had my Orders . . .'

The photograph shows German prisoners being marched down the line on 1 July 1916. For many of them, after a week of 'drumfire' and the trauma of sustaining the mass assault of nineteen Allied divisions, captivity must have been a relief. At least they would almost certainly survive the war.

But others were less fortunate. In some sectors the attacking battalions were told not to take prisoners. Certainly this was how Private Arthur Hubbard of the London Scottish saw his duty, as his letter shows.

Extract from letter from Private A. H. Hubbard, from the East Suffolk Hospital, Ipswich, dated 7 July 1916:

'... we had strict orders not to take prisoners, no matter if wounded, my first job was when I had finished cutting some of their wire away, to empty my magazine on 3 Germans that came out of their deep dugouts, bleeding badly, and put them out of their misery, they cried for mercy, but I had my orders, they had no feeling whatever for us poor chaps ...'

Private, later Sergeant, Hubbard committed suicide in 1929: the official verdict at his inquest was that his death was the result of shell-shock. The episode which above all preyed on his mind, according to his family, was this terrible incident on 1 July 1916. It is fair to say that the Somme continued to claim its victims long after the battle was officially over: Hubbard was one of them.

position I could be trampled on and regarded as dead. There was a machine gun post to my right manned by a gunner who must have seen me fall. He gave a reassuring call and said he would help me as soon as he could leave his gun which eventually he did relieving me of my kilt and staunching the wounds with iodine and bandages from a dead man. He wouldn't use mine saying I might need it.

Private Henry Russell, 5th Bn London Regt, went over with the first wave at Gommecourt. He was very badly wounded, became one of those figures 'lying down' in No Man's Land throughout that long summer day and was invalided out of the Army. It was to be many years before he felt himself able to write an account of what happened to him on 1 July 1916. He and his comrades of the 56th London Division began their advance under a heavy smoke screen; but then they found themselves beyond the smoke screen and they became an easy target for the German machine guns.

During our advance, I saw many of my colleagues drop down, but this somehow or other did not seem to worry me, and I continued to go forward until I suddenly became aware that there were few of us in this first line of attack capable of going on. At this stage I found myself in the company of an officer, Lieut Wallace. We dived into a flat shallow hole made by our guns, apparently both wanting to decide what we should now do ... I came to the conclusion that going on would be suicidal, and that the best thing we could do would be to stay there and attempt to pick off any Germans who might expose themselves. Lieut Wallace said, however, that we had been ordered to go on at all costs and that we must comply with this order. At this, he stood up and within a few seconds dropped down riddled with bullets. This left me with the same problem and, having observed his action, I felt that I must do the same. I, therefore, stood up and was immediately hit by two bullets and dropped down.

I must say that this action had a profound effect on me in later years. I had thought that a man who could stand up and knowingly face practically certain death in these circumstances must be very brave. I found out that bravery hardly came into it. Once the decision was made to stand up I had no further fear. I was not bothered at all even though I believed that I would be dead within seconds and would be rotting on the ground, food for the rats the next day. I did not even feel appreciably the bullets going through and this was to me something extraordinary. I am now convinced that when it comes to the last crunch nobody has any fear at all; it is not a question of bravery. In some extraordinary manner the chemistry of the body anaesthetizes it in such a way that even when fully conscious fear does not enter into the matter.

The worst experience I had was sometime later after I had crawled into another shell-hole some distance away and into which another colleague of mine had also crawled. He told me that he had been shot through the middle of the back and that the bullet had emerged through his left ear ...

168

We had not long to wait before a shell burst on the edge of our hole; it killed my colleague and injured me in such a way that I was virtually emasculated. I considered the situation hopeless and that even if a miracle happened and I did, in fact, get away, I would not be fit for anything in this world. I, therefore, decided to kill myself.

To this end, I was under the impression that I had three choices. The first was to explode a Mills bomb which I was carrying in my pocket. This seemed to be a silly procedure because it would only be doing what the Germans were already attempting to do. The second was to take a very large dose of morphine tablets which I believed to be in my pocket. Some time before, I had buried a doctor killed in action and on going through his belongings I had found a tube containing a considerable number of morphine tablets. I intended to take all these but when I felt in my breast pocket, I found that they were no longer there and somehow or other I had lost them. The third course was one which came to my mind as a result of a talk given to us by the Medical Officer before going into action. He said that, if wounded or bleeding, we should never take intoxicants, as the result would almost certainly be fatal. Before the attack I had bought a very large bottle of Worcester Sauce or Yorkshire Relish at an advanced NAAFI, emptied out the contents and filled it to the brim with rum. I therefore managed to get hold of the bottle of rum which I had put in my haversack and I drank the lot hoping that it would result in my death. In fact it did me no harm at all. It probably made me slightly merry and bright and rather stupified. It also probably caused me to drop off to sleep, though I am not aware of this. However, I came to the conclusion, when I had recovered my senses, that, in spite of my condition (my left arm being torn, my left thigh damaged, my right leg wounded and strips of flesh hanging down from my abdomen) it was still worth while making a serious effort to save myself.

Russell had to wait through the long hot day until 11 o'clock that night before he dared to make a move. He was found the following morning, when a Private of the Middlesex Regiment heard his feeble cries.

Even in those parts of the front where the battle had gone well—the extreme right wing of the attack, where the British had attacked side by side with five divisions of the French Army—men knew that they had been in a hard and historic fight. The remarkable Second Lieutenant Macardle, doyen of No Man's Land, devotee of 'splendid war', felt a touch of war-weariness as he and his fellow Manchesters sat it out in captured Montauban under the bombardment of the German guns. He wrote in his diary:

We got tired of the shock of their explosions making us reel and feel dizzy and numbed; we got sick of the reek of high explosives which is synonymous with dead and broken men; our cheery triumphant treatment of those most unpleasant situations changed. When the first day and a night were gone we were silent and grim and—yes—a little afraid.

The Surreys Play the Game — The Story of Captain Wilfred Nevill, Killed 1 July 1916

There could be no better example of the kind of man who went bravely to his death on the first day on the Somme than Captain Wilfred Nevill, East Yorkshire Regt, temporarily attached to the 8th East Surreys. Born in 1894, he became Head Prefect at Dover College, where he was a successful hockey player and athlete, and was reading for a degree at Jesus College, Cambridge, when war broke out. While on leave in England in May 1916, in anticipation of the long-awaited 'Big Push', he bought two footballs for the leading platoons of his company to kick into No Man's Land at zero hour. Shortly before the attack of 1st July he had one of the footballs inscribed with the words: 'The Great European Cup—The Final—East Surreys v Bavarians. Kick-off at Zero.' The other was labelled, in large letters: 'NO REFEREE'.

This gesture was not mere bravado: according to his surviving brother, the intention was to give the men something homely and familiar to concentrate on as they went into battle. At zero on 1st July one football was kicked off by Nevill and the other by a private. The East Surreys duly went over the top (this was part of the right wing of the British attack, where the British had the greatest success on 1st July), but Nevill himself was killed just short of the German wire.

Touchstone's heroic poem was first published in the *Daily Mail* on 12 July 1916. Not unnaturally it was reproduced in the East Surreys' Christmas Card that year.

Captain Wilfred Nevill (far right) photographed in the trenches with two fellow officers.

THE GAME.

A company of the East Surrey Regiment is reported to have dribbled four footballs, the gift of their captain who fell in the fight, for a mile and a quarter into the enemy trenches.

On through the hail of slaughter
  Where gallant comrades fall,
Where blood is poured like water,
  They drive the trickling ball.
The fear of death before them
  Is but an empty name;
True to the land that bore them
  The Surreys play the game!

On without check or falter,
  They press towards the goal;
Who falls on freedom's altar
  The Lord shall rest his soul.
But still they charge, the living,
  Into that hell of flame;
Ungrudging in their giving,
  Our soldiers play the game!

And now at last is ended
  The task so well begun;
Though savagely defended
  The lines of death are won.
In this, their hour of glory,
  A deathless place they claim,
In England's splendid story,
  The men who played the game!

TOUCHSTONE.

A Second Lieutenant who went over with Nevill described his death in a letter to Nevill's sister:

> Five minutes before 'zero' time your brother strolled up in his usual calm way & we shared a last joke before going over. The Company went over the top very well, with Soames & your brother kicking off with the Company footballs. We had to face a very heavy rifle & machine gun fire, & nearing the front German trench, the lines slackened pace slightly. Seeing this Wilfred dashed in front with a bomb in his hand & was immediately shot through the head . . .

A Sergeant, also writing to Nevill's sister, gave a slightly different version—the death of a very popular officer as it was seen by the men whom he had led:

> It is no disgrace to the men when I tell you they wavered. . . . The chaps had got 'the Wind up' so he just lit a fag and talked to 'em—you know the way he used to talk. Well he joked and laughed and smoked. Of course 'they' got him.

The story was to become legendary. Fully reported in the newspapers it caught the popular imagination. *Touchstone*, poet of the *Daily Mail*, celebrated it in the heroic style of Sir Henry Newbolt (see opposite). The *Illustrated London News* commissioned their most famous artist, Mr R. Caton Woodville, to commemorate it.

There is an interesting postscript to this story. For the British this was a shining example of bravery and *sangfroid*. The Germans saw in it propaganda possibilities of a different kind—the chance to show to the world that the British were a race of idiots. They circulated the Caton Woodville drawing with captions in ten languages—including Russian, Arabic and Polish as well as French, English and German—of which the English version read:

> An English absurdity: Football play during storm attack. All English newspapers laud the 'heroic deed' of an English major who ordered his men to rush a football and keep it moving in front of the lines while advancing to a storm attack . . .

The Surreys Play the ame!' Kicking Footballs wards the German enches under a Hail of ells.' Drawn by R. ton Woodville from aterial supplied by an ficer present at the tion.

12

Into Battle: 'The Most Horrible Invention that was Ever Known'

After the battle for Guillemont, September 1916. Wrecked trees, wrecked German strong point. The scene of the attack described by Second Lieutenant Blake O'Sullivan this chapter.

Acting Captain Reginald Leetham, 2nd Bn Rifle Brigade, saw the Big Push of July 1916 from the close vantage point of a battalion whose attack was cancelled at the eleventh hour because of the fate of the battalions that had gone before. He described his reactions to the battle in a brief but vivid diary. He realized from the moment he heard the rattle of machine-gun bullets overhead that 'fellows in the open must be being mowed down like grass'; and that day he saw three battalions practically annihilated. He wrote: 'They went into a greater hell and a worse valley of death than the gallant 600 the poem was written about.' He summed up his attitude in a series of brief, bitter paragraphs.

> I wonder if a Corps Commander eight miles behind the front line has any idea of what life is like in the front line.
> A modern battle is the most horrible invention that was ever known and as the war goes on each one gets worse . . .
> If we had heroes in previous wars, today we have them not in thousands but in half millions.

The previous chapter brought together a number of experiences all related to that one day which so appalled Captain Leetham and which had begun with such high hopes, the first day of the Battle of the Somme. In this chapter are collected a number of accounts of other actions scattered through the war, most of them subsequent to the great catastrophe of 1st July.

Broadly speaking, the writers are men, like Leetham, who have seen the face of battle and recognized it for what it is. 'War,' it has been said, 'was found out on July 1st', and certainly there is little emphasis on war as a superior form of ball-game or as some grand charade in which paper men faced painless deaths. There is even, as for example in Lance Corporal Roland Mountfort's description of an attack on Pozières, a positive disclaimer of the jaunty, cavalier attitudes of 1st July—and the attack he was involved in took place only fifteen days later!

> We moved off in platoons, overland, towards the front line. Then came the order to advance & before we knew where we were we were 'going over the top'. In the distance—a fearful way it seemed—was Pozières; & by now

we were attacking it. Then the crumps began & what proved our undoing, machine guns crackled from the village. We advanced at the walk. There was a good deal of shouting—'Keep up', 'don't bunch', 'Half left' & so on, but only necessary orders. We didn't dribble footballs, neither did we say 'This way to Berlin, boys' nor any of the phrases employed weekly by the *News of the World*.

Yet a caveat must be entered: the disenchantment caused by 1 July 1916 was by no means universal. For many it was simply the beginning of a new challenge. Now that war had been recognized it had to be lived with and mastered. Above all the German must be made to know that 1st July was a temporary aberration only. Britain had suffered a bloody nose; the next bloody nose would be the enemy's. And, for some, war could still be enjoyable. It is significant that one of the most vivid accounts in this chapter relates to the beginning of the Third Battle of Ypres, launched thirteen months after the opening of the Somme, and that the writer, a Guards Lieutenant, could still talk of battle as 'splendid fun'. And it is worth adding that this same young officer could write, in a letter written *only five days* before the Armistice, that a battle in which he had fought was 'the best that I have ever had, and I would not have missed it for anything'.

The truth is, surely, that we are dealing with many men in many situations, and that each man reacted according to character and circumstance and in tune with the men around him. A Guards Battalion would maintain its sense of superiority and its high standards whatever its casualties. A Pals Battalion, which virtually lost its identity and *raison d'être* in a morning—and had to be made up to strength by random drafts with none of the local connections of the original recruits—would find the rebuilding of morale and fighting capacity a much harder task. Equally understandably, some men—simply by virtue of their character and personality—saw nothing particularly extraordinary in the new brutal form of war, and accepted it, horrors and all; others, no less brave, found it so utterly inhuman that they felt moved to protest, disenchantment and, sometimes, despair. Over the years the latter view has won a hands-down victory. Now the vision of the Great War accepted by most people is of doomed battalions going endlessly over the top to perish hopelessly in mud, of men who died 'as cattle'. It is still possible, however, to find disputing voices among the last survivors, to hear the claim that there were men who 'died gaily'. Both views, I believe, must be respected.

If there is a further comment to be added, it is this, that though the argument discussed above usually centres around the trauma of 1st July, there were men who found war to be quite different from the heroic cavalcade it was widely thought to be from the first actions of August 1914. This book has, perhaps unfairly, concentrated on the volunteers who flocked to Kitchener's call in 1914 and 1915. But while the bands played in Britain and the queues waited good-humouredly outside the recruiting

174

stations, men of the Regular Army were fighting and dying at Mons and Le Cateau, on the Marne and the Aisne. They had the opportunity to appreciate the reality that was modern war almost two years before the Somme. It is perhaps fitting therefore that the first action described in this chapter should be the Battle of Mons, fought on 23 August 1914, as seen by a Corporal of the 120th Battery, Royal Field Artillery, Albert George.

His battery was well aware the previous evening that they would be in action the following day. Even at this early stage of the war there were no heroics.

> That night we formed a ring & had an open air concert, just to keep our spirits up & also to amuse the civilians which were gathered around us as if we were super human beings, being British Soldiers. Many a mind was far away that night while we were singing the songs which were comic, patriotic & sentimental and there was many a wet eye; men thinking of the wives, children & the Girl they had left behind. Nobody can imagine how a song, sung as some soldiers sing, will turn the stoutest heart or wet the dryest eye.

On the morning of the battle George's Battery moved into the town of St Ghislain to the west of Mons.

> In St Ghislain the people were just going & coming from the different churches & the scene was very peaceful. At 10-a.m. we put our gun in action behind the Mons Canal on a small hill & about 500 yards to the right of the Town Hall. All the gunners were busy barricading & digging gun-pits & about 11-15 when they were almost finished the order 'Action' came down & everybody went to their different duties & also we were very pleased to have a go at the Germans. About 11-20 a.m. four shells came whizzing through the air & all four dropped in the town, terrifying the people who started screaming & running in all directions & a panic started but our presence soothed them a great deal. At 11-30 a.m. our Battery opened fire & the war began in earnest.

They were soon involved in a brutal slogging-match. At one time they found the easy target of a mass of German infantry, 'advancing so rapidly that we were firing at the low range of 600 yards & every shell killing dozens as they were advancing in close order'. But the Germans were not to be held, and the Battery, 'sick & downhearted', retreated into the town, where they were able to link up with the infantry. A brief lull followed, after which the Major in charge resolved to have 'another go at the Huns', even though they were hopelessly outnumbered.

> All that afternoon we kept the Huns at bay, although they were about ten to one. About 3.0 p.m. the Huns got on our right flank & a few Uhlans sniped at us wounding a few of our horses. The worst casualty of the day occurred about 3.0 p.m. when our Major (Major Holland) was killed & everybody in the Battery thought that their last day had come as shells were

bursting above our heads & rifle bullets were coming from our flanks & behind us, but I think the prayers of our dearest friends were answered. At 6 o'clock the attack began to get hotter & hotter & nobody knows of the narrow escape we had, only our officers & men that were actually there.

Eventually retreat became unavoidable.

Our Captain though a brave man could see it was murder staying as we had only two guns out of six that would fire & the officers & men were thoroughly fed up; there were many white with fright & with tears in our eyes we resolved to try a retirement.

We started to retire at 7.0 p.m. with 4 guns out of 6. As we were galloping through the villages infantrymen with ammunition wagons & water carts left them & their horses & ran after our own wagons so as to get away as soon as possible. The civilians also were shouting & screaming & running in hundreds & little children were crying piteously. It was an awful sight & an awful ending to an awful day. We thought of Sunday at 7.0 p.m. in England & of what our friends were doing & we all envied them.

Captain Lionel Ferguson, 13th Bn Cheshire Regt, went into battle on the Somme front on 7 July 1916. There were no forecasts of easy walk-overs now; in fact his battalion was promised 'a hard fight with much bayonet work'. The breezy optimism prevalent before 1st July had vanished also. As they marched towards the front line he became aware that a fellow officer was in a very bad state of nerves.

I was marching at the back of No. 3 Coy, walking with Freddy Hall in charge of No. 4 Coy; his manner was very strange. He certainly felt the strain too much for him, also he had 'wind up', telling me he thought it would be his last show. He was killed next day.

Ferguson himself was ill at ease and not as in command of himself as he would have liked.

With nobody to talk to, as Freddy was now speechless, I had to keep my thoughts from getting the better of me. I confess now I was very frightened. Sweat kept running down my face and neck. I could have drunk the sea dry; also a lump in my throat seemed to nearly stop me breathing. I tried to talk and words failed me, in fact no condemned man could have felt worse.

However, when the time came for the attack he had mastered himself, in spite of the fact that he knew his battalion was 'going over the top of a square held on three sides by the enemy' and that 'those who had better ideas of "stunting" than I had were very pessimistic about the show'. Zero hour was preceded by an intensified half-hour bombardment, which produced a heavy enemy reply.

All sorts of dirt was flying about now and we had to lie very low to avoid

The Battle of the Somme goes on. Men of the Wiltshire Regiment going over the top to attack Thiepval on 7 August 1916. Thiepval finally fell ten days later. The battle, which the Prime Minister, H. H. Asquith, called 'the long and sombre procession of cruelty and suffering', continued until mid November. During it 1,200,000 men from Germany, France and the British Empire were killed or wounded.

being hit. The rim of my hat was punctured also a brick fell on it which thoroughly put the wind up me. My heart was once again in my mouth, but this time I knew I had complete self-control.... I had a few old hands round me, as I was taking a platoon over, and they kept me cheery. One man in particular was fine, keeping us all laughing by his wit. We gave out a good rum ration at 7.30 and it did us a power of good, as the waiting to go over is most unnerving work. I kept calling out the time. Five, four, three, two, one more minute to go. 'Over the top and the best of luck.' The barrage lifted and we were up to our front line before we knew it; but here we got it hot, Stewart in charge of no. 1 platoon was killed outright, the best officer in the battalion, I saw him a few moments later, quite dead, his lighted pipe still between his teeth. The Hun now could be seen all round, he had MGs mounted on 3 sides of us, it seemed as if our barrage had been ineffective. From this point we were just mown down. My blood was up

now, my fear had gone and I wanted to kill and rushed on. Col Finch I saw in the middle of No Man's Land, trying to direct No. 1 Coy who now seemed to have lost direction. It appeared all their officers were hit and he called to me to get on and lead them to the enemy machine guns, now doing so much havoc. I did my best and with my batman Brown ran up forward. I felt a pain in my shoulder and found my arm was useless. I did not realize I was hit but fell headlong into a shell hole, Brown following, beginning to tie me up with a bandage. I remember telling him off and began to fire at the MG crew, now not 30 yards away. Of course, I never hit them, but I kept seeing them fall, and quite had the idea it was my work. I must say I admired them, for no sooner than the man who was working the gun was hit, then another took his place on the seat of death; in fact, they seemed endless. At this point Brown was hit with a shrapnel ball in his cheek; it settled under his skin, giving him the appearance of having toothache: but I had to tie him up, and he informed me he was going back. Myself I did not want to go, but he said I was badly hit and was losing a lot of blood; this I could not see as it was running down my back. I was beginning to feel weak also, so decided to try and get back. We started by running, but after two falls, I rested in a shell hole. Brown ran on, getting safely into our old front line, from which he beckoned me to follow; I had fifty yards to go, and the ground all round was being torn by bullets, so I had grave doubts about doing it, but beginning to feel faint, and not wishing to be lying out I started to roll from hole to hole; in time reaching the trench.

Ferguson and Brown made their way back to the dressing station along with the other walking wounded, passing many 'awful sights' on the way.

It was a long walk and I was getting weaker and my mind was wandering. I would talk to the troops who were going up; telling them what to do and what we had done. At last we arrived in Albert and entered a large hall filled with wounded. I saw Captain Dean getting a dressing put on and other friends lying dead & dying; the sight was so cruel that my nerve went and I fell down on the floor and started sobbing. I had had no sleep and little food for 60 hours, also was weak from loss of blood, so had some excuse.

Ferguson's wound took him home to Blighty. So too did the wound sustained by Second Lieutenant Blake O'Sullivan, 6th Bn Connaught Rangers, during the attack on Guillemont on the Somme in September 1916. He wrote his account of the action from hospital in Chelsea in response to questions from his mother about the recent fighting in France. He had had a hard introduction to war; there had been many casualties before the battalion had any chance of engaging the enemy. He had even been showered with the 'wet dust' of the blood and brains of a man standing next to him in a dug-out entrance, and had seen the battalion MO go mad with shell-shock.

A typical sight during a battle: walking wounded hobbling back for medical attention.

Sitting here in my hospital bed my mind is obsessed by the shocks and sights and the sudden deaths of so many friends during those last awful days. By writing down all the details I hoped to exorcise some of the mental migraine.

Waiting for zero hour, wrist watch in hand, 'uneasily wishing for 12.03 to break the horrible apprehension', he had glanced at the waiting men and found it hard to avoid 'a morbid anxiety about their chances of surviving the coming hour'. But fortunately 'the waves of sickening fear' which had plagued him at various intervals during the morning had vanished. With the cacophony of the barrage around them and a piper 'blowing as if his cheeks would burst—though, pathetically, nothing could be heard of the pipes above the screeching din', the Rangers went over the top and 'astounded me by a concerted yell and cheer that could be heard even above the bombardment'. As the attack began, 'for me the surrounding frenzy gave the illusion of taking place in the midst of a raging ocean tempest; and going over the top, like running shivering into ice-cold water'. There was the inevitable, ferocious German response.

On the ridge we were greeted by a hurricane of machine gun bullets sounding like hosts of bees, whistling, swooshing and shrieking past our heads with blood-curdling intensity. What saved those cheering men from wholesale and instant death was the lucky miracle that the Boche fire was aimed a few feet too high. Coming over that high ground we presented such a perfect target that by rights not a soul should have escaped.

I started by leading them towards the quarries; but, suddenly seeing Tamplin's Company attacking the concrete strong point, veered and headed for that. The pulverized ground was soggy, and the cheering faded in the heavy going while the charge slowed gradually into a laboured jog-trot. The constant need to skirt the constellation of shell-holes broke up our wave formation which soon looked more like a post-match mob invading a football field.

The bombardment crescendo reached its climax with the onset of an intense shrapnel umbrella (probably British, as we were minutes ahead of time table). About 200 feet above us the air became stippled by swarms of brown-black splashes as the shells burst and scattered hell in all directions.

I glanced fearfully to right and left to see the effect of this new menace and was surprised to find that so many were still going strong, though here and there a man would suddenly huddle into a little bundle. Even as I watched, a corporal close behind me pitched forward with arms stretched out and hands clutching frantically at the mud.

We were already within a few yards of the looming strong point and still saw nothing of the enemy. The great concrete block was unscathed by all the strafing and two slits in each wall glowered at our onrush like cynical eyes. Some of D Company stood to one side of the loopholes in the north wall and tried unsuccessfully and dangerously to lob grenades through the slits. Guessing there'd be some sort of entrance at the back I spurred myself

180

Albert

Albert was to the Somme what Ypres was to the battlefields of Flanders—though unlike Ypres it fell into enemy hands, on 26 March 1918. It was liberated the following August. It was famous above all for its remarkable landmark—the 'Leaning Virgin'. Struck by a German shell in January 1915, it was secured in the bizarre position to which it had fallen.

The statue became a symbol, almost a kind of mascot to the soldiers here. The rumour grew that if it fell the war would end; but when it finally came down it was by British action, because the Germans were using it—after they had seized Albert in 1918—as an observation post.

Yesterday afternoon they let us out into the town for two hours. It is rather badly knocked about, especially the big church—I don't think they call it a cathedral—which is a pitiful sight. At the top of the tower stood a gigantic gilded statue of the Virgin Mary holding the child above her head, and this has fallen, but in a miraculous way the base has held fast or caught in something so that now the lady is in the act of diving into the street. ... There are few civilians left and only two or three small shops.
Roland Mountfort, 10th Bn Royal Fusiliers

The great basilica of Notre-Dame de Brébières was almost completely destroyed by the end of the war, as was the town around it. Now town and church have been restored—the church to the exact specifications of the original building.

for a final rush to get round to it from the south side, dashed past one of the west wall eyes and suddenly felt a terrific thump and a streak of burning pain across the shoulders; stumbled on for a few paces, tripped over some wire and fell flat on my face and realized that a bullet had got me.

I dragged myself and rifle to a shallow hole to assess the wound. Spit on my hands showed no blood from lung damage and only the shoulders and back hurt badly—though arms weighed like lead.

Looking along the wave I was aghast to see that my fall had been misinterpreted as a taking of cover. Everyone was doing likewise; even CSM Johnson close left was crawling into a convenient shell hole. In a frenzy I got up and shrieked myself hoarse but to no purpose. To signal with my arms was painful and slow, but by dragging the rifle by its muzzle and going forward at least indicated that the advance should go on. Moments later they were all up and going again.

The unrehearsed breather was a lucky chance, because once on their feet the men recovered the wild abandon of the charge just at the moment when the Germans began to emerge from shell holes and wrecked trenches. Behind the strong point a scuffle and scramble developed as a group put up a hectic resistance that was overwhelmed by the bayonet-stabbing onslaught; a vortex of shrieking; of yells and brutish grunting—then rushing ahead, leaving the crumpled bodies in a stink of blood and high explosive.

Some idiot exploded his p-bomb on my right front and a phosphorous cloud swept over and obliterated the shambles. Choking, and blasting the careless fool who had blinded and almost smothered me, I staggered out of the smoke. By the time my eyes cleared the tide of men had swept on and was already into the heart of Guillemont.

Private Albert Johnson, 11th Bn Royal West Kents, was in the successful infantry attack that followed the blowing of nineteen mines under the German front-line trenches in the vicinity of Messines in the early morning of 7 June 1917. As compared with the standard situation on the Somme resistance was minimal and by the end of the day the British had reached and held the German second line. Private Johnson wrote an account of his part in the battle in a letter of 10th June. For a long time he had been fascinated to know what being in action was really like.

I remember that whilst in England last year I read with active interest the first account of the Battle of the Somme* and tried to get my mind to imagine what a push was like but now having had the personal experience I realize the impossibility of it.

Waiting for the word for up and over I began to feel a trifle dozey but this speedily vanished when the mines went up. Our trench rocked like a

*The word 'Somme' was censored by whoever passed Private Johnson's letter, but can still be easily deciphered.

ship in a strong sea and it seemed as if the very earth had been rent asunder.

We started for Fritz and the land he occupied which is better known as the Ridge. What passed in that journey across No Man's Land was only a passing vision of moving figures intent on gaining their objective pausing only for a breather in a shell hole, for the vicinity was as if an earthquake had passed over it so great had been the havoc wrought by our splendid artillery. On we went until we came across our first opposition—a machine gun which began to spit very nasty from our extreme left. From this whilst lying in a shell hole I had my first reminder, a bullet hitting the earth four or five inches in front of me which sent the dirt flying in my face. Eventually the difficulty was overcome but I cannot vouch what became of gun or Germans.

There was a pause in the attack while they were waiting for the barrage to lift. Johnson took advantage of the lull to move to a more advantageous position:

but before I could reach my objective one of Fritz's shrapnel shells came over and burst immediately in front of me but for some unaccountable reason two of my comrades passed between it and me and therefore caught the full force of the burst while I was extremely fortunate only to get my right ear peppered. I found I was bleeding but not feeling anything I took no notice of it and carried on. We came to a wood where Fritz began to appear in large numbers. His morale was badly shaken however and he had no stomach for a fight and they threw equipment right and left and ran out towards us as hard as they could in order to get out of our barrage which had properly put the wind up them.

Lieutenant Alex Wilkinson, 2nd Bn Coldstream Guards, went into action on the first day of the Third Battle of Ypres, 31 July 1917. Exhilarated, content with his and his battalion's performance, he wrote in a letter to his father a breezy account of the opening phase of what was to become the great set-piece battle of the third year of the war. He went into the attack with one extra advantage: a complete confidence in the certainty of his own survival (Ch. 9), though soon men were falling quite near him.

A 5.9 pitched within about 5 yards of my leading half platoon, killing two and wounding one: two such good fellows. I heard this shell coming and saw it just before it pitched. If I had been on the right instead of the left of my $\frac{1}{2}$ platoon it must have had me. All I could do was curse the Hun and carry on.

As the attack developed his Company Commander was wounded. Wilkinson took over.

Crossing the open we deployed from artillery formation and extended to about two paces. Everything worked like clockwork—the men were

wonderful—and there we were in our position of readiness, just short of the third objective, well up to time and in touch with our flanks.

The advance continued steadily: everything was going according to plan.

Away we went reaching our final objective at 9.25. We were supposed to be there at 9.23! Arrived there, it was an imaginary line right in the open. I ascertained that the company was in line, the flanks secure etc., and then we dug in. It was at this juncture that we suffered most. Snipers were very active and several men were hit and then before we could get a proper line dug a Hun aeroplane came over and spotted us, with the result that we were immediately crumped and rather heavily, suffering further casualties. Eventually we got a fairly good line dug, linking up shell holes etc., and there we stayed.... I could tell you heaps more, various incidents, but I have given you a fair idea of the war side of it. The war side of it was splendid fun, we all enjoyed it immensely, but the weather side of it was very different. I never thought the human frame could endure such hardships.

The weather Lieutenant Wilkinson referred to in his letter was to be a persistent belligerent in the Third Battle of Ypres and to bedevil the British chances of success. This was its first strike.

At 6 p.m. the night we arrived at our objectives it began to rain and continued incessantly for 30 hours. In a proper line of trenches it would have been quite beastly, but in an absolutely new line with practically no means of revetting it, it beggars description.

They had more than forty-eight hours to go before they came out of the line followed by an 'awful walk back', but morale could not have been higher.

Never for a moment did the men lose heart. No men, even of the original expeditionary force, could have done better. ... The only thing they wanted was a chance to kill more Huns. They were rather too quick on our front; we couldn't see them for dust. It is said that no Huns can be induced to face the Guards Division and it looks like it. They knew we were coming! The men were praying for a counter attack and so was I, for then we could have fairly slaughtered them!

The War Drawings of Gunner Harry Bateman Royal Field Artillery

Harry Bateman was born in Bradford on 12 April 1896. At fourteen he enrolled at the Bradford School of Art, where he won a number of certificates and prizes. In 1915 he volunteered for service in the Royal Field Artillery. At his first parade, when the Sergeant asked any artist present to make himself known, Bateman remained silent, as he wanted to go and fight.

He was, says his sister, in 'top physical form' when he joined up, 'undergoing rigorous training at the Ripon, Yorks, camp without any strain'. He continued to draw during his training, producing a number of sketches of rural scenes in the Ripon area.

From April to November 1916 he served in France during the Battle of the Somme. He was in the Thiepval and Beaumont Hamel areas, serving first as Gunner and then as Signaller. His sister remembers him stating that his 'hottest spot' as a Signaller was 'keeping a wire going in a sunken road time after time'. It was his experience in this battle that inspired him to make the drawings reproduced here.

In November 1916, at the end of the battle, he was committed to hospital at Étaples with acute neurasthenia following utter exhaustion and shell-shock. He was subsequently in various hospitals in England and left the Army in 1918 with an honourable discharge. He was awarded a small war pension.

Harry Bateman as a newly joined volunteer.

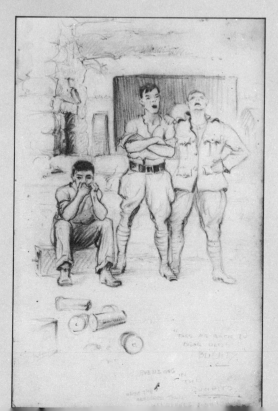

OUR DIGS AT METHIL

LEADERS SPOTTED

RUNNING A WIRE OUT.

BRINGING UP RESERVES.

After his discharge, on medical advice, he went to live in Scarborough, but never entirely recovered his health. He managed, however, to live as an artist. His main interest was in landscape and coastal scenes, but he was also an accomplished painter of portraits. He exhibited at galleries in London and in the provinces; examples of his work were purchased by galleries at Scarborough and Newcastle upon Tyne. He died in January 1976.

He scarcely ever looked again at his war drawings after his return to civilian life. His sister, Miss Doris Bateman (by whose courtesy a selection of them are here reproduced), sent them to me within weeks of her brother's death following my appeal for material on the Battle of the Somme. They are now permanently housed in the Imperial War Museum, London.

13

'The Terrible Price'

A dead British soldier in a trench at Guillemont, on the Somme front, September 191

Somewhere in Flanders,
19 : 7 : 16

Dear Ernest,

Thanks muchly for your letter d/12 : 7 : 16. So pleased to hear that you have landed home again, also that you are going on well.

Sergeant E. E. Lane, in hospital in England after being wounded in France, received a letter from a fellow Sergeant of the 6th Battalion of the Royal Berkshire Regiment, telling him how his battalion and its various members had fared on the Somme.

You remember that morning, I waited on the road for over an hour for the Ambulances, first one I saw was Sergt Thomas poor chap, I think he was pretty hard hit on the right shoulder, his jacket was pretty red I noticed, hope he is nicely tucked up somewhere in hospital. I heard from Medcraft, another of my chums, the other day, he is in Reading no. 4 War Hospital. If you would care to write to him, poor old chap, 'can't sit down', what a pity. But still, he's far away from Shrapnel and the like . . .

I am very pleased to say that both Woodley and Hawkins two more of my pals came out with a whole skin; Woodley brought Mr Brown, one of our Officers, back with him, he was badly wounded in both legs & arms, poor chap has since died. We lost Mr Hayes killed, Mr Haywood my Platoon Officer & Mr Child missing, & the Captain badly wounded, I hear he has since died. I am so sorry, although we had only had him with us a week or two, I am sure every man thought a lot of him. We had quite a number wounded in my platoon, Haycock, Wylde, England, Bullen, Wyles, Wood, Osborne, House, Nash, Robinson. Missing: L/Cpl Hilsdon my best pal, Pte Webb, Giles, Hudson, L/Cpl Searies. Pte Morgan killed. Corpls House & Tucker are missing & quite a number of L/Cpls and men of other platoons . . .

Well now old Chap, keep smiling and you'll get well again, kindest regards, all kind thoughts & good wishes, to you from us all, I will always remain,

189   Your Chum, Ivern Deacon.

My dear Hall,

I do hope you will not think me unkind or neglectful that I have not written to you before. Believe me, I have often thought of you, and have been living in hopes of hearing how you are getting on.

Captain H. S. H. Hall, 10th Bn Royal Fusiliers, lost an eye in his battalion's attack on Pozières in mid July 1916. In hospital in England, he received a letter from his Commanding Officer, Lieutenant-Colonel the Hon. Robert White.

First, let me thank you from the bottom of my heart for your splendid and gallant conduct, and for the glorious example of duty you set the men. Your loss is irreparable to me. I can only hope and trust that you may be spared pain and soon restored to health and to your family. You deserve all the rest and happiness that I hope is in store for you . . .

Well, we have paid a terrible price! Though very sad, I am filled with pride at the bearing of the dear 10th.

Poor Taylor and Bevir are gone, as you know. Dear little Haviland died at Heilly on the 16th very badly wounded. Heathcote followed him next day and they lie quite close to each other and not far from poor Hodding, who died on the 10th. To my great grief our dear Shurey died yesterday, and we all went over to his funeral in the same graveyard as the others, about 400 yards from the railway station and under a beautiful hanging wood. I am grateful to think that they were all nursed by nice English nurses, and tended by good surgeons.

Richards you know was also killed, poor fellow . . .

We are an attenuated little band. We lost 397 K. & W. in the two days, but full of cheer; doing our best to re-organize and hope to have another go at the Bosch soon.

In General Orders the Battalion and Brigade were complimented. The message ran—

'the 10th did all that gallant British soldiers could do'!

Do let me hear how you are getting on and where you are. I miss you sadly, but am very proud to have had such officers and men under me. God bless you! Every kind wish.

Your grateful Colonel,
Robert White.

P.S. I watched your grand advance from the Chalk Pit on the road.

The paying of a 'terrible price' on the field of battle—in particular by those most vulnerable of fighting men, the infantry—was a commonplace of the Great War. It was not unknown for battalions to be virtually annihilated. On 1 July 1916 certain battalions lost over 90 per cent of their attacking strength in killed and wounded.   190

Usually between 700 and 800 men went into battle: on the morning of 1st July—in a matter of minutes, though the full toll would not be known for some time—the 10th Battalion of the West Yorkshire Regiment sustained 710 casualties and the 1st Battalion of the Newfoundland Regiment 684 casualties. A sizeable proportion of every battalion, usually including a senior officer (often the second-in-command), was left behind in the safety of the base area, so that whatever happened its continuity could be maintained. But what guaranteed continuity could not guarantee continued identity. When men who had lived and trained together for many months marched into the savagery of a set-piece battle, there was the virtual certainty not only that there would be huge losses but that the unit with which they had come to identify themselves would never be quite the same again.

Captain Harry Yoxall, 18th Bn King's Royal Rifle Corps, wrote the following letter from a rest camp after the heavy fighting on the Somme in mid September 1916:

> Dearest Mater and All,
> ... Our brigade took its part in the general operations of the 15th–17th. I cannot give you any details as yet; but we reached all our objectives and held them till relieved, advanced for over $1\frac{1}{2}$ miles on a 500 yards frontage, captured a village and took 750 prisoners ...

The military cemetery at Heilly, just behind the battlefield of the Somme, where Haviland, Heathcote, Hodding and Shurey, all young officers of the 10th Bn Royal Fusiliers, lie buried (see the letter by Lieutenant-Colonel Robert White in this chapter). This photograph shows the cemetery as it was in December 1916.

Newspapers

HOW NEWS CAME HOME TO BLIGHTY—THE IMPACT OF A GREAT BATTLE

The standard message of the news and picture pages was at first one of optimism and success. Even *The Times* ran headlines like 'Heavy German Attacks Shattered', 'Great Day on the Somme' or 'Swift British Advance'. Meanwhile the casualty lists grew longer and longer: the vast majority on the lists printed opposite would be from the Somme, but there would also be the daily losses from the other sectors. The Navy (given pride of place as senior service) had its handful of losses printed here too.

How Bradford reacted to the First Day of the Somme

First reports were optimistic—'Splendid Dash—Great Attack Described—West Yorkshires Engaged' on 3rd July but by 7th July there was a more sombre note— 'Heavy Toll of the City Units', though even at this stage there was the hope that their much-loved 'Pals' battalions (the 16th and 18th West Yorks) had not been too badly hit. 'It is satisfactory that up to the present there have been very few deaths recorded,' wrote the *Bradford Daily Telegraph*. The Roll of Honour began that same day (the first name was Lieutenant Robert Sutcliffe, 1st Bradford Pals, whose last letter before battle is printed on page 137). As the lists went on through edition after edition it became obvious that a major tragedy had struck the city. *The Bradford Daily Telegraph*, and its weekly counterpart (see opposite), began to print double-page spreads of the fallen and wounded men. They were still printing them well into August.

A pathetic consequence of the heavy losses on 1st July—photographs sent to the local newspaper as part of the grim process of identifying dead soldiers. It would be all too obvious to relatives that their loved one must have been mutilated beyond recognition.

PHOTOS FOUND ON THE BATTLEFIELD.

This further selection of photos found on the battlefield—(there are fifty of them)—which have been forwarded to us with the view of identification, is typical of the varied interests which they make manifest, and emphasise the need of straining every effort to bring the war to a victorious and an early end.

No more 'Pals'

1 July 1916 put an end to what had seemed so grand an idea in 1914 and 1915—there were no more 'Pals' battalions after the Somme. Little thought seems to have been given to the effect on a local community of the annihilation of its own specially raised fighting force. It was a marvellous concept that friends from civil life should serve together in the new companionship of war; but what if they not only served together but died together as well? The newspaper reports given here and over the page are typical of many at that time, as local pride turned overnight to local grief. And many photographs put happily into albums or propped on mantelpieces or pianos in the early, heady days must suddenly have become unbelievably poignant.

> The companionship was marvellous, absolutely marvellous. Everyone seemed to help one another and agree with one another. It was lovely. We were all pals, we were happy, very happy together; and they were such good people. They were fine young men, the cream of the country. That spirit lasted until 1 July 1916. We had so many casualties that we were all strangers after that. The new men who came were fed up, they were conscripts and they didn't want to come, they didn't want to fight. Things were never the same any more.
>
> *Private George Morgan*

'Arrived here at 3.30 this morning all alive and well. Your loving son Bert.'

A postcard showing a platoon of Bradford Pals during early training in 'Blighty'.

The cemetery in France where so many Bradford Pals lie buried—Serre Road No. 1 (below, left).

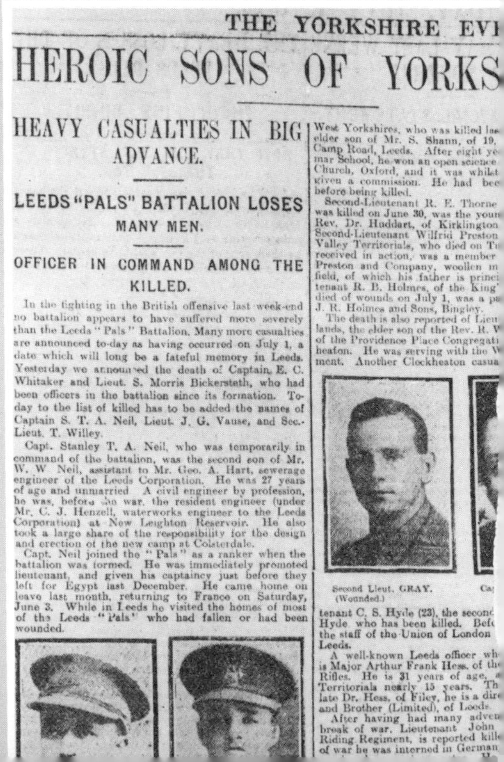

THE YORKSHIRE EV

HEROIC SONS OF YORKS

HEAVY CASUALTIES IN BIG ADVANCE.

LEEDS "PALS" BATTALION LOSES MANY MEN.

OFFICER IN COMMAND AMONG THE KILLED.

In the fighting in the British offensive last week-end no battalion appears to have suffered more severely than the Leeds "Pals" Battalion. Many more casualties are announced to-day as having occurred on July 1, a date which will long be a fateful memory in Leeds. Yesterday we announced the death of Captain E. C. Whitaker and Lieut. S. Morris Bickersteth, who had been officers in the battalion since its formation. To-day to the list of killed has to be added the names of Captain S. T. A. Neil, Lieut. J. G. Vause, and Sec.-Lieut. T. Willey.

Capt. Stanley T. A. Neil, who was temporarily in command of the battalion, was the second son of Mr. W. W. Neil, assistant to Mr. Geo. A. Hart, sewerage engineer of the Leeds Corporation. He was 27 years of age and unmarried. A civil engineer by profession, he was, before the war, the resident engineer (under Mr. C. J. Henzell, waterworks engineer to the Leeds Corporation) at New Leighton Reservoir. He also took a large share of the responsibility for the design and erection of the new camp at Colsterdale.

Capt. Neil joined the "Pals" as a ranker when the battalion was formed. He was immediately promoted lieutenant, and given his captaincy just before they left for Egypt last December. He came home on leave last month, returning to France on Saturday, June 3. While in Leeds he visited the homes of most of the Leeds "Pals" who had fallen or had been wounded.

West Yorkshires, who was killed las elder son of Mr. S. Shann, of 19, Camp Road, Leeds. After eight ye mar School, he won an open science Church, Oxford, and it was whilst given a commission. He had bee before being killed.

Second-Lieutenant R. E. Thorne was killed on June 30, was the youn Rev. Dr. Huddart, of Kirklington Second-Lieutenant Wilfrid Preston Valley Territorials, who died on T received in action, was a member Preston and Company, woollen m field, of which his father is princi tenant R. B. Holmes, of the King' died of wounds on July 1, was a pa J. R. Holmes and Sons, Bingley.

The death is also reported of Lieu lands, the elder son of the Rev. R. W of the Providence Place Congregati heaton. He was serving with the W ment. Another Clockheaton casua

Second Lieut. GRAY. (Wounded.)

tenant C. S. Hyde (23), the second Hyde who has been killed. Bef the staff of the Union of London Leeds.

A well-known Leeds officer wh is Major Arthur Frank Hess, of th Rifles. He is 31 years of age, Territorials nearly 15 years. Th late Dr. Hess, of Filey, he is a dir and Brother (Limited), of Leeds

After having had many adven break of war, Lieutenant John Riding Regiment, is reported kill of war he was interned in German

"COVERED THEMSELVES WITH GLORY."
BATTALION COMMANDERS WARM PRAISE.

...gh tributes are being paid to the heroic part which the lads of Barnsley and ...t have taken in the great offensive movement so ...cessfully launched and ...ed, and the following congratulatory message, coming ...om Lieut.-Col. Wilford, ...mand of the 13th York and Lancasters, the Barnsley First Battalion, to Lieut.-...ewitt, will be read with deep interest and pride.

FRANCE,
11th JULY, 1916.

...r Hewitt,

...e 13th Y. & L. have covered themselves with glory, and you who ...the Battalion should indeed be pleased.

...ey have added a page to history.

...e way the Regiment advanced through an intense artillery "carrage" ...chine-gun fire to the attack equals any deed done in the War.

...faltering or wavering, each man pressing on to his objective, and as ...y as if on parade.

...r casualties were very heavy, but we have the consolation they fell ...hour of victory.

...ould like you to let the people of Barnsley know that every lad who ...that day was a hero.

...e Battalion has been congratulated by many—the Corps Commander, ...visional General, and by our Brigadier on its gallantry, and I am the ...st man in France.

Yours sincerely,
E. S. WILFORD,
Lieut.-Col. Commanding 13th Y. & L.

Like the Bradford and Leeds Pals, the Barnsley Pals suffered in the attack on the German strong-point of Serre. Serre was never captured, but occupied in early 1917, when the Germans withdrew to better positions.

A group of Grimsby Chums (10th Bn Lincolns) photographed at Ripon just one year before the battalion suffered on the Somme. Six of these men were killed in action; the remaining two were wounded

The Leeds Pals was one of thirty-two battalions that suffered more than five hundred casualties on 1 July 1916.

The Effect on Ulster

The 36th (Ulster) Division—the former Ulster Volunteer force reconstituted as part of Britain's New Army—took virtually all of its objectives in the great attack, but, unsupported through the lack of success elsewhere, was finally forced to withdraw. It was involved in some of the fiercest fighting on 1st July, and suffered very heavy losses. An index of both those factors is that it was awarded four of the ten VCs won on that day. Nowhere is the memory of the Somme more zealously guarded.

THE VALOUR OF ULSTER.
NEW RENOWN FOR JULY 1.
THRILLING STORY OF BRAVERY.
CHARGED TO DERRY'S WATCHWORD.

Special Order of the Day by Major-General O. S. W. Nugent, D.S.O., Commanding 36th (Ulster) Division.

The General Officer Commanding the Ulster Division desires that the Division should know that, in his opinion, nothing finer has been done in the War than the attack by the Ulster Division on the 1st July.

The leading of the Company Officers, the discipline and courage shown by all ranks of the Division will stand out in the future history of the War as an example of what good troops, well led, are capable of accomplishing.

None but troops of the best quality could have faced the fire which was brought to bear on them and the losses suffered during the advance.

Nothing could have been finer than the steadiness and discipline shown by every Battalion, not only in forming up outside its own trenches but in advancing under severe enfilading fire.

The advance across the open to the German line was carried out with the steadiness of a parade movement, under a fire both from front and flanks which could only have been faced by troops of the highest quality.

The fact that the objects of the attack on one side were not obtained is no reflection on the Battalions which were entrusted with the task.

They did all that men could do, and in common with every Battalion in the Division showed the most conspicuous courage and devotion.

On the other side, the Division carried out every portion of its allotted task in spite of the heaviest losses.

It captured nearly 600 prisoners and carried its advance triumphantly to the limits of the objective laid down.

There is nothing in the operations carried out by the Ulster Division on the 1st July that will not be a source of pride to all Ulstermen.

The Division has been highly tried and has emerged from the ordeal with unstained honour, having fulfilled, in every particular, the great expectations formed of it.

Tales of individual and collective heroism on the part of Officers and Men come in from every side, too numerous to mention, but all showing that the standard of gallantry and devotion attained is one that may be equalled, but is never likely to be surpassed.

The General Officer Commanding deeply regrets the heavy losses of Officers and Men. He is proud beyond description, as every Officer and Man in the Division may well be, of the magnificent example of sublime courage and discipline which the Ulster Division has given to the Army.

Ulster has every reason to be proud of the men she has given to the service of our country.

Though many of our best men have gone, the spirit which animated them remains in the Division, and will never die.

L. J. COMYN,
Lt.-Col., A.A. and Q.M.G., 36th Division.

3rd July, 1916.

'In 1916 crying could be heard in the streets of Belfast and in the provincial towns and villages of Ulster. The sight of a uniformed telegram-boy sufficed to cause fear, so dread were the tidings of the Division's fate.' (Mr James Page)

But the cost was heavy. My own battalion was particularly unfortunate. ... Of those that one or other of you knows Major Fadd, Captains Lester and Langford are all killed. Each is a tragedy in himself. Fadd was the best of good fellows, an adored son and brother, and had had a meteoric career in the army. Then there is Lester's wife—poor girl, I can't bear to think of her. And Langford's only brother was killed at Ploeg Street last June.

I can't give you details of casualties, but four other officers, including the Colonel and the Adjutant, were killed and eight wounded.

I am still heavy with lack of sleep and fortunately perhaps can't realize what has happened. It seems impossible that all these people with whom I have lived and worked for all these past months are no more—just washed out as far as we are concerned. But it is so: and all that we that are left can do is to set to and pull the depleted battalion together and make it once more what it was. For it was a good battalion: not brilliant but hardworking and dogged: so that though we had, under the terrible shell-fire, to give up our third objective once and retire through the village we came again and held it till relieved ...

Friends, chums, colleagues 'just washed out'—this was the hard experience to which the soldier had to become accustomed. Second Lieutenant Kenneth Macardle, 17th Bn Manchester Regt, in what was to prove the last entry in his diary, written on 6 July 1916, mourned the loss of his friends who had fallen in the attack on Montauban on 1st July.

All the world was forever dead to Vaudrey, Kenworthy, Chesham, Sproat, Ford, and of the 'other ranks' we did not know how many. Vaudrey used to love rousing parades; Chesham had loved to hunt the buck in Africa when the heat was shimmering with the birth of a day.... Young Victor was killed—his problem of marriage to a woman six years senior to him finally settled. Towers Clark too was dead and Captain Law of County Down.... We are about 400 strong tonight—we who went in 800.

Macardle's attack had been a success and, depleted as they were, they were greeted with praise, cheers and handshakes when they returned to base. But what if a battalion—or a division—had suffered heavy losses with no compensatory achievement? Captain Lionel Ferguson, 13th Bn Cheshire Regt, moving up towards the front on 3 July 1916, saw the survivors of a Highland division coming out from a heavy mauling on the Somme.

It was a sight new to me to see really tired men, they were just walking along in twos and threes, holding each other up for support, unshaven, covered with mud, and war-worn, in fact never have I seen troops in worse condition. I met with them Major Popham, whom I had known in Bebington days, he had now a staff job with that division. He was pleased to see me, but told me they had had an awful time and that they were a smashed division.

196

All the accounts quoted so far in this chapter except the first have been the powerfully written statements of educated officers well capable of expressing their sense of grief and loss. Equally moving, surely, is the following letter by a young, unsophisticated soldier of the 36th (Ulster) Division, Herbert Beattie of the 2nd Bn Royal Inniskilling Fusiliers. The Ulster Division fought magnificently on 1 July 1916, but at an appallingly high cost. Under the shock of this terrible experience and stunned by the deaths of so many friends, Fusilier Beattie wrote home.

> Dear Mother,
>
> Just a few lines to let you know I am safe and thank God for it, for we had a rough time in the charge we made. Mother don't tell V. Quinn's mother or Archer's (mother) that they must be killed (or) wounded for they are missing from roll-call, and tell Hugh that the fellow who used to chum about with E. Ferguson, called Eddie Mallon (he used to keep pigeons— if Hugh does not know him, McKeown knows him) has been killed. Tell

Popular postcards, inevitably, portrayed the Tommy as eager at all times to have a go at the enemy, nonchalant in action and cheerful after it. Popular reporting of the time conveyed the same impression: a writer who visited the front in 1916 praised the 'sublime devotion and unparalleled cheerfulness [with which] our heroic soldiers are facing death Out There' (*Out There: Impressions of a Visit under the Auspices of the War Office*, by Charles Igglesdon, 1916). In a chapter on 'Tommy Atkins', Igglesdon wrote: 'I have come to the conclusion that we who stay at home are not fit to black his boots. I used to admire him, now I adore him. Out there in France and Flanders . . . he is proving himself a hero of heroes.'

In the same style, the caption on the postcard below reads: 'Before battle, in battle and after battle, our "Tommies" are ready for a fag. These men are lighting up after a scrap.' Somewhat nearer the truth (overleaf)

A "FAG" AFTER A FIGHT

them that there is not another Grosvenor Road fellow left but myself. Mother, we were tramping over the dead; I think there is only about 4 hundred left out of about 13 hundred. Mother, you can let Alfred know something about all this. Mother, I have some German helmets and sausages, and I am sorry that I could not send them home. Mother, if God spares me to get home safely, I will have something awful to tell you. If hell is any worse I would not like to go to it. Mother, let me hear from you as soon as possible, as I have had no word from you this fortnight. Don't forget to let me hear from you soon.

From your loving son Herbie*

* I am grateful to Mr James Page of Belfast for sending me a copy of this letter and for providing me with the version printed above, in which gaps caused by the fading of the original pencil have been filled in and one or two remarkable (but irrelevant) spelling errors corrected.

When a soldier lost his life, it was normal practice for someone in his battalion—perhaps most frequently of all his Company Commander—to write a letter of consolation to his next of kin. On 10 November 1915 Private Edgar Foreman, Civil Service Rifles, was killed during a routine spell in the trenches. Three days later Captain Arthur Roberts, officer in charge of 'D' Company, wrote to the dead man's father.

> Dear Sir,
>
> It is my painful duty to acquaint you of the death of your son killed in action on November 10th. He was killed together with two others by a shell & we buried all three together close by.
>
> There is little of comfort that I can add. Your son was a fine soldier, who always did his share & played his part cheerfully and well. He died doing his duty.
>
> It may provide you some small comfort to know that death was instantaneous; he suffered no pain. We all, officers & men, join with you in mourning his loss.

Captain Roberts himself was killed ten months later, in the fierce fighting for High Wood on the Somme. Letters of condolence to his relations have also survived, including this to his sister from a lieutenant of his company:

> It is with the deepest regret that I have to inform you that Captain Roberts was killed on September 15th.
>
> He was leading the Company and had crawled up to 20 yards of the enemy trenches when he rose to give the charge and was killed instantly.
>
> His loss is a great one to us who honoured and respected him for bravery and dauntless courage.

On 18 August 1916 Captain Goronwy Owen, 15th Bn Royal Welch Fusiliers, wrote to the widow of Private A. J. Salway.

> Dear Madam,
>
> I regret that pressure of work and illness have prevented me from writing earlier to express my sympathy with you in the loss of your husband, who met his death while gallantly doing his duty in action.
>
> He was engaged at the time in carrying water and rations to his comrades in the wood during the fighting. It was, indeed, a case of a man laying down his life for his comrades. His death was instantaneous and mercifully he suffered no pain.
>
> All of us, officers and men, mourn his loss. He was a good and conscientious soldier and did his duty nobly and well. No better testimony could be given to any man.
>
> We all offer you and your family our heartiest and sincerest sympathy. May God protect and comfort you and all that are near and dear to you.

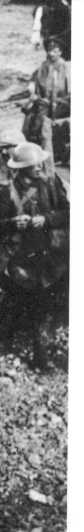

Men of the 4th Battalion the Worcestershire Regiment coming out from the trenches in the third month of the Battle of the Somme.

Killed in Action

THE DEATH OF PETER McGREGOR

Private Peter McGregor, 14th Bn Argyll and Sutherland Highlanders, was aged forty-four when he was killed on 13 September 1916.

From his last letter to his wife:

> ... How I long for Scotland and 'Green Fields of England'—oh to be in dear old Edinburgh—it's the loveliest place on the earth ...
>
> ... I am well and looking forward to the end of the war. I wish it would hurry up ...
>
> ... One of our men was caught by a sniper—he was standing at the entrance to his dugout, the bullet went in under his shoulder—alas! alas! ... When I was standing at the cook-house door I saw the stretcher which came along to take the poor fellow away—how sad that was, he was carrried out, wrapped up in his waterproof sheet, placed on this thing and whisked away. His passing didn't seem to cause much stir—crowds of chaps were standing about—of course we all came to attention as it passed—that was all. The business of the hour had to go on. A dead man is no use to the army, get him out of the way as quickly as possible.
>
> War is a terrible thing, and so few people realize it ...

From a letter to his widow by his platoon sergeant:

> I have been requested by the members of no. 6 Platoon to convey to you & to your family an expression of their most sincere sympathy with you on the death of your husband ... and of their sense of the great loss occasioned to you thereby.
>
> Your husband died quite instantaneously, while on duty, as the result of a shell bursting in the trench.
>
> I must say that his injuries were mostly internal and caused no disfigurement of the features ...

From a letter to his widow by his Company Commander:

> We buried him last night in the British Military Cemetery. It was a beautiful evening and the simple service was held while the guns were booming round us.
>
> May the one who governs all sustain you and your family in your heavy loss. 'Greater love hath no man than this, that he gave up his life for his friends.'

W 6938—2691 250,000 8/15 C.F.R. $\frac{21}{796}$

Army Form B.-101—82.

No. 13538.

(If replying, please quote above No.)

Infantry Record Office,

Perth Station,

23rd September, 1916.

Sir, Madam,

It is my painful duty to inform you that a report has this day been received from the War Office notifying the death of

(No.) 5/9072 (Rank) Private

(Name) Peter McGregor, (Regiment) 14th Argyll and Sutherland Highlanders which occurred at _____

_____ on the Thirteenth day

of September, 1916 , and I am to express to you the sympathy and regret of the Army Council at your loss. The cause of death was

Killed in action

If any articles of private property left by the deceased are found, they will be forwarded to this Office, but some time will probably elapse before their receipt, and when received they cannot be disposed of until authority is received from the War Office.

Application regarding the disposal of any such personal effects, or of any amount that may eventually be found to be due to the late soldier's estate, should be addressed to " The Secretary, War Office, London, S.W.," and marked outside " Effects."

I am,

Sir, Madam,

Your obedient Servant,

Mrs Janet McGregor.

6. Great Stewart Street,

Edinburgh

Gibson Fergularson

Major

for Officer in charge of Records.

No. 1. District

Formal sympathy.

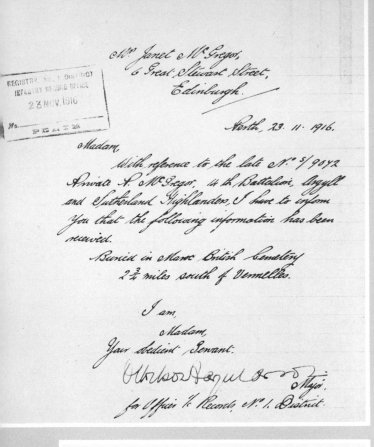

Mrs Janet McGregor,
6 Great Stewart Street,
Edinburgh.

Perth, 23. 11. 1916.

Madam,

With reference to the late No. S/9072 Private P. McGregor, 4th Battalion, Argyll and Sutherland Highlanders, I have to inform you that the following information has been received.

Buried in Maroc British Cemetery 2¾ miles south of Vermelles.

I am,

Madam,

Your obedient Servant.

Major.
for Officer i/c Records, No. 1. District.

Official notification of the whereabouts of Private McGregor's grave; and the grave as it is today.

'Death was instantaneous'; 'he suffered no pain . . .'—almost invariably this ritualistic consolation was offered to the mourning relatives. It could, of course, be true: many men were killed instantly by the bullet in the heart or brain or the sudden explosion of a shell. But there must have been countless times when this well-tried formula covered up a hideous and agonizing death. It was inevitable in such circumstances that reality should be softened by the admixture of a harmless fiction: what good would there be in telling the awful truth to a broken young widow or a grieving father and mother?

Death in fact was rarely tidy; rather it was ugly, degrading, dehumanizing. When Gunner Hiram Sturdy, Royal Field Artillery, saw his first death he found it a revealing and unforgettable experience.

> I crouch in behind some infantry holes (I won't call them shelters) and while there, one of the infantry is carried in. The top of the head is lifted off, a clean swipe whatever got him. His chum holds his head and I see him die. The first for me to see die, as they say, for his country, and it might be glorious, noble, brave, heroic, and all the rest of these beautiful words that sound so well on a platform or toasting your toes by the fireside, but it certainly is not a glorious sight to see a young fellow, with his face covered with blood, stiffening out in a hole dug out of clay. It isn't glorious, it's murder, was my thoughts when I saw my first infantryman die, and the years which I have lived since have only lowered the glories to the lowest depths and raised 'war is murder' to the highest pinnacle.
>
> The chum sits a little time looking at the bloody clay with a uniform on it, then buckles up, and goes out to the bloody war.

Second Lieutenant Blake O'Sullivan, 6th Bn Connaught Rangers, was mapping the trenches which the battalion had just occupied* on the Somme front in late August 1916 when he came across the body of one of their corporals, killed while coming up to the line the previous night.

> He was on his back with one knee crooked up and arms thrown apart, looking for all the world like a weary hiker. A gold wedding ring gleamed on one slightly closed hand and I wondered what thieving ghoul would eventually take it. A dreadful cloud of flies came buzzing up from him and I hurried past without looking any closer.

Earlier, while making their way to the front, their guide had lost his way and 'stupidly' led them into a trench which contained 'a snarl of telephone wires' and, in addition, was 'half full of liquid mud'.

> We waded slowly through the cold sludge, tripping and tangling in the wire, and stumbled over a dead man. Lying on his back and legs stretched out like an X. He was actually half afloat in the mud and nodded his head solemnly as each of us sloshed by.

203   * Prior to the attack on Guillemont described in Ch. 12.

Captain Reginald Leetham, 2nd Bn Rifle Brigade, while engaged in tending the wounded of 1 July 1916, came across a trench into which corpses had been heaped.

> The trench was a horrible sight. The dead were stretched out on one side, one on top of each other 6 feet high. I thought at the time I should never get the peculiar disgusting smell of the vapour of warm human blood heated by the sun out of my nostrils. I would rather have smelt gas a hundred times. I can never describe that faint sickening horrible smell which several times almost knocked me up altogether. To do one's duty, one was actually climbing over corpses in every position and when one trod on human flesh it sent a shudder down one's spine.
>
> Of the hundreds of corpses I saw, I only saw one pretty one—a handsome boy called Schnyder of the Berkshires who lay on our fire step shot through his heart. I wish his mother could have seen him—one of the few whose faces had not been mutilated.
>
> His eyes were open and he had a smile on his face; I suppose he died with the pleasure of knowing he had done his duty. His hair had not been ruffled and, unlike me, he had recently had a shave. There were no terrors of death on his face, poor boy.

Captain Leetham was himself killed in action, on 12 October 1917.

Fortunately for the sanity of the survivors, the very scale of the slaughter seems to have produced its own anaesthesia. It was possible for men to look on the most terrible of sights, to hear the most appalling evidence of pain and suffering, and still carry on. Corporal F. W. Billman, 9th Bn East Surrey Regt, on 25 September 1915, found himself in the dark, in the rain and under shell-fire on the battlefield of Loos: it was his first taste of war. Around him

> the ground was sprinkled with dead and dying heroes, but we had no time to stop and look at them, and soon got used to the ghastly faces, more so after midnight, as the moon shone out brilliantly. Many lay as they fell, some in an easy position, and one actually had a letter in his hand, as though he had managed to read it through before he died.

Private Archie Surfleet, on 16 November 1916, spent a night collecting badly wounded from No Man's Land after a 'show' which had produced many casualties. In his diary he wrote:

> Most of us have lost pals and some of them will never come back, but it is surprising how little 'brooding' there is about. . . . The lists of killed and wounded seem unending; yet practically everyone seems to take it all in an almost uncanny calmness. We are all looking forward to better times; God knows we can do with them.

It is necessary to add, however, that this capacity to 'soldier on' in spite of the deaths of friends should not be taken as a sign of indifference. 'When I think of my poor dear old chums who have fallen I could cry,' wrote Private Jack Sweeney in

Burial party near Monchy le Preux, 29 August 1918.

> We went out at night on a stretcher-bearing party. ... We first of all got in
> all the wounded we could find and scoured the whole area. I think it is creditable
> that *every* wounded man was brought in. ... There were dozens of dead bodies
> about; we collected all we could and stacked them in piles ready for removal
> to a decent burial further back. I am still amazed at the casual way we piled
> those bodies, like so many huge logs, without any horror at such a gruesome
> task; which seems to show we must be getting hardened.
>
> *Private Archie Surfleet, 13th Bn East Yorkshire Regt.*

A burial service on the
Western Front

The grave of Alex Macdonald
photographed in 1978.

On 25 January 1917 Private Tom Macdonald, 9th Bn Royal Sussex Regt, witnessed the funeral of his brother Alex, killed in an exchange of fire the previous night. The brothers were members of the same Lewis gun team. Tom Macdonald was slightly wounded and was taking another member of the team who was worse hit to the aid post when he heard a shout of 'Stretcher Bearers!' A hunch told him his brother had been hit. He asked stretcher bearer at the aid post to go with him and hurried back:

> It was pitch black. I had no torch and the Stretcher Bearer had his bag and gear. We went along the trench until we came upon Alex, the Stretcher Bearer just flashed the torch once and ran on saying he must get help. I just saw the sight my brother was, face down and the back of his head was hit. I was left in pitch black with him on my own. I was grief stricken. Later they took me to Advance Dressing Station and gave me an injection for the slight hand wound and this put me out for a while.
>
> The next day with my officer, Lieut Dudney and Padre Dodds, we left to bury him at the new cemetery at Philosophe near Masingarbe in the Loos Salient. I'll never forget, we had to go through long winding trenches to this village just behind the lines, it seemed the longest walk I ever had and the padre and my officer were kindness itself to me. It all seemed a dream and at the new cemetery the only ones were the padre and officer and a grave digger. My brother was just sewn up in hessian sacking and the padre gave the service. My 'bone' comes in my throat as I remember this and I can hardly write this but I feel I must for my sons and others to see the futility of war. When I returned again to this cemetery in 1918 there were hundreds of graves, then just wooden crosses. My brother's best pals had got a wooden cross and painted on it his name, rank etc. and 'one of the best'. They also loved him.

206

a letter home of 1916; and he was expressing a widely held sentiment. More, the grief men suffered was, in many cases, permanent. Anyone who has spoken to a survivor of a 'Pals' battalion, for example, will realize how deeply such a man can be moved at the thought of his fallen comrades sixty years after their deaths.

One thing that could disturb that 'almost uncanny calmness' referred to by Private Surfleet was an inability to cope with the agonies of the wounded. Death instantly put a man in a separate category; he was beyond help; in Captain Yoxall's phrase, he was 'washed out'. His body was merely a disposable piece of garbage, to be got under ground as soon as possible: the niceties could follow later. The wounded were different, as Captain Leetham, of the Rifle Brigade, after hours of attempting to help the survivors of the holocaust of 1 July 1916, wrote in his diary:

> It was the wounded that made the place such a Hell. I did not mind the dead. I could do nothing for them, but one felt so incapable of doing much for the wounded . . .
> Every now and then a wounded man crawled in. I shall never forget the agony in their faces, especially towards midnight when some had been out for 16 hours.
> Quite a number, for the time I hope, had gone stark staring mad . . .
> Stretcher bearers were frightfully scarce. What was the use of a handful of stretcher bearers to deal with literally thousands of wounded. It was two o'clock in the afternoon before I saw a doctor. All I could do was to give brandy and water to men we rescued from being buried alive; also to men who had to lie for hours with broken legs I gave morphia. I got rid of two tubes of morphia and two big flasks of brandy.

Private Tom Macdonald, 9th Bn Royal Sussex Regt, had a similarly frustrating experience on a similarly hot summer's day on the Somme: 'The worst part was when we could not get badly wounded back. Some were screaming for water and we could only moisten their lips with jam.'

But when men *did* rescue a wounded comrade, there was a profound satisfaction. Private Surfleet, 13th Bn East Yorkshire Regt, was near Oppy Wood in May 1917 when he and his friends

> noticed a chap stretched out on the strip of road, the Bailleul-Oppy road, which ran by the end of the bit of trench we were in. He waved an arm in our direction: Whole, Hurste, Bridge and I took a stretcher from the pile outside the MO's place and ambled along the road to him. Until we got right up to him we did not realize he must have been in full view of the enemy: he was just over the rise nearing Oppy Wood. We put him on the stretcher and brought him back to the Aid Post: he had been out there two days and nights with his leg shattered and had been trying to get back to our lines, using an old rifle as a crutch. I shall never forget that man's

A serious wound was often unbearable, and not only for the sufferer himself. Second Lieutenant Blake O'Sullivan, 6th Connaught Rangers was in front-line trenches on the Somme in 1916 when there was the sudden explosion of a random shell:

> The explosion viciously rocked the place and we hugged the side of the sap to avoid debris and then had to step aside to let a procession of stretchers go by. One of the passing casualties was an oldish man, and the distorted lump where his body should have been gave a horrifying effect; a wooden wedge was held fiercely between his teeth and his eyes flashed around with an extraordinary speed, implying such frantic agony that I had to look away.

Bringing in a badly wounded man after the capture of Guillemont in early September 1916. The incident described above happened in this sector a day or so before this photograph was taken. In the capture of Guillemont Second Lieutenant Blake O'Sullivan was himself wounded and subsequently sent to Blighty.

Not a subject for a popular postcard: the wounded are Canadians being transported in a motor ambulance in July 1917.

expression of gratitude when we got him safely to the shelter of the Aid Post; the tears in his eyes gave us an inkling of the hell he had been through. I know I had a peculiar feeling of exhilaration as he waved goodbye when the stretcher bearers took him away.

Behind the Aid Post was the Advanced Dressing Station; behind that the Casualty Clearing Station; behind that the base hospitals; and behind these the vast resources of the hospitals, nursing homes and converted country houses of Blighty. All these were linked by ambulances, both horse- and motor-powered, hospital trains, hospital barges and hospital ships, and run by that most important of military arms, the Royal Army Medical Corps. They might be the butt of soldierly jokes which interpreted RAMC as 'Run Away Mother's Coming' or 'Rob All My Comrades'; but these were the men whom the Tommy relied on to pull him through in time of trouble. At the time of a 'Big Push' their task was a heroic and a horrifying one, as they struggled to cope with a continuous tide of men with a vast and unpredictable range of wounds.

Private John Martin, RAMC, was an orderly at no. 9 General Hospital, Rouen, during the opening stages of the Battle of the Somme.

To begin with we had very little to do. We had got rid of every moveable patient and the wards were practically empty. Each ward held forty beds.

Then early one morning the signal went for 'convoy' and for the next 72 hours the order of proceedings was: lift the stretchers from the ambulances, carry into the ward till it was full, go round washing face, hands and feet where these still existed, feed them, lift them on to stretchers and carry them out to ambulances unless the surgeon forbade further movement. Then the same again and again. Three times in the first twenty-four hours we filled the ward and emptied it, thrice in the second day and again during the third. In between times we had to do the regular work of feeding and washing those who remained in the ward who as time went on increased in number till there were no vacancies. There was also the occasional extra of carrying a stretcher to the operating theatre and back if he survived.

There were also the walking wounded who were examined and sent on without getting a chance to rest.

There was an incinerator in the hospital and I remember an old sweat who operated it recounting the incredible number of arms and legs he had disposed of in one day.

I should estimate that during three days three hundred men went through our ward no. 20. There were nineteen other wards and a dozen other hospitals.

Was it a nightmare? No, because we had no time to stop and think. We were too hard worked to feel at all. The only appropriate adjective was 'bloody' and after it we were lousy as well from carrying discarded clothing to the incinerator.

Letters to a Burial Officer

When the fighting on the Somme was closed down in November 1916 Second Lieutenant W. N. Collins, 4th Bn Seaforth Highlanders, then aged nineteen, became burial officer in the Beaumont Hamel sector. Beaumont Hamel itself ('there was nothing left of it') was captured on the 13th, with his own battalion playing a crucial part but losing many men. There were also the dead of 1st July to cope with, corpses which had lain there for four months:

> I buried over 1000 men in shell holes, a lot of them of the Newfoundland Regt. killed on July 1st ... There was a rat's nest in the cage of the chest of most of them and the rats had already attacked our newly killed men of the 13th. Our men were collecting bodies of their own brothers and cousins and friends ... Afterwards I wrote to many of the parents and although shortly afterwards I was in hospital wounded I received replies and kept a few of them.

A Letter from a Bereaved Mother

I now write to thank you for your kind letter of sympathy you so kindly sent to me on my sore bereavement, it is too cruel to think my Darling Boy is gone for ever, I do miss his letters to me so regular and he never grumbled.

But it was a great comfort to me to hear from you and to speak so highly of him and I know very well that it is for a good cause we are fighting. But only if his sweet young Life had only been spared I cant realize that he is gone and that I will never see him again. Well Dear Sir I hope and pray that you may get through all right and that your nearest and dearest may be spared the terrible blow that the sad news brings for it just breaks a Mother's Heart ... I hope you will overlook the liberty I have taken in writing to you but I felt I must thank you.

A Letter from a Bereaved Father

On behalf of myself and family I have to thank you for your letter of Condolence to us in our sad Bereavement.

Arthur was the youngest member of our family and we feel his loss all the more on that account ...

He spent the major part of his life here with us at Home, but you, his Officer would see him passing from Boyhood into Manhood in those 4 months he was under your care in France.

We would be ever grateful to you if you could give us a little more information about the lad regarding how he died. Also if it is at all possible that we may have some little remembrance of him such as his Pocket Book or anything of a like nature, we would cherish and prize it above all things.

If it is not in your power to do such, perhaps some of the lads who were his Companions in France would oblige us.

Again thanking you for your kindness to us in our Hour of Sorrow ...

From a letter by former Second Lieutenant W. N. Collins written in 1976: 'No doubt there is nothing new to you in this but it is all very near to me 60 years later ...'

The Small Book of Lance Corporal Thomas Henry Farlam, 4th Bn, Grenadier Guards

On 15 September 1916 there was a major attack on the Somme in which the Guards Division was heavily involved. On that day tanks were used for the first time in war; on that day too the son of the Prime Minister, Captain Raymond Asquith, Grenadier Guards, lost his life in the fighting. On the following day (when in fact the worst of the battle was over), Lance Corporal Thomas Henry Farlam was killed by a shell. His body was never found. He thus became one of the 73,000 missing of the Somme.

When he went into battle, Harry Farlam left his 'small-book' behind with his other personal effects. This was finally returned to his widow, together with the information that in settlement of her late husband's accounts she was due the sum of £4–1–4d, for which due application should be made. The small-book was kept by his widow, and later by their daughter, just as it was. It included among other items her last letter to him and his, unposted, last letter to her. All that she added were the official documents she received relating to his death and a small newspaper cutting from his home-town newspaper. Some of the contents of the small-book are shown or quoted from here. They add up to a simple but remarkable memorial to one of the fallen soldiers of the Great War.

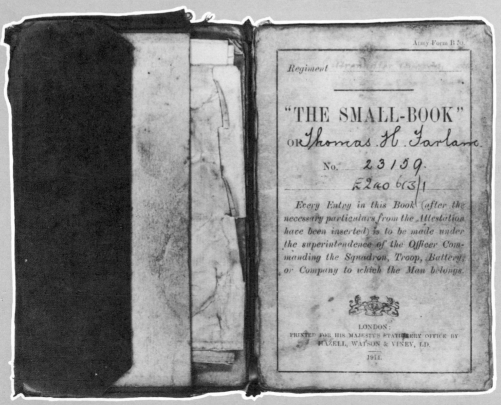

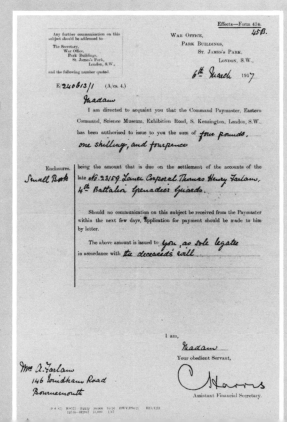

SOLDIER'S NAME AND DESCRIPTION ON ATTESTATION.

(REGULAR FORCES.)

Name *Thomas Henry Farlam*
Enlisted at *Chesterfield*
in the County of *Derby*
on the *24th Feb 1915*
at the age of *30* years _____ months
for the _____
for *3* years in the Army and *0* years in the Reserve.
Born in the Parish of _____
in or near the Town of _____
in the County of _____
Trade or calling *Grocer's Asst*
Last permanent residence _____
Height *5* feet *9½* inches
Complexion _____
Eyes _____ Hair _____
Marks _____

* Religion *Church of England*
† Signature of Soldier *Thomas Henry Farlam*

* This should be described under one of the following denominations, viz.:—" Church of England," "Presbyterian," "Wesleyan," "Baptist," or "Congregational," "other Protestant denomination" name of denomination to be noted;, "Roman Catholic," or "Jew."
† Whenever a Soldier who cannot write makes his mark in acknowledgment of having received pay or allowances, etc., such mark is to be witnessed by the signature of a witness (other than the pay-sergeant).

THE SOLDIER'S NEXT-OF-KIN NOW LIVING.
Any change becoming known is to be duly ____ with the date of each change.

Note. No entry on this page has any legal effect as a Will.

Nearest degrees of relationship.		NAMES.	Latest known address to be given in full.
1st.	Wife.	*Annie*	*51 London Rd Buxton*
	Children.	*Marjorie*	*51 London Rd Buxton*
2nd.	Father.		
3rd.	Mother.	*Anne*	*13 Torr Street Buxton Derby*
	Brothers† and Sisters.		
	Nephews and nieces, if children of deceased brothers or sisters.		
4th.	Other relations.		

Signature of Soldier *Thomas Henry Farlam*

Regimental number. _____ Date of Signature. *24 3 15*
Signature of Company, etc., Commander *C M Ellison Lieut*

† State whether brothers are younger or older.

From Annie Farlam's Last Letter to her Husband:

Just a line to say I have not had any P.C. or Letter from you this week, hope you are in the Best of Health, the news of the war does not seem much like coming to an end shortly, what does it seem like over there. I wish you could tell me where you are, I told you that your last letter had been opened so I expect it pays you not to say anything. Did I tell you Pilch Hall was dead, Poor old Pilch. I see Jack Heeling's young brother has been killed, I do feel sorry, he was our Willie's Pal and such a nice boy, he was only 20. When will you be able to get some leave, I don't expect yet.... I have not heard from our Willie lately but I expect he is still alright, it is good to think he is where he is, as Ned Williamson and young Porter are reported missing and his other Pals are all gone, so it is Lucky he is where he is (with) all those young Boys his Pals most of them gone. If this war does not stop soon I think every body will go mad. Hoping to hear from you soon with a Bit of News.

Your Loving Wife Annie.

Effects—Form 45B.
45B.

Any further communication on this subject should be addressed to—
The Secretary,
War Office,
Park Buildings,
St. James's Park,
London, S.W.,
and the following number quoted.

WAR OFFICE,
PARK BUILDINGS,
ST. JAMES'S PARK,
LONDON, S.W.,

6th March 1917

E/240613/1 (A/cs. 4.)

Madam

I am directed to acquaint you that the Command Paymaster, Eastern Command, Science Museum, Exhibition Road, S. Kensington, London, S.W., has been authorised to issue to you the sum of *four pounds, one shilling, and fourpence*

Enclosures.
Small Book

being the amount that is due on the settlement of the accounts of the late *No. 23159 Lance Corporal Thomas Henry Farlam, 4th Battalion Grenadier Guards.*

Should no communication on this subject be received from the Paymaster within the next few days, application for payment should be made to him by letter.

The above amount is issued to *you, as sole legatee* in accordance with *the deceased's will*

*Mrs. A. Farlam,
146 Windham Road,
Bournemouth*

I am,
Madam,
Your obedient Servant,

C Harris

Assistant Financial Secretary.

CORPORAL HARRY FARLAM.

Corporal Harry Farlam, another Buxton man, has given his life for his country. He was 32 years of age, in the Grenadier Guards, and went to France on New Year's Day, 1916. He was the son of the late Mr. Tom Farlam, manager of the Great Livery Stables, and Mrs. Farlam, of Torr Street.

The following is a copy of a letter received by his wife at Bournemouth from Corporal W. H. Finch, No. 2 Company, 4th Batt. Grenadier Guards, B.E.F.:—

"Dear Mrs. Farlam,—It is with the deepest regret I am writing to tell you that your husband, Harry, has been killed; he was killed by a shell on Saturday, September 16th. He was a great favourite of all who knew him, and all the Platoon will miss him greatly. Assuring you of our deepest sympathy in your great bereavement."

Corpl. Farlam was educated at Buxton Board School, and attended St. John's Church when resident in Buxton. He joined the Grenadier Guards in February, 1915, at Chesterfield. He was a very smart young fellow, and deeply respected by numerous friends and acquaintances.

To his wife and mother the deepest sympathy is extended.

A younger brother is serving with the North ... ds in F... somewhere in the Somme.

Mrs Annie Farlam.

From Harry Farlam's Last Letter to his Wife:

At last I have a few minutes in which to write to you; and I am pleased to say [I am] quite well.... I cannot tell you when I shall be coming on leave, as there are several to go home before me, but I may be lucky and get a chance soon, and we will have a good time together. I should like very much to get back to England and see all my old friends again. I am pleased to say I am jogging along all right as a Corporal, and have passed one stage, so I expect I shall be getting paid for them before very much longer.... You must remember me to all you people at home. I must say that we are having a pretty rough time at present but I keep coming through alright. I will now conclude with fondest love and kisses.

Your affectionate Husband
Harry.   *Corporal*

It is perhaps worth adding that the original of Mrs Farlam's letter, much folded as though read many times, is stained and discoloured with the distinctive colour of the mud of the Somme battlefield, and that the photograph of Annie Farlam had plainly been carried for a long time in the 'small-book'—it has the dog-eared look of a photograph much used.

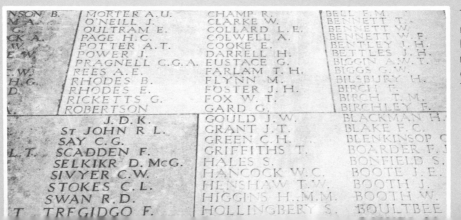

NSON B.	MORTER A.U.	CHAMP R.	BELL F.M.
M.A.	O'NEILL J.	CLARKE W.	BENNETT T.
C.	OULTRAM E.	COLLARD L.E.	BENNETT W.
CK A.	PAGE H.C.	COLWELL A.	BENNETT W.F.
W.	POTTER A.T.	COOKE E.	BENTLEY J.H.
E.W.	POWER J.	DARRELL H.	BETTLES J.H.
	PRAGNELL C.G.A.	EUSTACE G.	BIGGIN A.W.T.
.W.	REES A.E.	FARLAM T.H.	BIGGS G.W.
H.G.	RHODES B.	FLYNN M.	BILSBURY H.
D.	RHODES E.	FOSTER J.H.	BIRCH E.
	RICKETTS G.	FOX W.T.	BIRCH T.M.
	ROBERTSON	GARD G.	BIRCHLEY E.
J.D.K.		GOULD J.W.	BLACKMAN H.
St JOHN R L.		GRANT J.T.	BLAKE F.C.
SAY C.G.		GREEN C.H.	BLENKINSOP C
L.T. SCADDEN F.		GRIFFITHS T.	BOARDER F.J
SELKIKR D. McG.		HALES S.	BONFIELD S.
SIVYER C.W.		HANCOCK W.C.	BOOTE J.E.
STOKES C.L.		HENSHAW T.W.	BOOTH J.
SWAN R.D.		HIGGINS H.M.M.	BOOTH W.
T TREGIDGO F.		HOLLINGBERY S.	BOULTBEE

Thomas Henry Farlam' name, among others o his Battalion, on the memorial to the missin of the Somme at Thiepval.

There is perhaps a necessary postscript to this chapter. It has contained, inevitably, much harrowing material; but what is here printed was recorded by some of that handful of men who felt able to face up to the horrors with which they were confronted and write them down. For every one man that put pen—or pencil—to paper, there must have been hundreds if not thousands who wrote nothing, who simply indicated that they were 'in the pink' and resignedly carried on. And of those who wrote, how many would be prepared to *speak* of their experiences when they went home and mingled with people to whom the private world of the Western Front was entirely alien? The answer is, surely, very few. Their silence allowed people at home to retain their comfortable illusion that the trenches were, if dangerous, at least in some measure tolerable (an illusion that was in fact to produce a massive pendulum swing of emotion after the war when the reality was finally revealed) whereas in fact many of the khaki-clad figures whom they met in the streets of 'Blighty' had lived through enough horrors to last them several lifetimes.

14

'Take Me Back to Dear Old Blighty'

Men collecting in Poperinghe to go home on leave; the papers many of them are waving are leave passes. The date is 30 September 1917, when the Third Battle of Ypres (Passchendaele) was two months old and had another month to go.

I got a smack on my shoulder equipment and felt warm blood on my back. I went to the Dressing Station hoping I had got a wound that would put me in hospital in England. For that seemed the only hope of getting out of the war. We used to hope for a Blighty wound because we heard that the wounded were having a great time especially when convalescing. Taken everywhere, plenty good meals, etc. Therefore the only hope was a cushy flesh wound. Cushy meant easy and good.

Tom Macdonald, 9th Bn Royal Sussex Regt

A 'Blighty wound', otherwise known as a 'Blighty one', or simply a 'Blighty', became for many men, particularly those who had somehow survived long months in the trenches, a kind of ultimate ambition—provided it was not too serious and in the right place. Tom Macdonald was not fortunate on this occasion; his wound was attended to and he was sent back to his war. When Corporal, formerly Private, George Morgan, 1st Bradford Pals, finally got the wound which he knew had been coming to him for months, he *was* fortunate; it was a perfect 'Blighty'.

It was August 1917. We were in front of Vimy and I had just received a parcel with a tin of strawberries in it. We had been at 'stand to' in the front line and we came down the communication trench to have some breakfast. I dug a little hole out of the trench to make a seat to sit on and we boiled some tea in our mess-tins. I had just opened the tin of strawberries and was going to eat them when a shell came over. I was sitting there in my hole with my legs sticking out and there was a man going down the trench to the doctor's to have his eyes bathed (he had some trouble with his eyes) and this whizz-bang simply blew his head off—and a piece of shrapnel hit me in the legs. As for that tin of strawberries I don't know where it went to.

It was a wonderful 'Blighty'. I had often thought, where will I get hit? You can't go every day, month after month, just being missed. I didn't want it in my head—I didn't want to be barmy after the war—and used to think, I'd like it in my legs somewhere. And that was just where I got it. Everybody who saw it said 'What a lovely Blighty!' I went down to Rouen and then over to England, and everybody who came to dress my wound said 'What a lovely Blighty!' I think that was the best thing that ever happened to me.

George Morgan's wound was an honourable one, honourably obtained. There were less noble circumstances in which to earn that longed-for ticket home. Private Jack Sweeney, 1st Bn Lincolnshire Regt, wrote in a letter home in January 1917: 'My Captain has had to go into hospital, he was playing football and broke his knee, he thinks he is very lucky, so do we as it is a sure "Blighty one". No such luck for me.'

There were no absolutes in this matter; in a marginal case a ticket to Blighty might depend entirely on the whim of some doctor at the base. Indeed, there were doctors with a tendency to think of every soldier on sick parade who was not totally incapacitated as a malingerer for whom the only relevant treatment was another dose of life in the trenches. Lance Sergeant Elmer Cotton met such a doctor at a Divisional Base Camp in 1915.

> He used to line the men up and go along the line asking each one, 'Well, and what's the matter with you my man?'
> (1) 'Bad teeth, sir!'
> *answer* 'Well, I don't want you to eat the Germans.'
> (2) 'Consumption, sir!'
> *answer* 'Go up & spit at them.'
> (3) 'Short-sighted, sir!'
> *answer* 'How far can you see?'
>   'About 30 yards, sir.'
> *answer* 'The trenches are only *15 yds* apart at some places. Up you go & the best of luck.'
> (4) 'Shot in the leg, sir!'
> *answer* 'Up you go & shoot the man who shot you.'
> (5) 'Hit with shrapnel, sir!'
> *answer* 'Up you go & get your own back.'
> (6) 'Bad eyes, sir!'
> *answer* 'Just the man we want for listening posts.'
>   The result of this particular doctor's methods was that one man with a varicose vein and another with his trigger finger shot off were returned to the firing line.*

But there were other doctors who earned nothing but praise and admiration from their colleagues. Second Lieutenant Cyril Rawlins wrote home in a letter of August 1915:

> Our doc is a fine little Welshman who gave up a lucrative practice in Manchester to serve the country: he had a cellar full of patients last night and

---

* Harsh as this doctor plainly was, he may have had some justice on his side. Tommy was no saint and malingering by no means foreign to his nature. Tom Macdonald, convalescing at a Base Hospital after a gas attack, became aware that 'all kinds of rackets' were being tried by men eager to prolong their stay. 'My pal Johnny Bull had some soap pills he had made and reckoned if you swallowed them a little while before the Doctor saw you they would give you palpitations of the heart and he would not pass you fit.'

Wounded from the Western Front arriving at Charing Cross Hospital. The photograph was taken early in the war, in September 1914. What Lance Corporal Roland Mountfort called 'the fatheaded crowd' is present, as always, when train-loads of wounded were expected.

stood among the stretchers encouraging them and giving them cigarettes: see the eagerness with which the poor chaps reach out trembling hands for the 'Woodbines' and the grateful sigh as they sink back inhaling the first few puffs. But some can't smoke: they lie very still, staring at the smoky ceiling, wide eyed. Heavy wounds, these. . . . Two motor ambulances slide purring up to the entrance and the driver stumbles down the steps: 'Anything for us?' They take out the bad cases one by one, very tenderly: a shock-haired lad, not more than 19, heavily bandaged round the hand and arm, grins and looks down at the label printed on his blanket. 'Got my ticket for Blighty? Right O.' Envious eyes follow the boy as he is loaded into the car.

Captain Lionel Ferguson, exhausted by lack of food and the strains of action, weakened by loss of blood and shocked at the sight of the dead and dying, collapsed in the dressing station at Albert and broke into tears (Ch. 12). But after that the rituals of medical care took over and things began to go better. The first move was to Corbie, where the casualties were sorted. Ferguson was now destined for Blighty. He wrote subsequently in his diary:

219

Left Corbie by motor for the railhead, at which was a big canvas hospital, near Amiens; but we did not leave here till evening, watching many trains of prisoners leave first. Arriving at Boulogne early next morning we were taken to no. 14 General Hospital, having our wounds dressed and a good meal. I also managed to get some new underclothes, also a shave, a luxury I had not had for many days. We then rested till evening, getting called in time to be taken to the 'Blighty' ship. . . . The joy of a hospital ship is great, for those who are able to enjoy it, and as I was, I did. We got everything we could wish for on the way over. We were met at the dock by many kind people who bestowed gifts upon us. The delights of being home once more gave us a smile which was hard to get rid of.

His good fortune held. He found himself within a matter of hours at Wilton House, near Salisbury, a superb country house which the Countess of Pembroke had converted into a private hospital.

It was late evening when we arrived, but Lady P was most kind, coming herself to see to our comfort. We were given an excellent dinner, after which we were put to bed for 48 hours, whilst our clothes got fumigated. Eight officers were in our ward, in a beautiful room on the ground floor.

Army Form B 104–81A: the standard form by which next-of-kin were informed when a soldier was wounded.

Wounded soldiers at the home of the mother of two Grimsby Chums, shortly after the opening of the Somme battle. One of her sons had been killed on 1 July 1916 and the other wounded.

Ecstatic welcomes to the heroic wounded were standard, particularly at the time of the great battles. Some men could not stomach these ritualistic returns home, which seemed simply to emphasize the gulf of incomprehension which divided the soldier and the civilian.

> At Waterloo I was with the first party of wounded out of the train and they put us in private cars. There was the fatheaded crowd, just as you read about it, gaping and throwing cigarettes etc., and the whole ride was most detestable through the heart of London, with me perched up in front, not quite in such a bad state as on reaching Rouen, but nevertheless with two days dirt and beard, hatless and dishevelled, and a dangling sleeve.
>
> *Lance Corporal Roland Mountfort, 10th Bn Royal Fusiliers*

> Arriving home, covered in blood and mud, we were met by cheering crowds at Charing Cross Station. But we were in no mood to be entertained and were glad to get to hospital.
>
> *Lieutenant H. C. Lovely, 2nd Bn Bedfordshire Regt*

All these men were to survive their wounds and the war, but there were many thousands for whom a 'Blighty' wound was not just a temporary relief from the trenches;

221

for whom in fact it was the end of all prospects of a normal life; who might be doomed to long years in ex-servicemen's homes or hospitals; who would become the inevitable wrecks of a large-scale modern war—heroic and pitiable to begin with, later to be largely forgotten.

There was a less painful way of getting to 'dear old Blighty', even if it ensured only the briefest and most tantalizing of visits: leave.

> One evening I was told my officer had been to see me about going home on leave. Oh, what a feeling! No one but the Tommy knows what it is. After ten months of war and all its horrors, I was getting leave to go home, to dear old England, or rather, to call it by our favourite name, 'Blighty', for seven clear days.   *Corporal F. W. Billman, 9th Bn East Surrey Regt*

There was an unavoidable consequence of being informed that you were due to go on leave: suddenly you seemed to be especially vulnerable and the trenches especially dangerous.

> On Tuesday I hear that I am for leave on the following Saturday. . . . How well I remember the next two days. The old Fritz seemed to be after me everywhere and I certainly was more times in the fire trench than I need have been just to prove to myself that I wasn't nervy, but oh my! how I longed for Friday when I would leave the trenches. Nothing else mattered.
>   *Captain J. H. Mahon, 8th Bn King's Liverpool Regt*

The normal pattern for the journey home was a long walk to a railhead, a long wait for a military train and hours of kicking heels in Boulogne (or Le Havre) before being allowed on the boat for England. Captain Harry Yoxall and two fellow officers, going on leave in March 1917, attempted to add a few hours to their all-too-brief taste of home by aiming for the afternoon packet from Boulogne instead of the evening boat by which they would normally have sailed. When they reached Hazebrouck *en route* for the coast they did not wait for the military train but climbed on board the first civilian one.

> There followed an agonizing journey, in which the train crawled round and about Northern France at a pace amazingly slow and with halts every quarter of an hour: but eventually dumped our anguish-torn souls at Boulogne at 2.10 p.m. and after a frenzied rush to the docks we found that the boat—did not leave till 4 p.m.!!
> So we lunched in comfort, had a shave, went down to the docks again, slipped aboard when the press was at its greatest and with our tickets unexamined: and hay-ho! for England, home & beauty.

To set foot in Blighty after all those months of war was an overwhelming experience.

223 Sergeant Albert George, 120th Battery, Royal Field Artillery, landed in Southampton

on 1 December 1915 after 'sixteen months forced absence': 'Directly we landed we jumped into a waiting train which took us to Waterloo, and I am sure we were the Happiest men in England although our Happiness we knew was short-liv'd.'

Corporal Billman, who unlike Captain Yoxall and friends took the evening sailing from Boulogne, found himself in London at 12.30 a.m. on a Sunday morning, with a night and the best part of a day to kill before he could make for home. He felt conspicuously different from the crowds strolling the Sunday streets.

You can imagine how dirty I felt among all the people wearing their Sunday best, but that did not trouble me, as it was not my fault, and it showed that I had been doing my little bit for my King and country. Still, I had another journey to do, & this time it was to Norfolk, & to the best place on earth—home.

I arrived there at about 8 p.m., meeting my mother on the way as she was just taking a quiet stroll, and since I had not been able to let anyone know I was coming what a surprise it was for her! It was not long before I was sitting down for a good meal, and the kettle was singing, just the same as it used to do before this awful war commenced.

The soldier on leave was always a man apart; even in the later phases of the war, when the energies of Britain's young womenfolk were added to those of her young men in the great drive towards victory, he was still not without honour. Driver R. L. Venables, Royal Field Artillery, went home in September 1918:

The leave train from Folkestone arrives at Victoria Station, London.

We arrived safe and got to Victoria Station and I was delighted. . . . [But] only an old man with trolley of tea etc. Two years ago, there were tables of food and ladies serving cups of tea.

Tom Macdonald, 9th Bn Royal Sussex Regt, 1916

FRENCH MONEY EXCHANGED HERE

FOR

OFFICERS & SOLD IN UNIFORM.

The train from London terminated at Rotherham, and from there I went by tram to Mexborough; the tram was packed with women, many of them standing, and they were evidently returning home from some kind of men's work for their clothes, hands and faces were very dirty. As soon as I had pushed my way on to the tram, one of the seated women got up and told me, in a resolute manner, to sit down and I refused, whereupon all the other women called out 'sit down lad', so reluctantly I had to comply, not being keen on having a scrap with a lot of women.

But as those precious days of leave began, all too frequently a jarring note was struck.

Was I glad to be back in the bosom of my family? But one thing that annoyed me very much was to be met by the 'old uns' who usually said to me, 'What, home again? When are you going back?' We'd had quite enough of it without going back.

So wrote Private T. A. Bickerton, 11th Bn Royal Sussex Regt. Tom Macdonald, a fellow member of his regiment, recorded the same experience, with one other standard and equally insensitive question.

When I walked the old streets and met old friends, the first thing they would say was 'When are you going back?' and 'Do you like it over there?' They had no idea of the conditions and it was stupid to try and explain.

The two worlds—those of the soldier and of the people at home—were too far apart and the gap was unbridgeable. Civilians, fed by the heroic propaganda of the newspapers, perhaps even confirmed in their misconceptions by the natural restraint shown by most soldiers in their letters home, had little idea of the effect of their clumsy but quite natural curiosity on men who for a very brief while were trying to forget the awfulness of the environment from which they had been temporarily released. Not that there was much chance of forgetting; the reality of the Western Front was only a few days behind them and only a few days away.

London seemed as familiar as ever; I might never have left it; but at the back of my mind, whether I was sitting in a music hall or having dinner with friends, there was a vision always present—the contrast between that front line and the happy theatre.

Major R. S. Cockburn, 10th King's Royal Rifle Corps

Lance Corporal Roland Mountfort, 10th Royal Fusiliers, also found that he could not escape from his constant awareness of 'that front line' and that this made him bad company. Back in France he wrote to his mother in apology:

I am afraid you must have found my society a trifle dull. I realized at the time that I wasn't being exactly brilliant, but didn't seem to be able to help it. I think it was due in a large measure to the sub-conscious oppression of the knowledge of my imminent return to Army life, which after two years

I still loathe with all the hatred of which I am capable. We must have another holiday after the war, when the horizon is all clear.

Then, all too soon, it was over: time to go back.

> Those seven days passed quicker than any I have known. Oh those Good-Byes and that bone in throat feeling.
> *Private Tom Macdonald, 9th Bn Royal Sussex Regt*

> I shall never forget the parting from my wife and kiddies, it was cruel. But I would go through the same again for another leave, for we spent a very happy time altogether.   *Lance Corporal James Gingell, Royal Engineers*

Sergeant Albert George, Royal Field Artillery, who had thought himself and his comrades the 'happiest men in England' just a few days before, was now very much subdued. He wrote in his diary:

> Last walk round town, decide to catch the 12.25 up. Break down while saying Good Bye to Mr and Mrs Daniells—decide to go by earlier train—leave without saying Good Bye to Daisy and Annie—very childish of me. Go to station with S.—catch 11.40 up—very sorry having to leave dear old Watford—miserable ride to London. Very pitiful sight at Waterloo—many men and women crying—Bagpipes playing 'Keep the Home Fires Burning' etc. Enter train 3.45 p.m. thinking of the girl I was leaving behind & wondering if I should ever see her again! Train starts 4.0 p.m.—inwardly very downhearted—Good Bye London—Wish the Kaiser were dead and peace restored.

Then, once again, the soldier was on the boat bound for France—but going back from leave was worlds away from going to France for the first time.

> I remember on the after deck of the boat were troops returning off leave; they were mostly very quiet and deep in thought; and on the foredeck were men of a new draft going over for the first time. They were singing the latest songs and laughing and joking—they did not know what they were in for.
> *Private Tom Macdonald, 9th Bn Royal Sussex Regt*

For some, however, it was preferable to be in France than in Britain. Home sapped the vitality, muddied the certainties, and the incomprehension of the civilian made one a stranger.

> So my leave has gone; and I go back to the war for the third time. It was not so hard as I had expected. England is clearly no place to be in now: civilian opinion is disquieted and peevish: and I find there once more all the doubts of personal conduct and general policy, so it is good to escape from that atmosphere to one where one sees clearly and one's way lies straight ahead.

So wrote Captain Harry Yoxall, who had been so keen to add to his time at home   226

by catching the early boat from Boulogne. It was not the first time he had expressed such sentiments. At the end of an earlier leave he had written: 'Good as leave was, I have quite enjoyed getting back.'

But leave could be an embittering experience, returning a man to the trenches unhappy, frustrated and deprived. Sometimes the pages of a diary tell a tragic story: of a young man of intense vitality desperate to taste the pleasures of life before the opportunity is snatched from him and whose inability to find what he is looking for wrings from him a cry of protest. Such a diary is that of Second Lieutenant Kenneth Macardle, the brave young officer *par excellence* of the 17th Manchesters. He was just twenty-six when he spent what was to be his last leave in Blighty. Back with his battalion on the Somme, only a few weeks before his death, he wrote in his diary that he had 'seen a lot of people and a lot of plays and ate a lot of food and had a lot of baths—and on the day I left I had a long, delicious but solitary lunch at the Piccadilly.' But one element was missing.

> To thoroughly enjoy leave one should be engaged, or married (very newly married), or have—well—a friend with a delicate but overriding love of sensation. Failing this one has a rebelliousness; places one always loved seem intolerably dull; people one has found thrilling ere now fill one with dissatisfaction. Busy days have fallen flat. The ordinary dinner at the Carlton, box at the Gaiety, supper at Ciro's programme is tiresome and dull— it is hard indeed to keep up the illusion of enjoyment; one says 'Well goodnight, see you tomorrow' with a dreary feeling of stalemate & a sense of acting indifferently done. One enters the lift at one's hotel in a villainously bad humour.
>
> There are only nine days of leave after a hundred of war. A hundred of discomfort and hard work, plain necessary work, stupid necessary work. A hundred days and nights of uneventful dullness and of wearying strain; a hundred days & nights of 'keeping cheerful'—of pretending you don't mind dirt and discomfort and are quite used to being killed:—and then nine days and nights of leave. Surely they should be more than a holiday full of comfort and pleasure. One needs days of lazy dalliance and luxurious spending; eyes sleepy from adoring someone with a low laugh and inexplicable sunlight in her hair—someone with soft clothes; leading up to nights of madness—nights drunk with loveliness and love.
>
> But I must take a fatigue to clean trenches at Maricourt and it is a very wet night and the roads are very muddy; and first I must have my dinner on the door covered with newspaper and laid from a windowsill to a packing case, and sit on the carpenter's bench which it was such a stroke of luck to find & which makes the mess so perfectly top-hole!
>
> Cheer O! it's a jolly old war.

227

No. _19550/18_

(If replying, please quote above No.)

Army Form B. 104—82A.

RECORD OFFICE,

[stamp: INFANTRY RECORD OFFICE PRESTON]

_____ STATION,

_20·4·_ 1917.

SIR,

It is my painful duty to inform you that no further news having been received relative to (No.) _15552_ (Rank) _Pte_

(Name) _George Pickup_

(Regiment) _East Lancs_

who has been missing since _1·7·16_ , the Army Council have been regretfully constrained to conclude that he is dead, and that his death took place on the _1·7·16_ (or since).

I am to express to you the sympathy of the Army Council with you in your loss.

Any articles of private property left by missing soldiers which are found are forwarded to this Office, but they cannot be disposed of until authority is received from the War Office.

Application regarding the disposal of any such personal effects, or of any amount that may eventually be found to be due to the late soldier's estate, should be addressed to "The Secretary, War Office, London, S.W.," and marked outside, "Effects."

I am,

SIR,

Your obedient Servant,

A. Jacob

MAJOR FOR COLONEL

Officer in Charge of Records.

(9 38 72)   W 8777—2796   100,000   9/15   H W V(P 1521)   Forms/B. 104–82A/1

Official
notification
of death.

Missing, Believed Killed

Letter to the mother of Private Raymond Horace Turner, 'B' Coy, 7th Bn East Kent Regt from his Company Commander:

    I am sorry to say I cannot give you good news of R. H. Turner. ... He went out with us on the 13th but never returned.

    He had to be returned as 'Missing, believed killed' as none of our survivors saw him actually fall. He certainly was not taken prisoner, & if he had passed through the Casualty Clearing Station, his name would have been sent to us ...

    He was a cheery fellow & had no end of pluck. I saw him when he was wounded in January & although in pain, he jokingly said he deserved it as he hadn't his chin strap down. It was he who when some of our shells burst short said 'That's the worst of letting women make them, they must have been filled with cotton reels & baking powder'.

    A man like that with Turner's pluck & keenness is worth a deal.*

Official condolence.

The King commands me to assure you

of the true sympathy of His Majesty and

The Queen in your sorrow.

Derby.

Secretary of State for War.

* See the scroll of commemoration on p. 266.

Missing, Brought down by Enemy Action

On 24 October 1918 an RE8 Biplane of No. 6 Reconnaissance Squadron, Royal Air Force, was shot down behind enemy lines. The pilot was Lieutenant Ralph Cresswell—it was his first operational flight—and the observer was Lieutenant Ralph Silk.

Ralph Silk's account of the action, written in 1978:

> I had already made two flights over the enemy's lines that day, bombing, straffing and taking photographs, and had retired to my tent for rest when the Squadron Commander lifted the tent flap and said: 'Silk, you will have to go up again. The Huns are withdrawing their guns on the LeCateau road. I want you to blast the lot.' Feeling apprehensive, I remarked: 'I feel I shall not return this time'. 'Come, come,' he said, 'Your Guardian Angel will still look after you.' He gave me a gentle pat. 'But who's going to be my pilot,' I asked. 'Cresswell the new fellow.' I shook hands with him and rushed off to the waiting machine. Over the lines a number of enemy Fokker machines swooped out of the sun upon our four RE8 machines, the air was full of wings and bullets; when my machine gave a lurch, I turned my head to my pilot, he had slumped over the controls mortally wounded. Next I had a gun-shot wound in the head. The machine went into a spin and finally crashed upon some trees near LeCateau. I can faintly remember being lowered to the ground, then passed out ...

Silk was sent to a Prisoner of War camp at Stettin and finally repatriated through Denmark. He subsequently visited the father of Ralph Cresswell in Wakefield, who gave him the photograph of his son shown below as 'a reminder of that eventful time'.

Lieutenant Ralph Silk, Observer—Survived.

Lieutenant Ralph Cresswell, Pilot—Killed.

15

'Cheer O! It's a Jolly Old War'

Winter on the Western Front. Horse and motor transport in difficulties caused by mud and rain flooded shell holes: the Aveluy-Albert road, 16 December 1916.

Back in the trenches after his frustrating leave, in uncharacteristic low spirits at the prospect of resuming his role as the daring young officer of the 17th Manchesters, Second Lieutenant Kenneth Macardle summed up his reactions to the circumstances in which he found himself with the words: 'Cheer O! it's a jolly old war.' It is a significant and revealing sentence. It has a hint of world-weariness, of shoulder-shrugging resignation, but there is no defeatism and the generally accepted determination to slog on and see things through is quietly understood. It suggests a mug of scotch (or a mess-tin of tea) raised in a dug-out on a wet night in not-so-cushy trenches in the middle or later years of the war. This is not the naive crusading mood of 1914. The Army in France—a far cry from the tiny expeditionary force that had marched towards Mons—had become a vast and many-sided organism, a self-contained society, with its own rituals, its special disciplines, its own codes and attitudes. Soldiering on the Western Front was no longer a simple matter of firing guns and 'biffing the Boche'. It singled out successes and failures, made heroes of the strong, submitted the personalities of weaker men to often unbearable pressures, created huge animosities between one group and another, shook men's beliefs to their foundations.

What follows are not complete statements about these less discussed but vitally important aspects of the 'jolly old war'. A few episodes, a few fragments of experience, a few interesting comments and descriptions have simply been brought together.

Morale—and Leave
In 1916 Sapper Garfield Powell, Royal Engineers, wrote in his diary:

> As an army we are darned badly treated. Officers claim to get leave every three months and get it. Battalion and Company Sgt-Majors claim leave every four months and again get it (being called 'Sir' by their inferiors in rank not being sufficient sop to their self-love). In what army (barring the national armies of Germany or Russia) would such a system be in vogue? The officers in most regiments take very little more risk than their privates. Their bodies are not fatigued by constant and hard work and they are no more useful to the Army than privates. Why should the fools in higher command allow it? Why should 'gentlemen' take it as nothing less than their due? Ay, what fools we all are!

This is an eloquent outburst, all the more meaningful in that the writer was a university graduate with a B.Sc. in Chemistry and Mathematics who would almost certainly have been a candidate for a commission but for the social accident that he was a miner's son. Certainly in this case he is an intelligent commentator—no sheep accepting without compunction the patently unfair dispensations of his superiors. Everybody knew that ordinary soldiers might go well over the year without leave, even as much as eighteen months, while his officers seemed by contrast to be always making for Blighty. Some might accept that in this as in so many aspects of life at the front the officer did far better than the soldier. But for many this disparity in the highly personal matter of home leave became a real and growing grievance. This was privilege not on the military but the human level. It meant deprivation not only for the Tommy himself but also for his parents, wife, sweetheart, children; and this was an area where all men were, or at any rate thought they should be, equal.

Captain J. H. Dible, RAMC, wrote in his commonplace book in September 1917 that 'a very definite and serious current of discontent and dissatisfaction has indubitably come into existence'. He added that he was convinced that it was 'the question of leave which is at the root of the larger part of the discontent around us'. The entry in his commonplace book continues:

> The facts of the case at present, as for the last two years, are these. An ordinary officer gets leave, on an average, once in every six or seven months: the man gets his on an average of once in fifteen to nineteen months.*
>
> This is a perfectly inexcusable state of affairs and should not be allowed to continue for a minute. In the British army the officer, on campaign, is supposed to share the hardships of his men. Here there is a gross disparity between the treatment of the two.

The autumn of 1917 produced such a serious situation that questions were asked about the subject in Parliament and, Dible noted, circulars were sent round urging that 'every effort should be made to give leave to men who have not had it for twelve months or more'. In October Captain Lionel Ferguson was noting in his diary: 'We are trying to send on leave the men long overdue; men left my company today who have not been home for 20 months.'

Dible had one more inequality to record in his book: the almost inevitable fact that the Staff

> from the people who frame the leave regulations to the latest learner in the headquarters office who signs the leave tickets get their leave regularly every three or four months. The officer himself, well treated as he is by comparison with the men, has his own grievances in the superior treatment allotted to the Staff. He sees that they go on leave twice to his one; that the way is paved for them by special trains; that boats are reserved for their use by

*I have not attempted to reconcile these figures with Sapper Garfield Powell's. Disparity in the matter of leave was such that I have no doubt both statements were true within the experience of the men concerned.

One Man's Leave

July 25th (1917) Rather a wet day so we went and had our photos taken then came back and spent the rest of the day at home.'
From James Gingell's diary

James Brown Gingell of Bexhill was a married man of thirty-six with two young children when he joined the Royal Engineers in 1914; being married he was outside the scope of Kitchener's appeal but nevertheless he took the King's shilling and by May 1915 he found himself in France. He served on the Western Front for three years and eight months and only went home on leave three times.

His first leave was in December 1915; he returned to his unit just five days before Christmas. He wrote in his diary: 'I had to part from my Dear ones, yes it was a very hard task for us all but it had to be done. Good Bye till we meet again.' They were not to meet again for over a year and a half. Throughout the whole of 1916 his only leave was a two-day visit to Le Treport, where he found the 'grub' good but expensive, ran rapidly through a hundred francs and noted the 'beautiful sea breezes'.

It was not until July 1917 that he went on leave again. When he finally arrived in England his diary entries became quietly exultant and happy:

July 18th Left Victoria at 3.20 arrived at Bexhill, met my Dear Wife and son, I was overjoyed to see them also them seeing me, my little daughter was not there, as it happened her Sunday School treat was the same afternoon, so being childlike she went to the treat, then she had another treat when she came home ...

July 24th Just had a run round the town and done a little shopping, in the afternoon we went down the front and the kiddies and mother went paddling in the sea, altogether we spent an enjoyable time ...

But as always the last day arrives:

July 27th My train departs at 9.45 p.m. so I daresay I must say goodbye to good old Bexhill once more, I hope it won't be for long as I think we have all had enough of the war.

Once again he had more than a year to wait. He was not given leave until August 1918. Six weeks before he wrote what is possibly the only really angry entry in his diary:

June 17th Our Captain went on leave, I think it is a bit off as he has had four leaves to my one. I don't see why an officer should have any more leaves than their men, for certainly God only ordained them in the same equality as us, we are all flesh and blood.

which he is not allowed to travel. . . . On his return from leave the ordinary officer has to catch a train leaving Victoria at 6.50 a.m.: the gilded Staff travel down in comfort after their breakfast on a train which leaves London at 10.30 or thereabouts.

The soldier in the Middle East or Salonika would of course have one general comment on all who served on the Western Front, whether 'gilded Staff', officer or man: that they were lucky to have any home leave at all.

Discipline

In 1916 Private F. H. Bastable, 7th Bn Royal West Kent Regt, came out of a hard spell in the trenches and went into billets behind the line. The next morning, being mess orderly, he did not have time to clean and unload his rifle.

> When on parade for rifle inspection, after opening the bolts and closing them again the second time as it did not suit the officer the first time, I accidentally let off a round. I had to go before the CO and got No. 1 Field Punishment. I was tied up against a wagon by ankles and wrists for two hours a day, 1 hour in the morning and 1 in the afternoon in the middle of winter and under shellfire.
> There were two wagons with one soldier on each wheel. It was in what had been a French school, and I could hear the shells going overhead and was frightened one might land near as it was battalion headquarters. If one had we could not have got away or ducked down. But the worst part was the cold. After we were untied, the guard room sergeant who was walking up and down made us run round the playground to get us warm again. The Colonel who passed sentence said he had to as an example to the rest of the battalion.

Private Archie Surfleet, 13th Bn East Yorkshire Regt, saw a man undergoing Field Punishment No. 1 on the Somme front in July 1916 and found the experience horrifying:

> A lot of guns were lined up very regimentally and a number of limbers, spotlessly polished, stood beside them. At first, I could not believe my eyes, but as we came quite close to the guns, I saw that one of the artillery-men was lashed with rope to the wheel of one of the limbers. He was stretched out, cruciform-fashion, his arms and legs wide apart, secured to the wheel. His head lolled forward as he shook it to drive away the flies. I don't think I have ever seen anything which so disgusted me in my life and I know the feelings amongst our boys was very near to mutiny at such inhuman punishment. I have seen some Infantry lads lashed to trees at Warnimont Woods, sometimes as many as five or six, spaced out amongst the trees looking like so many American Indian prisoners about to be scalped and *that* seemed an anti-British sort of way to punish a man for any fault, but the expression on the face of this half-crucified gunner got us all groggy. I have never heard

such expressions of disgust from the troops before. I'd like to see the devils who devised this having an hour or two lashed up like that. The *milder*, No. 2 Field Punishment consists of full pack-drill; not ordinary drilling, but with a police-sergeant standing by, shouting 'Right turn, left turn, about turn . . .' one after the other, all done at something near the 'double'. It seems hellish that anyone should be treated like this and I am sure it cannot make them any better soldiers. I suppose troops on active service have to be dealt with severely, but these degrading punishments are only creating a feeling of utter disgust amongst the others; I am quite sure the corrective effect on the individual is more than negatived by its influence on his pals.

Field Punishment No. 1 was abandoned later in the war but military discipline never lost its harsh quality. Death by firing squad, as has already been mentioned, was not uncommon. In addition to the 332 cases of death sentences carried out, many men were condemned to death and later reprieved; it no doubt being part of the military psychology to assume that there could be no better incentive to a wrong-doer to improve his ways than the threat of being deprived of the opportunity to do so. Private Henry Bolton, 1st Bn East Surrey Regt, recorded in his diary how on 1 July 1915 he and his comrades

> were formed up to listen to 4 Court Martials of our own Regt they were all for sleeping at their post, the first to be read out was that of L/Cpl Wilson one of my old boys of Devonport, his crime was not serious as he was in support at the time when caught. The others were serious as they were on Sentry in the firing line & they were sentenced to Death but the sentence was not carried out, the good work of the Regt saving them.

An incident that particularly shocked the Bradford Pals was the execution of two members of the 2nd Pals (18th Bn West Yorkshire Regt) shortly before the disaster of 1 July 1916. Private George Morgan:

> These two men got drunk and they wandered away and got caught and were brought back and were charged with absenteeism on active service. If it had been in England they would have got seven days CB. They laughed it off, they thought wandering away was just something or nothing; but they were court-martialled and they were sentenced to be shot, subject to Sir Douglas Haig. He could have said no, but he didn't. So they were shot. They were described as being killed in action. Of course it was kept fairly dark, but their family got to know about it. I remember a letter years ago in the local paper, in which some lady was asking 'what happened to my brother?' That was what had happened to her brother.

To this story George Morgan added this footnote: 'They didn't shoot any Australians. They would have rioted. They weren't like us. We were docile.'

236

Sex

Private Archie Surfleet, 13th Bn East Yorkshire Regt, much quoted in this book, kept a diary during 1916–18, wrote it up in the 1920s and expanded and edited it forty years later. In a Preface to his final version he wrote:

> A lot of excellent books, films, plays and television productions have covered many aspects of life in the Great War.... There has been a lot of talk of blood and horror and devastation; some of it is true. Other accounts, written by much abler (and braver) authors, have given so much prominence to sex, there seems a danger that 'our war' may only be remembered as a series of drunken orgies interspersed with a few cases of rape and almost nightly immoral relations with every available French and Belgian female. This sort of picture is far from the truth. At times it *was* bloody and terrifying but, as for sex, most of the females were too old or too tired doing a man's job to be interested. There were 'Red Lamps' (brothels) in some of the bigger towns but they were, comparatively, little used. The propaganda against VD before we went out and later was good enough to deter the vast majority of overseas soldiers and those who 'caught a dose' suffered so much in so many ways their misery killed the 'urge' and discretion usually triumphed. I never saw any girl molested in any way; they were mostly treated with the utmost respect by the troops.

This is a comprehensive and important statement and perhaps goes a long way to explain why sex is a subject rarely touched on, even obliquely, in the diaries and

Bairnsfather as always went to the essence of the situation—the usual gross disparity between dream and fact.

Bystander copyright.   THE IDEAL AND THE REAL
What we should like to see at our billets — and (inset) what we do see.

letters of the time or in the later reminiscences of old soldiers—when they might perhaps have been expected to divulge more, say, than in letters likely at some stage to catch the censor's eye. The Western Front was inevitably a masculine and very public world. The sight of a female was a rarity and opportunities for any sexual relationship other than a commercial one were rarer still. Women were remote, occupants of a far-off idealized horizon. One young subaltern watched avidly at a station up the line as two young 'female guardians of a coffee urn' dispensed their sustenance to tired Tommies: 'For months to come we are going to a land peopled with one sex. Do they realize how much they stand for in our eyes?' (Lieutenant V. F. Eberle, Royal Engineers, 48th Division). In the same way a pretty young nurse at a base hospital would seem like a visitant from another planet; but unless you were an RAMC man you were only likely to see a vision at a time when you were incapable of doing anything other than dumbly admire.

Of course there were exceptions to Archie Surfleet's generalization about the unavailability of the young and attractive among the French or Belgian women whom the soldier met when out from the line. But all too frequently the customs of the French peasantry were too strict to allow of easy dalliance.

> There was a girl about 17 years old, I fell for her, her name was Madolien Vatblag. We could never get alone together, because the mother would always turn up. But love finds a way, in the evening we used to sit at the table with a book on French and English and I would point to sentences and she would read and point to answers and our hands would clasp under the table and we would press our knees together. It was frustrating, I could never get a moment alone with her (perhaps it's just as well). We corresponded years after. I had to send her letters to a friend in London to be translated.

But Tom Macdonald, 9th Bn Royal Sussex Regt, whose story this is, goes on to emphasize the rarity of cases even as innocuous as this. 'Many thought we had plenty of mademoiselles but at times months passed without a sight of civilian girls, especially on the Somme. And when we did get to a village where they were, there was too much competition.'

There were, of course, as Surfleet indicates in the statement at the head of this section, brothels; such institutions have always sprung into existence in the presence of great armies and in the context of the Western Front they were inevitable.

> One afternoon, whilst in camp, two or three of us decided, out of curiosity, to see what it was like, and with no intention of making the usual use of the amenities, to visit No. 1 'Red Lamp' Establishment. This was one of the French Government licensed brothels.
> We had been given to understand that, at such places, there was a bar, where one might sit and order drinks, like in an ordinary estaminet, without going any further. This place was a large house, with '1' painted on the door.

In we went, and took our places at a table in the bar. 'Madame' appeared, and we ordered drinks, but she intimated that they were not allowed to serve drinks until after 6 p.m., but said we could 'go upstairs' now!

We said 'No', and that we wanted drinks first, but Madame was adamant, and rang a bell. In trooped five or six girls, all most scantily dressed! I have never seen such an unattractive collection of females in my life! Not one was in the least pretty, though all were quite young. Some were downright ugly! I should have thought that it was enough to put anyone off completely, even if he had gone in with the usual intention!

Madame, and the girls too, all began saying that we should 'go upstairs' but we said 'No', and that we would come back after six that evening (having really no such intention), have drinks, and then 'go upstairs', after which we hurriedly left, to a torrent of abuse, in both French and English.

We were glad to get outside! At least I had added to my French vocabulary! In spite of the unattractive appearance of the merchandise, this establishment obviously did a good trade. We often used to watch ASC lorries drive up, stop, the driver disappear inside, and, in an incredibly short time reappear and drive off! This always intrigued us! 'Rapid Fire' with a vengeance! *Rifleman H. G. R. Williams, London Rifle Brigade*

Brothels inevitably meant that there was the danger of venereal disease. That danger implied the necessity of VD inspections. Here is Private Surfleet again, describing such an inspection in 1917.

Yesterday we all lined up before the Medical Officer for what the troops call a 'short-arm inspection'. It could only have been for one purpose which, four years ago, would have made a young man flush with shame. But, today, it does not seem degrading and I must confess as we lined up *facing each other* with only our shirts on, the thought flashed through my mind that it was better for us all to show, however crudely, the absence or presence of that horrible disease the Doc. was looking for. That shows how much we have changed and God only knows how much more we shall change before the end of this blasted lot.

One other subject is worth touching on in this section, even though it is worlds away from 'Red Lamps' and venereal disease. The writer is that idealistic young officer, Second Lieutenant Cyril Rawlins, and his theme is the paramount importance of marriage at a time when the flower of the nation's youth was subject to the possibility of death or injury on a massive scale.

I consider it the duty of every fit man to get married, whether he is at home, or a soldier only home on five days leave. The 'marry after the war' idea is very nice, but then the blunt fact is that for many there will be no 'after the war'. Our best and finest men are daily being killed and wounded, all our best blood going to waste and our race is bound to suffer terrible

depreciation in consequence and we ought to do all in our power to lessen this for the sake of the country's future. If the best happens, every single man will have to marry 'after the war': if the worst happens, don't you think it is better for a man to leave behind a young widow and a robust child, duly provided for by Government, than an unmarried fiancée, who, moreover, will *never have the chance of marrying*? In my mind there is no doubt of this: it is cold sense.

Medals

After heavy fighting on 11 April 1917 in the vicinity of the new Hindenburg line ('The Lincs went like bulls for it') Private Jack Sweeney wrote home:

> There were over 100 men recommended in the last battle including myself, 40 of them are dead and I think that there are too many for all of us to get a medal. I suppose that the dead men will get one at least their parents will, they deserve one more than all of us that are alive.... All the boys deserved a medal as I am sure they all did as much as one another but those that were recommended were seen by the officers to do these things.

There was a reasonably generous distribution of medals and honours in the war: over 31,000 Military Crosses for officers, over 110,000 Military Medals for NCOs and men. In addition and more rarely there were Distinguished Conduct Medals for NCOs and men and Distinguished Service Orders for officers—and, an honour out on its own, the Victoria Cross, which could be won by any officer or man for bravery of a particularly outstanding kind. Over five hundred were won in France and Belgium.

The problem with the distribution of honours was that it was, as Sweeney's letter implies, distinctly arbitrary. Often the most courageous acts went unrewarded simply because they were not seen by an officer. As George Morgan commented: 'We couldn't be recommended for bravery for July 1st 1916 because there were no officers left. There was no one to recommend us, only ourselves.'

The other major source of grievance was that those who were well clear of danger seemed to fare substantially better in the matter of awards than those who were doing the fighting. George Morgan again:

> A friend of mine could type—he used to work in Bradford Town Hall— and he got a job down at Divisional Headquarters. I met him one day and he said: 'George, I've been mentioned in despatches!' So I said, 'You what?' 'I've been mentioned in despatches,' he said. I said, 'What the hell for? You never saw a trench!' I was staggered: he had never been further than a typewriter 30 or 40 miles away from the trenches. Medals were ten a penny down at the base. A chap got the DCM for baking bread down at Étaples. You could get a DCM for *washing the general's dog*!
>
> I had another friend, Joe Calvert, who was awarded the French *Médaille Militaire*. I said, 'What have you done for it?' He said, 'I don't know, no more than anybody else.' Joe went on leave and afterwards a copy of the

local paper was sent out to the trenches to a neighbour of his, a friend of mine called Whitworth. And there it was in the paper: 'WAR HERO COMES HOME ON LEAVE. . . . The modest hero refused to disclose how he had won the coveted honour . . .' And my friend Whitworth was reading this out of the local paper and he was rolling laughing, because, of course, Joe *didn't know*!

Of course, countless medals were won fairly and at the place where they were meant to be won, in the centre of the storm. Captain Harry Yoxall, 18th King's Royal Rifle Corps, was recommended for an MC after the fighting on the Somme in September 1916 ('I did some fairly useful work getting the bombs up: on one occasion too I got back three wounded and a German machine gun'). He registered quiet pleasure in his diary when the news that the recommendation had been accepted came through:

> I am now officially Captain H. W. Yoxall, MC. This I learnt from Col Potter over the phone after dinner. And very nice too. I'm very glad, principally for the people's sake. But it's a very lucky one. How many better deeds went unrecorded and unrewarded that day it is impossible to say.

In March 1917 he went to receive his medal from the hands of the King himself.

> This morning I attended the investiture at the Palace. It was a very dull show; we were kept waiting a long while in a very stuffy atmosphere and then filed up like a lot of school boys for prizes. The King, with wonderful originality, asked me which battalion I belonged to and he shook me by the hand.

In February 1918 Second Lieutenant E. J. Ruffell, 342 Siege Battery, Royal Garrison Artillery, found himself (in a flurry of 'spit and polish and speculation as to who

Presentation of medals—to men of the 56th Infantry Brigade.

was to be honoured') at a ceremony at which certain Belgian awards were to be made to various deserving British officers. The occasion, albeit held in a muddy field, was lavishly adorned by 'mighty ones'. Among those present were 'the 2nd Army General and our own General and a Belgian General representing the King of the Belgians, [with] trailing behind them Brigade Majors, Staff Captains and Red tabbed subs with blue eyes and no ambition'. It was going to be an occasion of some embarrassment: the whole of Ruffell's Brigade was there. 'The RSM "broke" the flag at the masthead. The Colonel hoarsely "shunned" the Brigade. The Brigade then presented "aps" without any casualties and "serloped aps"* again with a sob of relief.' Then one by one those to be honoured were called forth.

> '2 Lieut E. J. Ruffell, 342 Battery'—'Chevalier de l' Ordre de la Couronne' with palm and 'Croix de Guerre'. Blushing and feeling a silly idiot I jerked myself forward, saluted, had the ironmongery pinned on my stomach—shook hands with all the Generals, saluted, 'about turned', nearly fell over my feet and wobbled back. A half cheer—quickly suppressed from my battery. And then on top of that, we the Decorated ones had to stand alongside the Brass hats while the Brigade marched past giving us 'eyes right'—never felt such a fool in my life. I felt so sorry for the poor chaps—as they marched by with their heads and necks in a permanent crick. It was a particularly muddy piece of ground and they couldn't tell where their feet were going. I felt as if I had lost a shilling and found sixpence! because I knew that several of our men whilst with the Belgian Army had been recommended for a Decoration for bravery, and it seemed to me so unfair that only I, because I was an officer, had got anything.
>
> However, I am pleased to say that later in the Official Gazette when my name appeared, the following June, their names appeared as well for the 'Croix de Guerre', but unfortunately by that time we had lost about half the men recommended by wounds or sickness.

However, most men's attitude to medals would have coincided with that of Private Sweeney, who, having told his wife that he had been recommended for an award (which he felt, rightly as it turned out, that he would not get), added: 'Blow the medals, as long as I live to scrape out of this war I shall be satisfied with a tin medal.'

Front Line versus Staff
Second Lieutenant W. N. Collins buried a thousand men after the capture of Beaumont Hamel in November 1916 and subsequently collected their paybooks into sandbags and delivered them to Brigade Headquarters. 'Brigade H.Q. amazed me. It was in a deep dug-out in the chalk with electric light, officers very immaculate, parcels from Fortnum and Mason. The contrast with the front line and No Man's Land shocked me.'

---

* i.e. presented arms and sloped arms.

Captain Harry Yoxall, a month after being involved in the hard fighting on the Somme for which he won his MC, found himself for a day or two 'living in luxury in a château'. It was a billet like no other. He commented:

> One can understand that those people at Army and Corps headquarters behind the line some thirty miles, with nice chateaus in which to live, are in no hurry to end the war. It was nice to sleep in Mme la Contesse's room & dress in her boudoir—though one felt it was rather an intrusion.

However, his spell of staff work was not the easy ride that most men in the front line thought it to be: 'You know the old jest—*Question* "If bread is the staff of life what is the life of the Staff?" *Answer* "One long loaf." Well, it isn't true. I've never been so busy in my life.'

Nevertheless the reputation of the staff was unredeemable. Captain J. H. Dible, RAMC, expressed the standard viewpoint when he wrote of staff officers 'who are all too frequently nincompoops who think to hide their vacuity behind an eye glass'. And Major R. S. Cockburn, 10th King's Royal Rifle Corps, was moved almost to a litany of protest when out 'on rest' in June 1917:

> I get one football field at St Hilaire, but it is very small.
> There seems to be no help forthcoming in anything from the Staff. They tell us to play football and put us where there is no ground to play on. They actually order sets of cricket things but there is nowhere to play.
> They tell us to bathe, and there is nowhere to bathe.
> They tell us we shall be in very comfortable billets and several officers have no beds: three sleep in one tent.
> They give us no material to improve the billets and make beds with, when we ask for it.
> They are miserably inefficient.*

The odium against those who had a permanently 'cushy' war rose to such a point that in March 1918, Captain Arthur Gibbs, 1st Bn Welsh Guards, could write home:

> I wonder if you have heard of the list of Stormtruppers which I am told is going the round of the club in London now. To be a member of the Stormtruppers it is essential to have been in the army since the beginning of the war, and never to have been in the trenches with one's regiment, in other words to have a real soft job for the whole of the war. It caused no ordinary flutter, I believe.

One particular grievance was that the 'high-ups' never put themselves in any danger of being hurt. Captain Yoxall noted, not without dry amusement, the visit of General S. T. Lawford, 41st Divisional Commander, known to his men as 'Sydney', to the proximity of the front line.

---

* It is perhaps fair to add that in checking and revising his account of the war Major Cockburn deleted the final sentence.

A sight displeasing to
Sergeant Cotton: Staff
Officers at Hazebrouck.

Sydney went round the trenches. I hear they chased him up a communicag-ger-tragger with whizzbangs and oil jars* and that he didn't stay to investi-gate where they were coming from. But after all you don't want a first chop divisional commander taken off by a miserable Minnie:* it's not his job.

Perhaps for a final comment one might turn to that remarkable reporter of Western Front conditions, Sergeant Elmer Cotton, of the 5th Northumberland Fusiliers:

To see some of the officers of our army lounging about & 'swanking' in somebody else's motor car, & in such large numbers at Hazebrouck and such like towns well behind the line, would disgust the average & energetic business man.

* Oil-jars, or oil-cans were German trench mortar shells. Minnies were the bombs fired by the German Minenwerfer, their formidable Mine or Bomb thrower. They were also known as footballs, rum jars, or Christmas puddings.

244

Why doesn't God stop the War?

Plainly this question worried the mother of Lieutenant Cyril Rawlins, as it worried many people at the time. In his letter of 1 July 1915 he wrote:

Dear Little Mother,

I too have wondered why God should allow such a catastrophe as the war: we cannot guess at the purpose, and as you say it is taking all our, *everyone's* best men. We are fighting for the right, and more than this, we are fighting for our very life as an Empire and as a nation against a foe without mercy, and whatever happens, whatever sacrifice we have to make we *must* beat him. This we have always before us. *The enemy must not take Calais!* If they could, our Empire built up for us by centuries of toil and sacrifice, our nation, would cease to exist, we should be lost as surely as if England sank beneath the sea. You in England cannot realize this as we do who live as it were shoring up a dike, holding back the pitiless sea of brutality and slaughter.

For Rawlins there was no doubt: God was on England's side. In an earlier letter to his mother he had written: 'Another day: the 312th day of the war! three hundred and twelve dawns since this horror came upon the world.... Thank God a new day dawns in my fair green England undefiled.'

Private Archie Surfleet, however, saw an insoluble problem in the fact that the enemy was claiming divine support at the same time.

Saw some fellows with a German helmet, quite a massive affair with a spread-eagle and a scroll saying *'Mitt Gott für Koenig und Faterland'*. Strikes me God must think we are a pack of fools: surely he can't be on both sides. What a christian world this must be.

What about the Tommy? What did Christianity mean to him in this world of deliberate slaughter? Archie Surfleet's diary has this to say: 'Not many of us are religious in the true sense of the word though a lot of us turn to God for help and comfort when we are afraid: that does not make us religious.' But he added: 'One thing does strike me as significant: there have been several confirmations out here in France.' He also had nothing but praise for the chaplains whom he had met, one in particular:

All the Padres I met were good men, but there was something different about Capt. Lynn. The most foul-mouthed chap in the companies was pleased to call him a friend. I think it was his kindly interest and thoughtfulness for *every* man in the Battalion, regardless of sect or creed, which made him such a favourite with us all. I know I felt he was a man doing a grand job in accordance with the views he must have felt when he was ordained.

Sapper Garfield Powell, brought up to attend church 'occasionally' in his native Cardiff, received a kindly letter from his home church which 'after talking a lot of the usual rot' offered to confer on all their 'soldier adherents the boon of a fortnightly

The Waste of War

Men were often profoundly moved by the sight of a ravaged battlefield or a shattered town or village and wrote accordingly. Such scenes were also natural subjects for the camera. In this section a handful of descriptions and photographs—not necessarily strictly related—are brought together. The photographs were taken on an illicit camera—by Sapper Jaboor, a linesman of the 2nd Divisional Signal Company AIF, on a vest-pocket Kodak camera which he carried round in the leather case of his telephone.

As far as you can see is a wilderness of torn up soil intersected with ruined trenches: it is like a man's face after small pox or a telescopic view of the moon. The shell holes overlap and run into each other; some are mere scratches, some would hide an average haystack; here and there a few distorted posts form all that remain of a barbed wire entanglement. But the most startling feature is the debris that is lying scattered on the surface and thick in the trenches. Sets of equipment, rifles, bayonets, shovels, shrapnel helmets, respirators, shell cases, iron posts, overcoats, groundsheets, bombs (in hundreds)—I don't suppose there is a square yard without some relic and reminder of the awful waste of war.

Lance Corporal Roland Mountfort, 10th Bn Royal Fusiliers, July 1916

The woods had changed hands by repeated German counter attacks and shelling and it had been difficult to bury the dead. The trees were criss-cross, with shattered, splintered limbs, and the stench was awful, and we could hardly put a pick in the ground or shovel but what we would strike a buried body and clothing. The ground was pock marked with shell holes everywhere and one place we found a whole machine gun team buried by shell fire.   *Tom Macdonald, 9th Bn Royal Sussex Regt, August 1916*

Delville Wood, 1916.

In front of Ypres, 1917.

The stark and shattered scene: flayed tree stumps, wastes of mud and great pools of water, reminded me of an ocean floor suddenly exposed and tensed for a crashing re-engulfment. Not a sign of life anywhere—but an obsession of human eyes, watching ...
Second Lieutenant Blake O'Sullivan, 6th Bn Connaught Rangers, August 1916

Would that every brick and stone there [Ypres] could be swallowed up in the earth tomorrow, if that would help us to forget what they have seen! Those narrow streets of ruins, the crumpled water tower, the daredevil prison standing up there until it should be knocked down; the dingy cellar where we played the gramophone; the mangled bodies of those two officers who were killed in the street outside the door that afternoon; the abandoned switch canal all covered with long weeds; and, leaning miserably over all, the gaunt, maimed cathedral tower and Cloth Hall, left to be as great a mockery of civilization as the world will ever see. I suppose that men will flock to see the ghastly remains of that city. Let them walk with reverent and humble step.   *Major R. S. Cockburn, 10th Bn Royal Rifle Corps*

A ruined village on the Somme, ▶
autumn 1916.

Scenes in Ypres, 1917.
▼

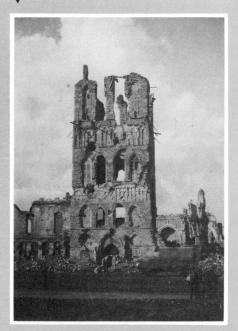

letter'. He was in a quandary: they would expect a reply in like terms, but like many of his fellow soldiers in France he had felt the strain of the contrast between the innocent values of home and those of the war-zone.

> What am I to do? I am not sincerely religious and care not a rap for theology as they teach it. As far as I can see at present I am like all my friends—an agnostic. Most of my friends are Church members and are therefore hypocrites as well. Shall I tell them that I am *trying* to believe but cannot or shall I tell a lie? I'll temporise.

It should be added that there were many who came through the war with their faith unimpaired, men to whom such questions as 'Why doesn't God stop the war' seemed irrelevant and naive. Yet a shattering of beliefs and a sense of profound spiritual shock were inevitable in a conflict of such enormity, of which the essential act appeared to be the continuing sacrifice of the best youth of the combatant nations. Wilfred Owen's vision of an Abraham who spared the ram

> but slew his son
> And half the seed of Europe, one by one*

was daring, shocking, but brilliantly apposite. George Morgan, sixty years after, put the same point in his own way: 'Such splendid youth: it seemed such a pity that they had to be killed.'

* 'The Parable of the Old Men and the Young.'

16

'Guerre Finie! Boche Napoo!'

Dawn at Passchendaele, 1917.

The war had been in progress for almost three years when Second Lieutenant E. J. Ruffell, 342 Siege Battery, Royal Garrison Artillery, saw the front line for the first time. It was in that depressing part of the fighting zone where the trenches ran through the coal-mining area centred on the industrial town of Lens. Ruffell was taken to an Observation Post in a ruined pit-head.

> Cautiously crawling up ladders which had more rungs shot away than remaining we at last came out on a small platform with sandbag sides and with a $\frac{1}{4}$-inch steel plate on the outer wall and we observed through holes made by shell splinters.
> I shall never forget the disappointment of my first view of the 'front'— shell pocked ground, ruined houses, rusty barbed wire everywhere and a maze of trenches and No Man's Land—not a soul to be seen, and not a sound except a solitary 'plop' of a sniper's rifle. And yet hundreds of men were living in those trenches and hundreds of eyes were watching for the slightest movement on either side—the slightest exposure over the top of a trench and 'plop' goes the sniper's rifle, and another man gets a 'blighty' or is sewn up in his blanket.

A greater source of disappointment for anyone who had held these trenches in the early days of the war would have been that after so many months the line was still where it was. To begin with it had been possible to hope that the Western Front was a temporary phenomenon only, that what Henry Williamson was to call 'that great livid wound across Europe' would soon be healed. Now such hopes seemed threadbare indeed. As early as August 1916 Driver R. L. Venables, echoing a wide-spread point of view, had written in his diary: 'When the war began everybody thought it would be over in a few months, now we are wondering if it will be ended in our lifetime.' Almost a year later relatively little had happened to counter such pessimism.

A major shift in the log-jam was, in fact, just about to happen. On 7 June 1917— probably the very day that Ruffell climbed his rickety ladder and looked down on the front line—the British seized the Messines Ridge after the explosion of nineteen mines: it was, for once, almost a walk-over. This was to be the overture to the Big Push of 1917.

Flanders was the place chosen for the great set-piece attack that year. The attacking battalions went over the top on 31st July. Like the Somme, this battle was to continue with small gains and huge losses until November. Like the Somme, it was to become the subject of fierce controversy at the time and unceasing argument ever after. Officially known as the Third Battle of Ypres, it was to achieve its bitter fame under the name of the little Belgian village which represented the high water mark of the British advance, Passchendaele.

This was to be a battle in which—even more than on the Somme—rain and mud were to prove a crucial belligerent, and they were not on the British side. Hindenburg even felt 'a certain feeling of satisfaction when this new battle began'. Experience had shown that with the onset of the wet season 'great stretches of the Flanders flats would become impassable, and even in firmer places the new shell holes would fill so quickly with ground water that men seeking shelter in them would find themselves faced with the alternative, "Shall we drown or get out of this hole?" This battle too must finally stick in the mud.'

The wet season began on the first day of the attack, causing an immediate setback after early success. 'Had we only had a dry wicket we could have forced the Hun to follow on, as it was the rain came down and the match had to be abandoned' (Lieutenant A. C. Wilkinson, 2nd Coldstream Guards). The abandonment was only temporary; all autumn the British fought slowly forward, while, in Churchill's words, 'the vast crater fields became a sea of choking fetid mud in which men, animals and tanks floundered and perished hopelessly'.

This battle produced much bitterness among the men who fought it. There was no place for idealism or even humanity in this brutal, bludgeoning campaign.

> There's no manœuvre, it's only batter the enemy—if you kill them we go forward a little, if not, we don't. Surely a private or a gunner could do that. It's not brains; it's blood. I never thought that we, British, would allow our good boys to be put in such a slaughter as this, so callous. No one thinks of another's life now, it's his own and to hell with everybody.
> *Gunner H. Sturdy, 162nd Brigade, Royal Field Artillery*

Private Jack Sweeney, 1st Bn Lincolnshire Regt, was almost distraught when he wrote to his fiancée in the last week of the battle:

> Our boys are having a terrible time in the trenches, up to the Waist in Mud and Water. Just like a ditch full of water. Each side of the Menin Road there are dead horses and men, cars, motor lorries in their hundreds, it is death to go off the road, as the mud is so deep. It is nearly death as it is as he is shelling all along the road ...
> The Somme was bad enough but this is a thousand times worse.

This agonizing second half of 1917 was a hard season on the Western Front. It was at this time that Captain Dible, RAMC, expressed his profound concern over the matter of home leave. Leave, however, was only one part of what he saw as a general

Passchendaele (The Third Battle of Ypres)

Official British casualty figures—British 244,897; German approximately 300,000. These were not finally assessed until long after the war and went counter to all previous assumptions, as for example in Churchill's *World Crisis*: 'The German losses were always on a far smaller scale. . . . They always took nearly two lives for one.' But the German Official History admits that 'the battle led to an excessive expenditure of German forces' and it has been forcibly argued that without this harsh battle of attrition the war might well have gone on until 1919. Yet this was the time, according to Sir Philip Gibbs, the famous war correspondent, when 'the British army lost its spirit of optimism'. Whatever the outcome or the effect, this battle was intolerable—indeed incomprehensible—to the men who were required to fight it.

In August 1917 Sergeant F. W. Billman wrote in his diary:

> For three days and nights it rained, as it only can rain in Belgium, and although it was the first week in August, it was as cold and dreary as November. The battlefield was turned into one huge quagmire, into which were sucked men, horses, guns, it being an impossibility to extricate them, when once they were in the grip of this terrible mud.

A Sapper, Corporal James Gingell, wrote in his diary at the height of the battle: 'I thought the Somme bad enough but this Flanders is cruel.'

From a letter written in the Ypres Salient 31 October 1917:

> . . . This awful place, a mass of shell holes, no trees or grass—only ruins, pill-boxes, rain, mud, and dead men, broken rifles and splashes of dark brown on fly-clotted crimson, discarded equipment—everlasting guns 'pooping off' day and night (ours though—Bosch sends little back, almost 1 to our 20), rain, mud, wind and general desolation and misery. I am also very busy, and am not spiritually at leisure at all—I am frankly depressed with my surroundings, although the war is going *awfully* well here.
> *Second Lieutenant James Dale, 2nd Bn Liverpool Scottish Regt*

> I remember the Passchendaele scene as always with grey, low, leaden skies. That is the great impression: hopeless greyness, a landscape with only one colourless colour, the dun greyness of mud below and of a pall of cloud above. *Lieutenant H. E. L. Mellersh, 2nd Bn East Lancashire Regt*

> I had to go up to the salient yesterday and the sights I saw there—well I could write a book of 50 pages. I saw motor lorries sunk in the mud over the wheels, also horses with just part of their heads showing above the swamps, also 2 Tanks which were in the Push. I must not tell you the tale of those 2 Heroes—the men who were in them were the Heroes, they were still in them yesterday and will never be able to tell the tale of the fight but they did well.
> *Private Jack Sweeney, 1st Bn Lincolnshire Regt, September 1916*

This photograph was taken on 11 August 1917, just a few days after Sergeant Billman made the comment left. The water-cart has gone over the edge of the brushwood track and is stuck in Flanders mud up to the axle.

Australian Advanced Dressing Station, 20 September 1917.

The notorious Menin Road, 20 September 1917.

Road through Château Wood, October 1917.

The Passchendaele battlefield in its final state—what Churchill called 'a sea of choking, fetid mud'.

Passchendaele village from the air before and after the fierce fighting of autumn 1917. By the end of the battle it was merely a 'brick-coloured stain' in the shell-pocked surface of the ground.

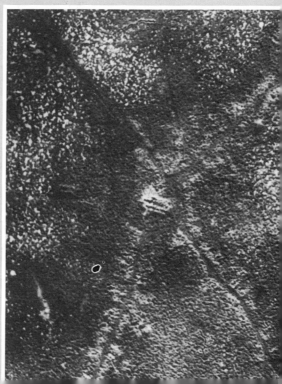

and growing disaffection—a malaise that had its own roots quite apart from the horrors of the battlefield. It is significant that he wrote the following at Étaples, where the notorious base camp and 'Bullring' had earned not a less but a more objectionable and tyrannical image as the war went on.

Men, accustomed to what the Englishman has fought for for generations, personal freedom, are suddenly deprived of this greatest of possessions. They are being worked seven days a week for long periods without rest or change. The strain is wearing tempers thin, and the breaking point is often very near. Anomalies of pay are proverbial and staring. (Two men in the ASC working side by side on the same job may receive 6/– and 2/6 per diem respectively depending upon the different periods at which they enlisted; and the man who enlisted first is often the worse paid.) The tobacco ration is deficient. Officers and NCOs are often unable to differentiate between discipline and tyranny. These and a hundred other smaller matters are jarring on already rawed nerves.

There the matter stands. What is being done? Nothing. There are two schools which have sprung into notice during the last week, in which some definite trouble has shown itself here in Étaples. The one school says 'Bring down a couple of battalions and shoot the swine!' 'Send a regiment of cavalry to charge through them.' 'Stick 'em up against a wall, etc. etc.' That is the attitude of the old time soldiers. I am convinced that it is a fatal and suicidal one: you cannot treat the Englishman like that. Your battalion might refuse to shoot or your cavalry to charge. You cannot take the risk. The other school says: 'Find out what are their grievances and remedy them' and that is the only modus operandi to which I can subscribe. I confess I have every sympathy with the men.

The simmering discontent has recently come to a small head in this area. It began with the killing of an inoffensive man by an excited military policeman; developed into an outburst which swept every policeman out of the district and resulted in some of them being badly mauled in the process; and culminated in the temporary abolition of all discipline. Confusion reigns in all the camps and rank insubordination in some of them. It is a sign of the times. A small upheaval indicative of the potential volcano below the seemingly firm crust. The volcano is more than potential, it exists and is actively working; whilst the higher powers seem to live in total ignorance of, and are certainly outwardly ignoring, its existence.

1917 was the year of mutiny in the French Army. A policy by Pétain of simultaneously improving conditions and executing ringleaders without compunction restored the situation by the end of the year. The British Army avoided the ultimate crisis but certainly was not without its strains and crises.

Meanwhile the Third Battle of Ypres was closed down after the capture of Passchendaele by the Canadians on 6th November. This was followed shortly by the brief elation of Cambrai, on 20th November, when nearly four hundred tanks broke 256

through the German line and advanced five miles. The next day church bells rang out in London for the first time since the start of the war, but within days German counter-attacks put the line back much where it had been before.

On 31st December Captain Dible was once more confiding his distress to his commonplace book:

> The war is getting more and more desperate. On every hand one sees unrest and dissatisfaction rampant and nothing sensible done to ameliorate grievances. We are living on a magazine.

A few weeks later Private Archie Surfleet was describing the same mood, though in terms perhaps more world weary than alarmist:

> February 8th. We have been in camp near the wood at Écurie for some days now and a more miserable existence it would be hard to imagine. There is nothing but unrest and uncertainty and everyone here is absolutely fed up to the teeth.

But the perspectives of the war were changing. America had been a belligerent, if to begin with at a distance, since April 1917. The shift of her almost limitless potential from a benevolent neutrality to active participation on the Allied side meant that ultimate victory was all but guaranteed. In addition Germany was suffering crucially, both on the battlefield and, most painfully of all perhaps, by blockade. Her leaders were, however, by no means defeated. They resolved on a massive offensive on the Western Front—to bid for victory before the Americans could affect the balance of power. The 'Kaiser's battle', as the Germans called it, was launched on 21 March 1918—and its principal target was the British Army. The attack began with a brief hurricane bombardment, with the initial strike upon the British batteries, strong points and command posts.

Second Lieutenant E. J. Ruffell's 342 Siege Battery took part of the brunt of the first onslaught:

> I was awakened at 4 a.m. by the most terrific gun fire I have ever heard. Only by shouting on the phone could I find out that all Batteries were answering on SOS Targets. The front line was one blaze of exploding shells and high bursting shrapnel, 'Very' lights and every coloured rocket imaginable. Long range guns were 'sweeping' the back areas and about ten minutes after the firing started a shell burst just outside our dug-out and blew up all the telephone lines to Corps HQ and to Batteries!
>
> As none of our Infantry were seen we concluded they had been wiped out ...

The 2nd Battalion of the Essex Regiment was one of the infantry battalions overrun in this great March attack. Private Thomas Bickerton, formerly of the Royal Sussex Regiment and now a Lewis gunner with the Essex battalion, described what happened in his memoir.

At day-break we could see the Germans advancing down the valley. We let loose immediately with everything we had got. I frantically filled magazines until my fingers could hardly move. We had a system of Very lights to send up immediately we were attacked and this would call for artillery fire on No Man's Land. We sent up Very lights but no artillery fire came. The artillery had been withdrawn and it appeared we were going to be sacrificed. The Germans had broken through on our right hand and on our left, but owing to our commanding position, we seemed to be able to hold them at bay. We sent back runners to Battalion Headquarters for instructions. The first two runners were either killed or taken prisoner; the third runner came back to tell us the Germans were cooking breakfast in our Battalion Headquarters. By this time we were mentally and physically exhausted and wondering what the end would be—it was obviously very near. I went into the next bay to see if our platoon commander was there, and he was sitting on the fire step in the corner with a revolver in his hand. I think he had shot himself rather than be taken prisoner.

The Germans were almost up to our trench and a Corporal tied his white handkerchief to his bayonet and stuck it over the trench. The Germans called on us to come out. Our Number 1 had stripped the gun and taken the spare parts over the back before giving himself up, so that the Germans should not be able to use it on us. Those of us who were gunners had torn our Lewis gun badges off our jackets because we were afraid of what might happen to us. All arms had to be abandoned and we were instructed to run with our hands over our heads towards the German rear. I had not got far when I was pulled up by a German flourishing a dagger. Fortunately I had the presence of mind to whip out my pocket wallet which I thrust into his hand, and whilst he was looking at it I ran on. Our heavy machine guns were still firing and my next encounter with a German was when one of them pulled me down into a shell hole. I wondered what was going to happen, but he was anxious that I shouldn't be shot! He indicated to me that we were both in danger from this machine gun. I quote these instances to indicate the difference between Germans—some good, some bad. On the way back we passed a heavy German Battery which was being shelled by some of our long range artillery, and many of our fellows were called in to help pull out the German guns.

Eventually we reached the first Collecting Station—a very crude barbed wire enclosure. Here we were addressed by a German Intelligence Officer who informed us that we'd been a damn nuisance and that we'd held up their advance for over three hours.

Tom Macdonald's 9th Battalion of the Royal Sussex Regiment was more fortunate; it managed to squeeze clear of the German attack:

We were ready to defend our position, when further along to our right the Germans were pouring through and getting around behind. We had orders

to pull out and as we retired to the road there were big cracks as ammunition shell dumps were exploded and it was an inferno.

We got back to dead ground. The remnants of us formed up and were marching when some Brass hat came from nowhere and our CO ordered about turn and we were put in a small wood to hold it. All were fed up and hungry, no rations. We were told it was a planned retreat and the cavalry were to close in on flanks. All propaganda to cheer us up.

I think a lot were destroyed on the first day. Half the time one did not know where our front was, as the Germans were putting all the force in one sector and working around behind. You could see the Very lights going up in daylight behind us to signal to their artillery where they had got to.

Having avoided the German net Macdonald's battalion pulled back to a town which had just been hurriedly evacuated by its panic-stricken population.

They had left in a hurry. It was a sad sight really. Furniture etc. in houses was intact and clothing too. The men went wild with looting. They killed a calf and were cooking lumps of it and searching through the drawers for little pots of food, rice, etc. Hoarded down in the cellars under the houses were stacks of black bottles, I think it was cider. Of course they were all having their fill, lying on good beds with all filthy clothes and boots.

They killed all the Fowls catching them at night by light when they were on the perches.

The Germans advanced thirty miles in a week and almost reached Amiens. The 1916 Somme battlefield was totally engulfed. But the British, though they yielded, did not break and by the end of the month the worst threat was over. Fierce fighting, however, continued well into April with prodigious losses. In the month following 21 March 1918 the British sustained 250,000 casualties, as many as those at Passchendaele.

Now began the slow but final turning of the tide. The historic moment was 8th August, when the British, using tanks as the spearhead with the infantry advancing behind, and with the support of a large number of aircraft, punched an eleven-mile gap in the German line. Following this 'black day of the German Army' (Ludendorff's phrase) the enemy was forced steadily backwards; but the price was always high and the enemy's spirit by no means broken.

Captain Lionel Ferguson, 13th Bn Cheshire Regt, was a participant in this hard August fighting. On 21st August—it was a not unfamiliar situation—his battalion found itself advancing under 'hellish' machine-gun fire:

We could find no cover or trench of any kind and we were walking through a hailstorm of MG bullets. Men fell right and left and we were quite unable to give them the attention required. . . . I noticed one of the men threw down his rifle and equipment, which angered me greatly but before he had time to run I forced him to put them on again, in fact if he had hesitated I would have shot him and he knew it.

Tanks — 'The Devil is Coming'

A tank in acti

> One stared and stared as if one had lost the power of one's limbs. The monsters approached slowly, hobbling, rolling and rocking, but they approached. Nothing impeded them: a supernatural force seemed to impel them on. Someone in the trenches said 'The devil is coming', and the word was passed along the line like wild fire.*

So wrote a German correspondent who saw the first use of tanks in modern war.

Tanks were essentially a response to the stalemate of the Western Front. Both sides now realized that in conditions of static warfare based upon lines of trenches laced with machine guns and interwoven with barbed wire entanglements, defence was always likely to wear down attack and attackers were likely to suffer enormous losses; but it was the British who saw the answer. The virtue of tanks was that they could cross trenches, break through barbed wire, force their way over shell-pocked ground and be impervious to, and deal with, machine guns. They were not in the first place seen as auguries of a new war of movement; they were to aid the infantry to do what modern conditions of war were making it increasingly difficult for them to do.

It is fair to say that the impulse to create tanks did not come from the War Office. Once the idea had been suggested it was Government, particularly in the persons of Churchill and Asquith, who pressed for the military establishment to take it seriously. The first real tank as the term is understood today was tried out in January 1916; by September 1916 tanks were in action on the Somme.

Taken to France under wraps, their very name a camouflage, they created an immediate sensation.

> One morning the Battn was paraded, and addressed by the CO. He told us we were about to be shown a very new secret piece of apparatus, which would have the effect of shortening the war—*provided that the secret was maintained.*
>
> These new pieces of equipment were known by the code name of 'Tanks'. Naturally we were all agog to learn what sort of things these 'Tanks' could be.

* Quotation taken from *The Ironclad of Cambrai* by Bryan Cooper.

We marched to the area where this demonstration was to take place, and there, before our astounded eyes, appeared about six of the first 'Mark 1' tanks, lurching about the country on their caterpillar tracks, and performing various manœuvres, bursting through hedges, crossing trenches, demolishing walls, and even snapping off small trees.

Rifleman H. G. R. Williams, London Rifle Brigade

They were first used in the attack on Flers and Courcelette on 15 September 1916. A Canadian soldier, Private Magnus MacIntyre Hood, 24th Bn Victoria Rifles of Canada, was a witness:

In the dusk of the evening we saw something never before seen in warfare. . . . A party of us had to rush up with more ammunition bullets and grenades to the 21st Battn, lying in shell-holes in front of the refinery at Courcelette. As we reached them we saw a tank—what we then called a landship—named the LS Crème de Menthe, pass ahead, and go right up to the walls of the refinery, its guns blazing. It seemed to lean against one of the walls which collapsed, and the monster roared into the fort, while we could see the Germans streaming out behind it, offering an excellent target to the riflemen in the shell-holes.

Lieutenant T. Glyn Platt, 11th Bn Royal West Kent Regt, also saw them on this occasion. In a letter to his parents he wrote: 'The caterpillars or tanks as they are called are wonderful things. . . . They are painted all colours like a snake, & look awfully funny going along. No wonder the Bosch ran!!'

Their success on the Somme was more psychological than strategic: they were too few in number and too prone to breakdown. Their first effective use on a large scale was at Cambrai in November 1917 and by the summer of 1918 they became a major factor in the final rounds of the war. The Germans did not appreciate the virtue of the new weapon—yet; that was to come later. The German General von Kuhl admitted that the secret of the great British breakthrough in August 1918 was that factor which had played so little part on the Somme and at Passchendaele—surprise: and that in this surprise 'the most important & decisive factor were the tanks'.* Thus were the blitzkrieg campaigns of the Second World War and the tank battles of the Middle East in 1967 and 1973 foreshadowed.

* Quotation from General von Kuhl from Liddell Hart, *History of the First World War.*

They 'keep on a' shufflin' along'.

Yet earlier that day Ferguson had seen a portent of the future nature of land war. Advancing through the fog of that summer morning

> we overtook a large tank which had lost direction. The officer in charge was inclined to let the fog clear; but I informed him (that) a number of our troops were ahead and that we must press on. An enemy MG opened up on our right at that moment, and the old tank went right for it, firing a round of big shot as it advanced; we stopped to watch the scrap, a sight for all the world like a big dog going for a rat: the MG was firing the other way and before the Boche gunners had time to escape, the huge monster was upon them, finishing them for ever. It was the first blood we had seen that morning and for us spectators a most thrilling moment.

But on Saturday 24th August he had a glimpse of the kind of war envisaged in pre-Somme days: 'The Cavalry were now going forward in large numbers, and we have lived to see the day of the cavalry in action. Every moment of the last few days have been wonderful and we feel we are making history.' That day he walked over the ground of their failed attack of three days earlier 'to discover what had been our undoing'.

> The trenches I came to were an eyeopener; now to me it is a wonder we ever escaped; on the hill were forts of MGs and TMs (Trench Mortars), one every 25 yards, these still lie in position in the trenches with the story of their capture told all around. . . . The slaughter in this trench had been awful, in front of each MG were the bodies of 5 or 6 British soldiers, and in the trench itself the Boche were lying two and often three deep. We are indeed fighting a wonderful enemy; his trenches, his ammunition, his equipment, etc. are very much better than ours, although in these times not such a good quality.

Now at last the Allies were moving towards the end-game. In September Walter Vignoles, formerly of the Grimsby Chums, now a Lieutenant-Colonel with his own battalion, the 9th Northumberland Fusiliers, wrote to his wife:

> It is very interesting in the front line just now; continually chasing the Boche, moving forward every day, no billets, no shelters, everyone just sleeping under hedges or in shell holes. The Boche is burning all the farms, and as $\frac{3}{4}$ of a French farm is wood it doesn't leave much.
> There is no doubt that Fritz is in a great mess.

At the end of September the Hindenburg line was broken. The advance continued against the background of the political disintegration of Germany and the first suggestion of an armistice.

> October 1918. Gerry was falling back and we were following on. The barrage was timed, so we were told, for 4 o'clock next morning. We stayed up waiting. It was a beautiful moonlit night. I had a watch with me and I remember a few of us were on the top of a hill to see what happened. At exactly 4

o'clock one gun fired—and then all the guns opened up all the way along the line, and there was a curtain of fire from horizon to horizon as far as the eye could see. It really was a magnificent sight. I remember someone saying, 'Not a cat could live in a barrage like that'. I suppose the fire-curtain wasn't above a man's height from the ground, but it was intense and continuous and accompanied by the non-stop roar of the guns. So there we stood with this world of moonlight around us and this world of flame in front, until the sun came up. That was a marvellous sight—the rising sun behind the curtain of flame; and as the sun gained in power the curtain of flame seemed to get ever paler, until in the full light of day it almost died out.

We moved on again after that.

Private W. G. Brown, 2/3rd Field Ambulance, 59th (North Midland) Division

On 23rd October Lieutenant Ruffell's battery trundled into Solesmes.

Up to this point in the advance, the Germans had driven the French civilians back with them, but this last push was rather too much for the Hun and he left the inhabitants in Solesmes and having evacuated the town, promptly shelled it.

The poor French people were pathetically grateful to us and their tales of Hun brutality were horrible—for the first time we realized that the newspaper reports of brutality etc. were quite true and in fact—very mildly written.

It was very embarrassing at first for us, for whenever a British officer passed a 'Civvy'—the 'Civvy' stepped into the gutter and removed his hat 'profoundly' (German order). We felt that this was not due to gratitude, and on questioning them, found that it was the result of four years of Hun discipline. Of course, we stopped this practice.

There was vigorous and sacrificial fighting right up to the end. It was on 4th November, just one week before the Armistice, that Lieutenant Wilfred Owen was killed at the crossing of the Sambre and Oise Canal, with the unhappy consequence that his parents received the telegram announcing his death as the bells of peace were ringing on 11th November. For Lieutenant Alex Wilkinson, 2nd Bn Coldstream Guards, it was by contrast a good time. He wrote to his father on 6th November that the battle in which he had just been engaged was

the best I have ever had and I would not have missed it for anything...

We were right on top of the Huns before he could get his MGs to work & we got a nice few prisoners & MGs straight away. And a nice few Huns were killed there too. I had sworn to shoot the first one I saw, but I could not bring myself to do it. I am a sentimental ass. Having sent the prisoners back, on we went at a tremendous pace. The men were perfectly splendid, and showed amazing skill in the use of their Lewis Guns and rifles.... But what I call the battle discipline left a great deal to be desired. The men got out of their formation unless carefully watched, and were inclined to lose

ARMISTICE!

The Canadians reached Mons—scene of the first fighting of August 1914—on the
very day that the war ended. (Above) Their triumphal entry.

    From letters by Gunner J. H. Bird, Royal Garrison Artillery: attached Canadian forces

> I walked into Mons in the afternoon of 11 November and oh what excitement,
> we were mobbed and nearly lost all our buttons. It was indeed a great day
> for Britain as well as France. It made one feel glad to be alive & to think that
> after four years hard fighting we had at last reached the places where our troops
> were in 1914 and also to think the war finished the same day!

This was the climax of many days of brisk advance in which the people of the liberated
towns and villages received the allied armies with acclamation:

> By Jove, we did get a reception, all the French people in the villages had the
> tricolour out & kept cheering & the kiddies wanted to ride on the motors. . . .
> During the afternoon a Band belonging to the Canadians played in the square
> & the inhabitants kept cheering & throwing wreaths of Flowers on the
> Bandsmen. You have no idea of the delight of these people.

direction, and too much time was wasted searching prisoners not only for arms but also for souvenirs. Even so it was most amusing to see practically every man smoking a cigar after we had passed the first objective...

I think it is safe to say that it cannot be much longer. The Huns we met were certainly nothing to fear, and they thought of nothing but peace. They fully realized that they were absolutely beat to the world.

And then at last, from its ultimate source in the woods of Compiègne, where the German plenipotentiaries had been brought to sign Marshal Foch's uncompromising armistice terms, the expected news came.

On the 11th November at about 8 a.m. we received a wire from Corps HQ to say that 'at 11 a.m. hostilities would cease, but no fraternization etc. would take place'.

11 o'clock came, and a sudden silence!

It was impossible at first to realize that the war was over. About 11.30 a.m. we realized that it was no longer necessary to wear our steel hats or gas-masks!

So Lieutenant Ruffell ended his war.

Belgium
12.11.18   7–0 p.m.

Dearest Mother and Father,

Hostilities ceased yesterday at 11–0 a.m.! It's jolly hard to realize and Phil and I have been selfishly shaking hands with ourselves for coming through with a whole skin.

We've had a great time in the last few days. The Civilians have all been going mad with delight and treat us awfully well. That swine of a bosche has finished all their live stock etc., left them absolutely nothing but a few hens.

It seems impossible to realize that the war is all over, sort of leaves you gasping! Every one is quite mad with delight here and the troops have been behaving, as usual, in a magnificent fashion. I'm quite certain there is nothing to surpass the work and guts of my own gunners and drivers. They are perfectly priceless.

Well it will be great to get home for a bit. I do hope they'll sling some month's leaves around.

Best love to all the family and I hope they are all as pleased as I am that this ruddy old war is over.

Très fatigué
Your most loving son
Dick
Captain R. R. Stokes, 83rd Battery, RFA

Certificate of demobilization—
for those who survived.

Scroll of commemoration—
for those who did not.

He whom this scroll commemorates was numbered among those who, at the call of King and Country, left all that was dear to them, endured hardness, faced danger, and finally passed out of the sight of men by the path of duty and self-sacrifice, giving up their own lives that others might live in freedom. Let those who come after see to it that his name be not forgotten.

Pte. Raymond Horace Turner
East Kent Regt.

A SOLDIER
OF THE GREAT WAR

KNOWN UNTO GOD

Gravestone—for those whose bodies
could not be identified.

Monday 11 November 1918 was one of the most remarkable days of modern times: 'the greatest day in the world's history', Queen Mary described it in her diary. Shortly before 11 o'clock the Prime Minister, Mr Lloyd George, emerged from 10 Downing Street and spoke to a boisterous, flag-waving crowd. 'It is over!' he said. 'They have signed! The war is won!'

On the stroke of eleven, the capital went wild with joy. Maroons exploded, the 'All Clear' was sounded from the plinth of Nelson's column in Trafalgar Square and, in Churchill's words, 'the strict, war-stained, regulated streets of London became a triumphant pandemonium'. Crowds thronged the approaches to Buckingham Palace and when the King and Queen appeared on the palace balcony they were vociferously and repeatedly cheered. The weather deteriorated as the day wore on, but nothing could spoil the ardour of a people released from fifty-two months of war. That night the lights went on for the first time in many months. There were bonfires and fireworks. The theatres, restaurants, buses and tubes were thronged with revellers. But here and there across the nation were those who did not celebrate, for whom the coming of peace brought home more bitterly than before the thought of loved ones and friends whom the war had taken away. One such was Robert Graves, poet and soldier, who went walking alone along the dyke above the marshes of Rhuddlan 'cursing and sobbing and thinking of the dead'. Another was Vera Brittain, who had lost a fiancé and a brother killed, and who walked through a carousing capital with her heart 'sinking in a sudden cold dismay'. For as she looked on the 'brightly-lit, alien world' around her, she realized the unhappy truth that 'as the years went by and youth departed and remembrance grew dim, a deeper and ever deeper darkness would cover the young men who had once been my contemporaries'.

In some sectors of the front there was fighting right up to eleven o'clock. At Lessines a squadron of the 7th Dragoons was sent forward to attack a bridge over the River Dendre at 10.50 a.m., so that in the very last minutes of the war men fell for their country. Elsewhere artillery fire went on sporadically for some time after 11 o'clock, as various batteries vied with each other for the distinction of firing the last shell. By midday or thereabouts, silence fell.

Men received the news of the cessation of hostilities in a variety of ways. For many there was unashamed relief; for others a numbed incredulity; yet others felt dismay that their victorious advance was to be halted just as they had got the enemy on the run. For Major R. S. Cockburn, now with the 63rd (Royal Naval) Division, who were, as he put it, 'probably nearer to Berlin than any other British troops', the news of the Armistice was 'as if the sun had forced its way through a bank of cloud'. But, he added, in his letter describing the occasion, 'on the whole the men took it philosophically. One of them said to me, "Well, that *is* a good thing, sir, isn't it!"'

As for the others whose experiences have been important in the making of this book, it is perhaps worth attempting to say where some of them were on this most memorable and longed-for of days.

War Cemeteries on the Western Front

French:
Notre Dame de Lorette.

German: Fricourt.

British: Blighty Valley

Lionel Ferguson was in England nursing a Blighty wound received in the fighting of October 1918.

Tom Macdonald was learning to be an instructor at an Army Training School at Berkhamsted and having a hard time with his Sergeant-Majors.

Roland Mountfort, after serving for some months in British East Africa, was training in an Officer Cadet Battalion, and would receive his commission in March 1919.

Archie Surfleet was undergoing training as a pilot in the Royal Air Force.

George Morgan, now a Sergeant, was taking new recruits through a musketry course at Whitley Bay. The moment the news came through training was abandoned and everybody drank 'pints galore' in the canteen.

Thomas Bickerton and a crowd of other prisoners of war, 'dirty, lousy and uncared for', were making their way on foot towards the Allied lines, having been sent packing by German guards only too glad to get rid of the responsibility of looking after them. When they finally reached friendly territory they formed fours and marched proudly down the road singing 'It's a long way to Tipperary' at the tops of their voices.

Jack Sweeney, walking down the main street of a village in Nottingham, saw the flag being raised over the local church and hearing that the bell-ringers were at work he and five others got together and rang the bells ('or at least made a terrible noise') for an hour and then went and had a drink.

For Corporal James Gingell and his Road Construction Company it had been a hard autumn, as they moved steadily eastwards in the wake of the advancing front. From nine days before 11 November he had begun every entry in his diary with the words 'Work as usual'. Armistice Day brought no relief. 'Hostilities ceased at 11 o'clock,' he wrote. 'But we are working as usual, and what is more we are moving forward tomorrow to Mons, I think.' 'Work as usual' was to be Gingell's standard diary entry until well into January 1919.

Cyril Drummond was outside Buckingham Palace. He and everybody else in uniform had to stand at attention for what seemed like an hour while the Guards Band

When I go back there I feel I'm on consecrated ground. That ground has been trod by all those lovely friends of mine, who never came back.
  I think that poem

    'They shall grow not old, as we that are left grow old:
    Age shall not weary them nor the years condemn.
    At the going down of the sun and in the morning
        We shall remember them.'

I think it's marvellous. Because that's just how it is. You imagine them as they were then—not as they would be now—young, and in their prime, and never grown old.
                                                                George Morgan (died 1977)

at the Green Park gateway played the national anthem of every possible ally. 'When at last the final one had been played and we all took our hands down the whole area around the Victoria Memorial suddenly became a sea of waving white handkerchiefs.'

Arthur Hubbard was serving as a Sergeant in the King's African Rifles in Nairobi. This for him was a happy time, but he would never recover from the effects of his war service and would take his own life a little over ten years later.

Hiram Sturdy, home in his native Scotland and having survived a bout of influenza, went to Glasgow and saw 'singing, dancing, yelling people . . . the pent-up feelings of four years of waiting, sorrow, loneliness, misery, wickedness, crimes and cruelty of unbelievable magnitude being sung, drunk and danced out'.

Harry Bateman was with his family recuperating after the complete nervous collapse that had followed his hard experiences on the Somme.

Cyril Rawlins, who had suffered a severe head injury in a minor railway accident while working as his battalion's transport officer, was convalescing in England but would never be restored to full health.

Walter Vignoles was with his battalion on parade in France when, to his annoyance, the Adjutant galloped wildly on to the parade ground waving a message to say that the Armistice had been signed. The men cheered a good deal, but Lieutenant-Colonel Vignoles subsequently spoke to each of the four companies in turn and explained that an armistice did not necessarily mean peace and that it 'behoves us to keep on with our work and ensure that really good terms of peace were made before we could put down our arms'. The parade then continued. Vignoles added in his letter describing the occasion: 'When we read how the news had been received by the people at Home and Abroad and how they went wild with excitement it made us think what a difference there was between those that were out doing the fighting and those who viewed things from a distance.'

Henry Bolton, Willie Clarke, Harry Farlam, Edgar Foreman, Kenneth Garry, Roland Ingle, Reginald Leetham, Kenneth Macardle, Peter McGregor, Arthur Roberts, Horace Turner, George Buxton, Ralph Cresswell and Robert Sutcliffe were dead. So too were more than a million other men from Britain and her Empire who had gone to war between 1914 and 1918.

Index